D0713107

Routes of War

Routes of War

THE WORLD OF MOVEMENT
IN THE CONFEDERATE SOUTH

Yael A. Sternhell

HARVARD UNIVERSITY PRESS

Cambridge, Massachusetts, and London, England · 2012

Library of Congress Cataloging-in-Publication Data

Sternhell, Yael A.
    Routes of war : the world of movement in the Confederate
south / Yael A. Sternhell.
        p. cm.
    Includes bibliographical references and index.
    ISBN 978-0-674-06442-3
    1. United States—History—Civil War, 1861–1865—Social aspects.
    2. Migration, Internal—Confederate States of America.   3. Confederate States
of America. Army—Mobilization.   I. Title.
    E468.9.S86 2012
    973.7'13—dc23
    2011035038

For my parents

לאמא ואבא

Contents

Maps

Routes of War

Prologue

Murders and Movements

In the epilogue to *War and Peace*, his magnum opus on the Napoleonic Wars, Leo Tolstoy makes the following observation: "All we have to do is admit that far from knowing the purpose of the convulsions that shook European nations we know only the facts—a series of murders committed first in France, then in Italy, then in Africa, Prussia, Austria, Spain and Russia—and also that movements from west to east and from east to west constitute the essence and the aim of those events." Tolstoy's distillation of war into a series of "murders" and "movements" rings true not only for the European conflicts of the early nineteenth century, but for virtually every large-scale war in history. While circumstances may vary greatly across time and place, the two constitutive elements of war-making remain the systematic employment of violence and the mass movement of people across space.[1]

Indeed from the age of the lance to the age of the aircraft, the processes lying at the core of armed conflict materialize in the motion of the human body. The mobilization of armies, the conquest of territory, the displacement of civilians, and the remaking of state authority are inherently contingent on the movements of large numbers of people. Examples abound: Mobility was central to Hannibal in his quest to vanquish Rome, as it was to Napoleon's drive to subjugate Russia. Movement was the essence of the Crusades, a series of epic military journeys that shaped medieval Europe, transformed the landscape and history of the Holy Land, and left imprints on regions and communities from England to the Middle East. Sherman's March to the Sea carried the wrath of civil war to the Deep South, transforming both the physical landscape and the social makeup of a region that had remained stable for nearly four years. German armies in both world wars embarked on vastly ambitious territorial campaigns that aspired to nothing less than the reinvention of Eastern Europe as part of a Teutonic empire. Ideologies and vehicles may change, but the execution of war rests on the motion of men and on their commanders' ability to use it effectively. The mobilization of armies has had a crucial impact not only on the soldiers who wage war but also on the citizens who stay behind. Mustering a mass army of citizen-soldiers refashions relations of power within families and necessitates a reorganization of economic structures. Well into the twentieth century the departure of soldiers wreaked havoc on the home front as governments took away the strongest workers, impressed the most valuable farm animals, and confiscated precious food supplies. Mobilization has also often unfolded as a defining moment in the histories of societies at war. The leave-taking of European men in August 1914 brought out enthusiastic crowds who bade the soldiers a festive farewell and celebrated their nations' decisions to go to what most people assumed would be a brief and effortless war. The scenes of men marching off remained etched in contemporaries' memories for years as symbols of self-delusion, false hopes, and warmongering.[2]

Once an armed conflict gets under way, movement becomes even more important to the wartime experiences of civilians. From the dire circumstances of noncombatants in the Assyrian Wars of the ancient Near East to the desperate plight of refugees in contemporary Darfur, the fate of men and women caught in the upheaval of armed conflict is closely linked with various forms of forced mobility. Dislocation, deportation, and exile have shaped the fortunes of societies at war in every corner of the globe and at every point in time. World War II set a standard of its own in this area: forty-six million people were uprooted in east-central Europe alone between 1939 and 1948 through evacuation, flight, resettlement, and forced labor. The aftermath of war left thirty million displaced persons, who roamed through Europe's ruined land looking for a home. One refugee moving eastward through Germany in 1945 described roads that seemed like "swollen mountain torrents in the spring, a Babel of people and languages, all former slaves of the Third Reich." The Holocaust itself was an offshoot of an earlier Nazi initiative to remove European Jewry into confined spaces in the east; the emergence of murder as an alternative to movement provides a particularly chilling example of the way Tolstoy's two distinct categories are in fact inextricably intertwined.[3]

Movement often plays an equally salient role in the collapse of political authority during wartime. Serbia ceased to exist as a sovereign state in the fall of 1915, when its government fled Belgrade. Only a year earlier this small central European nation was able to hold its own in the face of multiple attempts by the Habsburg Empire to invade its territory. But a renewed effort by German, Habsburg, and Bulgarian forces was more than the Serbians could handle. After having suffered a crippling blow, the army set out on a hurried retreat toward the Adriatic Coast, accompanied by the government and large numbers of civilians. In June 1940 similar scenes were repeated in France. The flight of the French government from Paris signaled the end of state resistance to Nazi aggression and the beginning of a new era in the life of the nation. Prime Minister Paul Reynaud, his cabinet, and what was left of their administration joined five million refugees on a panicked rout south that demolished their ability to either govern or fight. Within days France surrendered and accepted German rule. Governments do not always run in the face of an impending defeat, but when they do their withdrawal makes for a uniquely striking symbol of national collapse.[4]

Hence movement, in all its shapes and forms, is a critical component in the wartime experiences of men and women, combatants and noncombatants, individuals and nations. While we have come to think of armed conflict as taking place either on the battlefield or on the home front, much of the reality of war transpires on the road. The mobility of soldiers, deserters, stragglers, refugees, and deportees is the sum and substance of armed conflict, equally significant in the realm of grand strategy and in the private trials of a soldier on a night march or a civilian forced out of her home. Marching, retreating, fleeing, and straggling are simultaneously physical actions and psychological conditions, personal undertakings and mass endeavors, transformative political processes and mundane occurrences. Together they create the vortex of war.[5]

Despite the centrality of movement to armed conflict, it has figured in the historical literature only in very specific ways. Indeed some of the most popular and influential writing about war through the ages consists of soldiers' accounts of their travels to foreign lands; armies' mobility predominates in the work of military historians, who analyze campaigns, maneuvers, and strategy. The displacement of civilians garners much attention from social historians interested in population shifts, state formation, and the material conditions in nations at war. Yet even if movement enjoys a substantial presence in the vast corpus of works on armed conflicts, it has not received the same careful analysis shown to violence in the past two generations of historical writing, and one would be hard-pressed to find a study that concentrates on the phenomenon of wartime motion or attempts to create a synthesis of its different dimensions.[6] Students of armed conflicts often take it for granted that soldiers move from home to military camp, from camp to battlefield, and from battlefield to a hospital, a prisoner of war facility, or the next killing ground. They assume that wide-ranging conflicts propel civilians in the line of fire to flee their homes and unsettle the social order by creating new divisions of labor, new allocations of resources, and new geographical partitions. Scholars realize that mobilization, invasion, dislocation, and demobilization are all undertaken through the movements of a large number of bodies, but only rarely have they dwelt on the meanings of these motions, on the ways they shape experiences and perceptions, and on the social, political, and cultural consequences of the vast surges of human mobility created by war. The movement of people during wartime often remains in the background, as either a prologue or an epilogue to more exciting events, a matter of logistics or tactics rather than a pivotal aspect of how war is actually lived.[7]

Mobility is, of course, hardly unique to life during times of war. As Ira Berlin has recently suggested, geographic movement "has been and remains the normal condition of mankind."[8] Yet even as migrations of all sorts receive ever-growing attention, only rarely does wartime movement find its place in historical narratives. Armies on the march do not fit easily into narratives about dislocation and diasporas, and deserters and runaways are rarely counted in the formation of identities, cultures, and institutions so crucial to the study of population movements. Even Berlin excludes the story of slave flight during the Civil War from his comprehensive account of black mobility in American history. The marginalization of movement in wartime does not derive from scholarly misconception or neglect; it is a reflection of the fact that wartime movement is a different historical phenomenon than migration, an independent area of inquiry. As such it deserves to be studied on its own terms.[9]

As Tolstoy began work on *War and Peace* in 1863, a conflict raging halfway across the world in the United States demonstrated the profundity of his observation on the nature of war. "Murders" were no doubt both an essence and an aim in the Civil War, a conflict that cost the lives of at least

620,000 men and made death a formative experience for an entire generation.[10] But so were "movements." The sectional conflict thrust millions on the
roads and transformed the South into a land teeming with motion. The Union
and the Confederacy mobilized roughly three million men, who left their
homes, traveled to the front, and proceeded to walk, ride, and sail through
the great expanses of Southern land until discharged from the army and released back to their homes. The war was won and lost in a series of territorial
campaigns, which sent entire armies rushing back and forth across the land
until the overwhelming might of the Northern invasion finally overcame the
Southern advantage of interior lines. From the outbreak of war to the summer of 1865, the pathways of the South were inundated with men on the move
and with their animals, vehicles, weapons, and stores, the instruments of
nineteenth-century armies at war.

Yet as dramatic as the motion of armies was in the Confederate South, it
does not fully account for the place of human mobility in the realities of the
sectional conflict. The mayhem of war instigated a massive surge of movement
among enslaved Americans, who for the first time in generations could flee
from farms and plantations and find refuge in the camps of the Union army.
As many as 500,000 men, women, and children were behind Union lines by
the end of the war, and an untold number made bold if eventually unsuccessful attempts to escape. On the roads and in the woods, runaway slaves were
joined by as much as a quarter-million white refugees who were flying from
enemy occupation and seeking safety behind Confederate lines. An even
larger crowd of itinerant Southerners comprised hundreds of thousands of
deserters, stragglers, and skulkers, who dropped out of the Confederate army
and attempted to reach their homes or to find a place where they could rest
from the rigors of armed service. For these men and women, soldiers and civilians, enslaved and free, movement played multiple, shifting, and often contradictory roles. At times it was an act of liberation, at others an unwelcome
choice; the open road was for some a pathway to freedom, for others a journey
to death. Orders, threats, necessity, and hope threw people on the road and
created the mobile universe of the Civil War South.[11]

The following chapters are organized both thematically and chronologically,
each exploring one dimension of wartime motion during a particular part of
the conflict. Chapter 1 centers on the role of soldiers' mobility in the transition

of the South from a section into a nation. During the first few months of the war, the journeys of volunteers from different points in the Confederacy to the front lines in Virginia played a crucial role in the emergence of a national sentiment and in the mobilization of the population for the war effort. In the climate of uncertainty that prevailed in the slave states after secession, men on the move provided the first tangible proof of the Confederacy's existence. Their appearance on the roads of the South embodied the new nation and infused meaning into the notion of Southern independence. In hundreds of communities across the slave states, the raw recruits provided the focal point for elaborate civic rituals that allowed both soldiers and civilians to perform their new political identities. We will follow the soldiers as they leave their homes and travel to Richmond, examine their encounters with the civilian population, and interpret the full meaning of mobilization to the process of state formation that took place in the South in the wake of its sudden rebirth as an independent country. In 1861 soldiers traveling to the Confederacy's northern border were essential not merely as physical barriers between Union invasion and Southern soil, but also as living symbols of a nation on the rise.

Once the rebellion matured into a full-blown war, movement became even more significant to life in the Confederate South. Chapter 2 leads us into the world of military motion that emerged in Virginia in 1862. The peripatetic nature of warfare in this arena transformed peaceful towns into hubs of motion, country roads into avenues of destruction, and farmhouses into supply stations for armies on the march. We will accompany the soldiers as they embark on grueling territorial campaigns and as they retreat after having been defeated in battle. We will delve into the physical experience of life on the move and into the uneasy relationship between the citizenry on the roadsides and the men on the road. We will also trace the evolution of movement as a language in which both civilians and soldiers interpreted the realities of war. Southerners scrutinized men on the road closely and drew far-reaching conclusions from the speed, demeanor, and physical appearance of their columns. As time went by, marching, straggling, and fleeing evolved from simple modes of movement into powerful personifications of victory and defeat, hope and despair. The armies' ability to advance and retreat determined the course of military events as well as the ways these events were perceived. It governed the most quotidian realities of daily life while molding the citizenry's conceptions of soldierly valor, martial prowess, and national resilience. In the eastern theater, movement was the crux of the Confederate experience for civilians and soldiers alike.

At the same time, the pathways of the Confederacy formed essential sites for the social revolution that was sweeping through the region and shattering its oldest, most unyielding paradigms. For nearly 250 years the South had existed as a society based on the freedom of white men and the subjugation of their black slaves and female dependents. This social and political order remained remarkably stable in the face of powerful forces like territorial expansion, economic development, and antislavery agitation. Yet it could not withstand the shock of war. The mobilization of white Southern men and the invasion of the Union army shook this rigid social hierarchy to its core. It created new opportunities for bondspeople to attain their freedom while subjecting their masters to equally novel demands and constraints. Free men who had ruled their households with an iron hand were now nothing more than lowly soldiers; the women who had relied on them for subsistence and protection were left to fend for themselves. In many ways the fullest incarnation of these radical challenges took place in the realm of spatial mobility, for the Civil War transformed the South into a land of runaways. The experience of flight incorporated slaves who left their masters, deserters who abandoned their military units, and refugees who escaped the enemy. The gargantuan wave of motion that swept through the Confederacy challenged the laws and customs that governed movement in the antebellum years and subverted structures of power that determined which Southerners had the right to move at will and which did not. Chapter 3 follows Southerners on the run and those who went after them. It looks into the intricate and unacknowledged connections between desertion and emancipation, slave patrols and military police, refugee convoys and contraband camps. The slave society, in effect, collapsed on the road.

Even as the old order was slowly disintegrating, avid Rebels still clung to the hope that the South could emerge victorious on the battlefield. If the two warring sides met for one last, grand engagement, they believed, the Confederacy surely would be able to repel the invasion and attain its independence. Yet the decisive battle never took place. Instead Confederate armies were ultimately defeated during a series of long and chaotic retreats that destroyed their ability to fight. From Mississippi to Virginia, military units escaping the advancing enemy dissolved on the move. Thousands of men collapsed by the roadside, while numerous others left the columns and began to walk home. In 1861 these soldiers embodied the rise of the Confederate nation; four years later their journeys back from war symbolized the failure of the cause and the humiliation of the South. Chapter 4 discusses the dissolution of the armies as well as the flight of Jefferson Davis and his government from Richmond and the final breakdown of slavery with the massive exodus of black Southerners from plantations and farms.

What is gained by leaving behind battlefields, plantations, and other traditional sites of Civil War history, by turning our gaze to the routes that ran between them, is a new understanding of how war is lived, how it is experienced by the human body, and how the most mundane action of going from one place to the other translates into complex processes of political change, social revolution, and the evolution of wartime culture. Looking at seminal events like mobilization, invasion, and emancipation through the prism of motion reveals how physical acts attain symbolic meanings and how abstractions such as nation, freedom, and victory emerge out of the physical reality of war. It exposes hidden links between phenomena that seem entirely disparate but are in fact intimately linked. Grasping the different meanings of movement during wartime, the different ways movement figured in the lives of individuals and in the undertakings of society as a whole, restores to our view a crucial dimension of armed conflict. It is essential for comprehending the human condition in the Civil War South.

Movement in the Confederate States of America took place throughout a territory approximating one million square miles, a great, sprawling expanse. Naturally it did not have the same impact in every county and every state. This book focuses on the heartland of the Confederate war: the area that stretched between North Carolina in the south and Maryland and Pennsylvania in the north, between the Atlantic Ocean in the east and the Appalachian Mountains in the west. Across this tract of land, the eastern theater of the war, hundreds of thousands of soldiers marched during four years of extensive campaigning, and many thousands more moved on its roads as stragglers, deserters, prisoners, and hospital patients. The continuous presence of Northern armies enabled large numbers of slaves to liberate themselves from bondage by fleeing to Union camps; at the same time, Federal invasion instigated heavy traffic of refugees from occupied regions into

Confederate-controlled areas. The pathways of this region were perennially overrun with men and women, mules and horses, wagons and trains, all making their way through a chaotic, volatile landscape of war.

Focusing on the eastern theater does not imply that significant mobility did not take place elsewhere in the Confederacy. The western theater was a remarkably dynamic arena of military motion, starting with the early campaigns to capture forts on the Mississippi River and culminating in Sherman's March to the Sea. Since operations in the two theaters were closely entwined, and since both civilians and soldiers often moved between them, the west figures in what follows in several important ways. At the same time, while movement was upending some regions of the South, there were also areas where armies were rarely seen, where slaves had nowhere to go, and where white civilians had little to fear. In these quarters mobility played a role far less significant than that described in the following pages. Yet this study does not aim to cover the Confederacy in its entirety nor to make claims about the endeavors of every single man and woman living in the South during the Civil War. Rather it is preoccupied with the region where the sectional conflict was a constant, overwhelming, and inescapable presence, and with the people who encountered it in the most direct and visceral way. It is concerned with those parts of the South where the mobilization of local men, the arrival of enemy forces, the uprooting of civilian populations, and the transience of state authority fundamentally undermined the order of things. This is a study of a war land, a space where armed conflict was not an idea but the defining feature of life, a place where all aspects of day-to-day reality were determined by the success or failure of the Confederate army to hold its enemy at bay. It could not have been written about all countries engaged in armed conflict, but only about a region where war was actually fought on the ground, where the combined force of violence and motion tore through homes and fields, roads and woods, towns and cities, forever transforming the land and the people caught in its path.

Space is an actual geographical reality, yet it is also a construct, an idea that changes across time and place. Confederate space was the object of the military struggle, the setting for epic campaigns and ferocious battles between two armies who believed that control of territory would win them the war. Conquering space was also the challenge facing the region's numerous runaways, whether their goal was getting to a Union contraband camp, to a well-defended Confederate city, or to a remote farm where a wife and children awaited. Yet no less important, space loomed large in the minds of Southerners as a locus of ambitions and desires. The founding of the Confederacy was an act of spatial imagination, in which the territory of one section within the American Union was redefined as the Confederate States. As the war expanded and escalated, Confederates facing the might of the Union army pinned their hopes on the enormity of Southern spaces, believing that the very size of their country would prevent it from being vanquished by an enemy force. In what follows, space will figure in all its hard concreteness and all its elusive abstractness, from the course of territorial congealing in the early days of the war to its gradual fracturing over the subsequent four years. We will observe the relationship between the material and metaphorical dimensions of Southern expanses and the ways space and movement continually remade one another.[12]

The following journey along the Confederacy's routes of war aspires to yield a new understanding of process: the process of state formation, of social revolution, of the transformation of white Southerners into a people at war and of their land into a theater of operations, and of national disintegration and its eventual outcome, defeat. In all of these areas the issue at heart will be the physical execution of historical change by bodies in motion and the multiple, fluid, and shifting effects of motion in its various forms. By anatomizing the movements of Southerners, we will recover this crucial dimension of the Confederate experience and incorporate it into our vision of the war.

This new interpretation of the wartime South owes a great deal to the vast and varied historical literature on the Civil War and to the numerous scholars who have studied the conflict's social, political, and military aspects. Indeed it would have been impossible to undertake this study without the wealth of research on issues ranging from the African American war experience to battlefield tactics, from the plight of women on the home front to patterns of desertion from the army. Yet while many events and themes explored here have been studied extensively by other historians, the concept of movement has remained hidden in plain sight. Its explanatory power has never been utilized; its omnipresence has never been systematically analyzed nor properly understood. Hence as we zoom in on the men and women treading along the dusty roads of Dixie, we will watch some of the best-known episodes in Civil War history take on new meanings and come together as a new whole.

More broadly, studying the Civil War as an experience of movement furnishes us with an important and revealing prism through which to examine conflicts across a wide spectrum of time and place. The particular configuration of movement in the Confederacy emerged out of certain social, political, geographical, technological, and cultural conditions, but the pervasiveness and significance of bodies in motion were by no means unique. Marching, straggling, fleeing, and traversing deserve all the attention that wounding, killing, dying, and mourning have received from historians of war. We might be well served by following Tolstoy's cue and focus not only on death and dying, but on movements too.

1

Nation Building on the Road

In May 1861 Cornelia McDonald was following the preparations for war in her town of Winchester, Virginia. Only a few short weeks had passed since the firing at Fort Sumter, and Virginia had yet officially to secede from the Union, but in the northwestern part of the state the impending conflict was already looming large. "Troops were now pouring into Winchester on their way to the gathering of the clans at Harpers Ferry," she remembered years later. At first these were local men, farmers from the nearby countryside, and students from the University of Virginia. But soon the town was greeting soldiers who had come all the way from the cotton states: "The first regiment that came from the South was from Alabama; a splendid body of men, and a grand welcome did they receive as they came marching through the streets of Winchester, all along the length of which the windows streamed with banners, and expectant crowds awaited them. Loudon Street from end to end was draped with Confederate flags."[1]

Over the next four years the residents of Winchester would bear the full brunt of a bitter civil war and would become intimately acquainted with death, hunger, and the devastation of property. Soldiers on the move would become a nuisance and a threat to civilians living in their path. But in those first few months, when the harsh realities of war had not yet set in and the idea of Southern independence was still a thrilling novelty, the appearance of the first Confederate soldiers caused a sensation in Winchester and in virtually every other community they passed through. The mobilization of the Southern army amounted to much more than the mere transport of men from the home front to the battlefield. Soldiers on the move played a pivotal role in transforming the South from a section into a nation and in remaking Southerners into Confederate citizens. In more ways than one, their motion on the roads of the South helped bring the Confederate States of America into existence.[2]

Despite the widespread enthusiasm that swept the South in the wake of secession, there was in fact nothing inevitable about the sudden emergence of the Confederate nation. The idea of an independent South had been in the air since the 1832 nullification crisis in South Carolina, but until the late 1850s its popularity was largely limited to a group of planters, intellectuals, and politicians aptly nicknamed Fire-eaters. The great majority of Southerners considered secession a radical delusion and never expected it to materialize. The white population living below the Mason-Dixon Line was fiercely patriotic and easily combined a strong sense of sectional loyalty with a deep devotion to the United States of America. Southerners fought in their nation's wars, revered its Constitution, and dominated Washington for the better part of the antebellum period. Though regional tensions often ran high, white Southerners did not aspire to separate nationhood, but were willing to fight vehemently for their rights within the Union. Most of the time they were extremely successful. The slave society thrived and expanded under the protection of Federal laws, and Southern planters grew to be the richest and most powerful men in the land. The United States of America had been good to the South and to its peculiar institution, and few white Southerners felt the urge to betray it and strike out on their own.

The idea of an independent Southern nation gained public support only when Southerners became convinced that something had changed. Enmity between the sections began to escalate toward full-fledged conflict in the wake of the Mexican-American War, which added to the Union a large swath of territory and forced a discussion about the future of slavery in the new states. While the great majority of Northerners had no intention of meddling with slavery in the places where it already existed, a growing consensus above the Mason-Dixon Line demanded that there be no further expansion of the peculiar institution. This mind-set encountered fierce resistance in the South. By midcentury white Southerners had come to perceive any attempt to curtail slavery's growth or question its legitimacy as both a severe threat and a grave insult. In both slaveholding and nonslaveholding states, a new politics of acrimonious sectionalism was rapidly taking hold.

As the decade of the 1850s progressed, the debate grew violent. Northerners and Southerners openly fought each other in newly settled Kansas, where killing, burning, and pillaging became a fact of life in the struggle over the entry of slaves into the territory. Northerners refused to obey the Fugitive Slave Act, which forced them to assist in capturing runaway slaves, and Representative Preston Brooks of South Carolina won great acclaim in his section after beating Senator Charles Sumner of Massachusetts almost to death in the Senate chambers. In 1859 a decade of strife culminated in John Brown's raid on Harpers Ferry. The attempt by a white man to start a slave insurrection in Virginia and the support and sympathy his acts drew in the North shook Southerners to their core and provoked a regional wave of hysteria.

The victory of the Republican Party in the presidential election the following year, on a platform of stopping the expansion of slavery to new territories, confirmed for many the suspicion that their section no longer enjoyed a secure position within the Union and that their way of life was in danger. Even though Abraham Lincoln had vowed to protect the constitutional right to hold slaves in the South, his election expressed an explicit rejection of the institution of human bondage and the society that nurtured it. For those who saw slavery as the basis of their existence, there was little reason to trust the guarantees offered by a man who had openly declared slavery to be a "monstrous injustice," nor was there much cause to pin one's hopes on a rapidly growing Northern populace that no longer needed Southern votes to elect a president. The Union, Southerners now believed, was turning against slavery; full-fledged abolitionism was only a matter of time.

Hence Southerners did not abandon the Union because they had developed a coherent, separate national identity. The emergence of any national sentiment is more often than not a convoluted process, rife with uncertainty and happenstance. Hardly any group of human beings possesses an intrinsic sense of belonging to a preordained nation, and historians have long recognized the importance of armed struggle as a catalyst to the inception of a national consciousness. This was definitely true in the case of the Confederacy. Nationalism had not simmered in the South for decades, preparing the population for the moment of separation, nor was there a blueprint for what a Southern nation would look like. While the panic that swept through the region in the aftermath of John Brown's raid and the explosive election of 1860 went a long way toward convincing Southerners that their time in the Union had run out, there was no ready-made national identity that could serve as an alternative to their long-held allegiance to the United States. Southerners still spoke the same language as Northerners, believed in the same God, and worshipped the same Founding Fathers. They perceived themselves as the true inheritors of the legacy of the American Revolution, a sentiment they expressed in multiple forms, including placing George Washington on Confederate stamps and currency and scheduling the inauguration of Jefferson Davis on Washington's birthday. Four years of common sacrifices would do a great deal to create a viable nation out of the slave states and to inculcate in large parts of the population a sentiment of nationhood and a commitment to the South's independence. But in 1861 the process of nation building was on an extremely unsure footing. Unionist feeling remained strong across Dixie, and in many counties the majorities that voted for secession were strikingly small. Disunion, as one historian has written, "was often a tenuous choice of an emotional moment."[3]

And yet the moment had come, and South Carolina was the first to seize it. The most radical of Southern states seceded on December 20, 1860, and was followed by Mississippi, Florida, Alabama, Georgia, Louisiana, and Texas. Once the seven Deep South states were out of the Union, the Confederate States of America was launched at record speed. On February 4, 1861, fifty delegates convened in Montgomery, Alabama, where they founded the new nation, elected a provisional president, and wrote a constitution. Within days a new political entity was born and began to operate. A month later, on March 6, the Confederate Congress authorized the enlistment of 100,000 volunteers to defend the South from Union invasion. On April 12 the South Carolina militia fired on the Union garrison stationed at Fort Sumter in Charleston, prompting Lincoln to issue a call for 75,000 volunteers to suppress the insurrection and pushing the Upper South States out of the Union and into an alliance with their sister slave states. By May the new Southern nation was united, up and running, and preparing for war.

The most visible manifestation of the Confederacy's emerging war effort was the mobilization of the Southern army and its conveyance to Richmond, the Confederacy's new capital city. Only a hundred miles lay between Washington, D.C., and the Confederate seat of government, and it would simply be a matter of time, Southerners knew well, before a Union army would cross the Potomac and attempt to capture it. Roughly 62,000 men had enlisted in

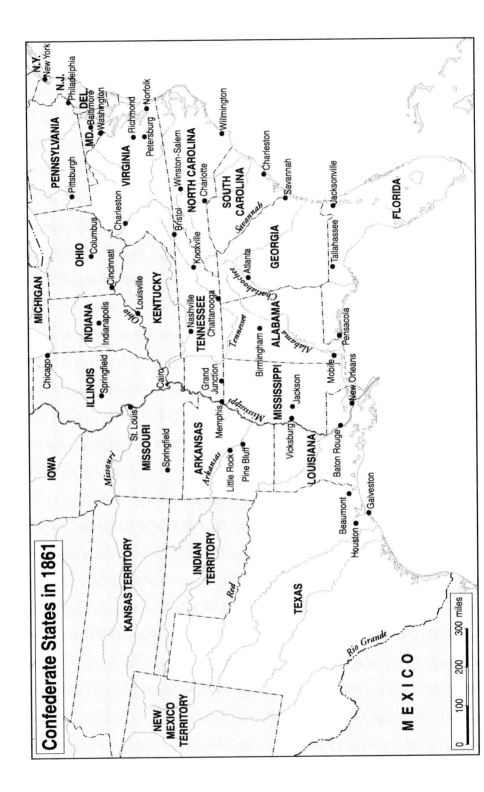

Confederate States in 1861

the different states by April, either through the conversion of state militia into Confederate units or through the organization of volunteer companies in localities from the Atlantic Seaboard to the far outreaches of the Southwest. As soon as hostilities broke out in Fort Sumter, many began making their way toward Virginia.[4]

In the spring and summer of 1861, towns along the main routes to the front lines were inundated with thousands of soldiers from every corner of the South. "Troops! troops!! They have been pouring in yesterday and to-day, principally from Southwest Virginia and Tennessee," exclaimed a diarist from the Shenandoah Valley in early August. "Trains, crowded, with troops from all directions, met at the junctions, and there had to lay over for hours, or days," observed Thomas DeLeon, a writer who spent much of the war traveling across the South. An army chaplain who had made a 1,500-mile trip from Texas to Virginia reported a slow and tedious journey, with roads "thronged with soldiers from New Orleans to Richmond, and the whole country presented the appearance of a vast camp." Roads and railways were packed with men in arms who used every means of transportation available in the South, making travel in the region even more tiresome than usual. A Louisianan soldier who traveled from New Orleans to Richmond in May was "detained a great deal by misconnections," as "the trains on every road were filled with soldiers." These clogged transportation routes and overcrowded trains were not simply an inconvenience for other travelers; they were an unequivocal sign that life in the South was beginning to change. Soldiers on the road were the harbingers of the impending conflict, a demonstration of "the mighty revolution going on in the country."[5]

Even more important, troops on their way to the front embodied the South's inception as an independent country. The frenzied nature of the secession process and the breakneck speed of events during the spring of 1861 meant that when soldiers started taking the road to Virginia the Confederate nation was only two months old, a nascent political entity whose existence was anything but certain. For a time soldiers going to war were the only proof civilians had that a great upheaval had taken place in remote state capitals. Men on the move were the emblems of the new order; they turned the Southern nation from a political abstraction into a tangible reality and created a living symbol around which the Southern citizenry could unite. Before the Confederate postal service began to operate, before impressment agents began to requisition food, before any other indication of Confederate sovereignty had made its appearance, volunteer units on their way to the front announced that the Age of the Confederacy had arrived and gave civilians on the roadside the opportunity to partake in the revolution.

The celebration of the South's newly minted armed force commenced with ceremonies to honor the troops on their departure. In hundreds of locales across the region, residents gathered to bid an emotional farewell to the soldiers who were about to embark on their journey. They showered them with food, flowers, and gifts and watched in tears as they marched away. "The whole community, far and near, assembled to see us off," remembered a soldier from Liberty County, Texas, who departed in late June. "We had a big dinner, barbecue hog and beef." Emma Simpson, who was enslaved in the neighboring Walker County, was summoned to a "great big dance and supper in Huntsville" to part with local men. "Both white and black were there to tell the soldiers boy good by, cause they knew some would not come back no more."[6] The entire city of New Orleans seemed to congregate to escort the first units leaving for Virginia: "The stores were closed on the day of our departure, the streets were crowded to suffocation, the balconies lined with crying and smiling women." All over the South local bands played "The Girl I Left Behind Me" and other favorite tunes, civic leaders gave patriotic speeches, and ministers led solemn public prayers for the safe return of the men and the success of the cause. "Gloomy indeed it seemed as we were standing in the church yard, when marching before us were the sad looking faces accompanied by the drum and fife," wrote Amanda Edmonds of Fauquier County, Virginia, in her diary. One soldier called the scene of parting "a day that can never be described, never be forgotten."[7]

The highlight of most events was the presentation of a battle flag, sewn by local women and offered to the company by a young lady. "We formed in double ranks in front of Hall's Hotel," remembered W. D. Pritchard of the 1st Texas Infantry, "and received from the hands of Miss Sarah Jane Monroe in an appropriate and touching address a beautiful Confederate flag, the gift of the ladies of Crokett, which was received in a gallant and characteristic speech by Cap. J. H. Wootters." When Joseph Polley's company left Texas in late June it was a Miss Narcissa Brahan, "one of the most lovely types of Southern womanhood," who presented "a beautiful banner made by the fair hands of Cibolo ladies accompanying the presentation with a most elegant and appropriate address delivered with a fervor which but nerved our arms with great strength and inspired our hearts with renewed zeal and patriotism in the good cause."[8]

It was not only Miss Brahan's patriotism that attracted the attention of Joseph Polley, who was twenty-one, single, and on his way to war. She also displayed "strong lips and teeth that seem in their rosiness and whiteness the cleft bud of some lovely prairie flower with the white petals bursting forth between with her small lilly like hands clasping the staff of that banner." Nor was he the only one paying attention to the presence of the ladies. A journalist reporting from Holly Springs, Mississippi, described one colorbearer as "a young lady of fourteen summers, dressed in a military frock, cap, stockinet leggins and gaiter-boots. She looked wicked and created quite a sensation."[9] Indeed it was hard not to notice the women who participated in the ceremonies, as they were so highly and uncommonly visible. Soldiers' departure to the front gave white Southern women an opening into a political world that had been utterly closed to them in a region where the civic networks into which Northern women had made inroads were lacking. The celebrations, which revolved around feminine motifs like flowers, food, and dancing, allowed them to showcase their Confederate patriotism and prove that they too were actively involved in support of the war effort. For the first time their responsibility for sewing flags enabled them to speak in front of entire communities and articulate both their enthusiasm and the expectations they had for the men going to war. In public rites all over the South women took center stage and functioned for a moment as political actors, not merely as symbols of Southern purity and virtue.[10]

For both men and women, the soldiers' departures created an occasion to take their first steps as members of a new political body. As they stood en masse, watching the new flag being raised and praying for the success of their country, those who not so long ago had been loyal and patriotic subjects of the United States of America enacted their transformation into the proud and belligerent citizens of the Confederacy. While legislators and clerks in Richmond were scrambling to put the Confederate government in working order, the process of nation building was gaining momentum in hundreds of communities across the South, where public send-off ceremonies served as highly effective instruments of mobilization and self-persuasion.

The departure rituals were only the beginning of what awaited the troops along the way. From the moment it started, movement to the front instigated a popular carnival that revolved around the volunteers as the physical realization of Southern nationalism. "Within the last two weeks more than 15,000 southern troops have passed through here on their way to the seat of war," wrote John Wilson, an ardent secessionist from Knoxville, in mid-May. "I reached home about 8 o'clock on Thursday morning, and found several thousand persons at the depot, including the ladies and the military. This was intended as an ovation to some four thousand Confederate troops who were momentarily expected on their way to Virginia. . . . I had the pleasure of seeing them arrive, and a nobler, manlier set of fellows have seldom marched to the sound of the fife and drum. They were not like the Northern soldiers, but on the contrary were the very flower of the land." Wilson and other excitable Rebels in east Tennessee embraced the volunteers in the cars as a vivid personification of the Southern nation, projecting their hopes and dreams for martial glory and national sovereignty onto the bodies of the men making the journey east. One regiment that drew particular attention was the 1st Kentucky, commanded by Colonel Blanton Duncan. "They numbered eight hundred and were the finest looking men that have yet made their appearance. They were mostly six feet high—weighing on an average about 170 pounds and were dressed in blue hunting shirts. They will give a good account of themselves in battle."[11]

During the first months of the Civil War, similar scenes took place in numerous locations along the roads leading to the front. Soldiers on the move made for an enthralling spectacle, drawing crowds of admiring men and women and providing a riveting image of Confederate independence and military might. "At every town and station citizens and ladies were waving their handkerchiefs and hurrahing for Jeff Davis and the Southern Confederacy," wrote Sam Watkins, who journeyed from Nashville in July. "It was one magnificent festival from one end of the line to the other. . . . At Chattanooga, Knoxville, Bristol, Farmville, Lynchburg, everywhere, the same demonstrations of joy and welcome greeted us." A similar reception was in store for Thomas Gorree, en route with his Texas unit in June: "At every depot the platform was crowded with men, women & children & Negroes to welcome the troops. Every lady almost had a bouquet for a soldier. I received several. In the country, as we passed houses, the men would hurra, and wave their hats, the Ladies their handkerchiefs, and the children their flags."[12]

Milton Barrett traveled 600 miles, from Georgia to Richmond, during the first days of August and enjoyed every minute. "We had a fine time of hit," he wrote to his siblings back home. "We was cherd all a long the way by croud of sitecens. a flag was a waven over most ever house and every winder crouded with ladys and the sides of the road linde with them throwing appels and bouquets of flowes in the cars. the best and warmest and best fealing was shound to us all the way." "Had there ever existed any doubts in the country as to the feelings of the people of the South before this in regard to Secession, it was entirely dispelled by the enthusiastic cheers and good will of the people along the road," wrote in hindsight another South Carolina soldier, whose brigade was one of the very first to arrive in Virginia. "The conduct of the men and women through South Carolina, North Carolina, and Virginia, showed one long and continued ovation along the lines of travel, looking like a general holiday. As the cars sped along through the fields, the little hamlets and towns, people of every kind, size, and complexion rushed to the railroad and gave us welcome and Godspeed. Hats went into the air as we passed, handkerchiefs fluttered, flags waved in the gentle summer breeze from almost every housestop."[13]

Traveling the same route in June, Mary Chesnut noticed, "Every woman from every window of every house we passed waved a handkerchief, if she had one. This fluttering of white flags from every side never ceased, from Camden to Richmond." Farther west, where soldiers often traveled by boat as they rushed to the front, civilians stood on the shores of the waterways to get a glimpse of the Confederacy's new army. "The people along the banks of the river continue to cheer us vociferously," wrote Louisianan David Pierson to his brother as he was sailing down the Arkansas River. "At Pine Bluff a few minutes ago the banks were lined for a half a mile with human beings shouting and waving flags & handkerchiefs."[14] The troops did their best to contribute to the festive atmosphere by hollering at the spectators as they went along. Volunteers, complained an officer who traveled with one company from Georgia to Virginia, had "the insane idea . . . that it was the patriotic duty of each and every one to hurrah and yell on passing through any settlement." On the Arkansas River, David Pierson's travel mates made "the woods and banks fairly roar with the shouts of the 3rd Regiment for Jeff

Davis & the South": "I never saw so much excitement and so much enthusiasm before."[15]

Just as in the ceremonies back home, women continued to figure prominently among the crowds. Mary Chesnut described "parties of girls" who "came to every station simply to look at the troops passing," and Myra Inman, the teenage daughter of a slaveholding family in east Tennessee, recorded in her diary regular outings to watch the troops passing by. Lizzie Hardin, a twenty-two-year-old Confederate from Kentucky, was in Abingdon, Virginia, when troops began streaming to the front. For a few days she "and the whole town" waited in vain at the train station for soldiers to come through, until she was tempted to believe "this whole ado about Southern soldiers a myth."

> Until one morning we were awakened by tremendous shouts for "Old Virginia" and answering ones for the "Kentucky boys." We caught only a glimpse of the passing cars but that was wonderful to us; they were ladened with troops. . . . The next morning while I was eating my breakfast a gentleman hurried in to say that two or three heavy trains of soldiers would be at the depot directly. Several of us dashed off at full speed and out of breath arrived at the depot a few minutes before the cars. It was an Alabama regiment. I have rarely seen a handsomer or more elegant looking body of men, and very rarely a gayer set.[16]

For Lizzie Hardin and countless other Southerners who spent their days waiting on the roadsides, the movement of troops had the air of a carnival, a welcome disruption to the routines of country life, and for some young women, an even more welcome display of attention from men. Yet at a time of political revolution these encounters had a deeper effect. The sights and sounds of mobilization created a powerful emotional experience that infused meaning into the notion of an independent South. The men going to war were not mere travelers passing by; they were the Confederacy in the flesh, and their arrival instilled in the population a triumphant mood and a sense of national pride.

Wherever they stopped to rest or switch trains, soldiers were treated to princely receptions in which the locals lavished them with food, drink, and female attention. "In those places where a stop was permitted, long tables were spread in some neighboring grove or park, bending under the weight of soldiers' appetite," wrote a South Carolinian. "The purest and best of the women mingled freely with the troops, and by every device known to the fair sex showed their sympathy and encouragement in the cause we espoused." A Louisianan who left New Orleans in late May remembered, "At every depot there would be gathered the most beautiful ladies of the place, who would enthusiastically stream out and welcome us." Women offered "flowers, cold chicken, gloves, aprons, and knic-nacs of every sort. Sometimes the reception would be at a regularly laid table, as it was in Huntsville—sometimes in a ball room, as at Iuka Springs, and then after fifteen minutes of waltzing of fast city youth and bashful girls . . . the cars would again move on." Deep in the rural South, where soldiers walked long distances before boarding a train or a steamboat, civilians invited the weary men to their homes, hosted them for the night, "and gave them all the nice fixings you can think of." Showing kindness and hospitality to men en route to battle allowed those who stayed at home to participate in the war effort when it was still a glamorous en-deavor that required few real sacrifices. Welcoming the traveling soldiers, making them food, throwing them parties, and putting them up introduced Southerners to their new role as a citizenry at war. In the time before battle-field news and food shortages, they embraced it with joy.[17]

Governments facing internal or external threats often stage elaborate mass liturgies to enhance allegiance to the state and to convey an image of martial strength. Whether it be the monarchies of early modern Europe, Mussolini's Italy, or Israel after the Six-Day War, autocracies and democracies alike have utilized the powerful impact of military parades, performative drilling, and aerial demonstrations as tools in managing both domestic policies and for-eign relations. But in the Confederate States of America the central govern-ment was barely in existence and had neither the means nor the intention to initiate and control the public rites that took place in the early months of the war. The ceremonies were the independent creations of citizens who sought to celebrate the founding of the new nation and to further their own trans-figuration from Americans into Confederates. In the absence of visible state institutions to rally around, soldiers on the move were the only ready repre-sentation of national authority that could serve as the linchpin for these com-munal events.[18]

The soldiers' ability to mobilize the population in support of the Confed-eracy was especially crucial in the border states, where the citizenry was divided and public opinion open to Northern persuasion. East Tennessee was a particularly vexing problem; the region had voted against secession by a large margin and remained staunchly Unionist even after the state had joined the Confederacy. While some soldiers who traveled through this troubled region encountered its passionate secessionist minority, others received a decidedly cold welcome from the bulk of east Tennessee's hostile populace. Regardless, Confederate officials insisted that the movement of Southern soldiers could help ease the tension between local civilians and the Confederate government. John B. Floyd, the commanding officer in western Virginia, suggested to his superiors in July 1861 that the army establish a large depot for Southern troops in east Tennessee. Apart from the practical considerations, Floyd argued, the plan was worthwhile: "The march of our people through the quarter of the State . . . will have, I have no doubt, a very salutary influence. I think Confederate bonds may be made to purchase that will be wanted for the service after the people become a little familiar with them."[19]

The mobilization of the Southern army thus evolved from a logistical enterprise into an important political process, whose consequences reached far beyond the transportation of troops from one point to another. Soldiers on the move made a crucial contribution to cutting the emotional cords that tied white Southerners to the United States and to creating an atmosphere of devotion to the Confederate States of America. Men en route to war, wearing uniforms and carrying guns, confirmed that the Southern nation was in fact a viable entity with an armed force defending it. In the volatile climate of the postsecession South, they provided civilians with a dynamic and rousing image to identify with and galvanized them for the struggle ahead. Their departures and arrivals served as focal points for elaborate civic rituals in which communities experienced and conveyed their new identities as Confederate polities, and in which a sentiment of Southern nationalism could grow and cohere. Soldiers going northward brought the Confederacy to life, and the South, in the early months of the war, rallied around them.

The irony underlying this mass adulation of Southern volunteers in 1861 was that the men on the road had not fought in a single battle, nor had they undergone any sustained military training. While civilians were enamored with their uniforms and martial bearing, the soldiers' journey had very little to do with organized military movement. The volunteers of 1861 elected their own officers, brought their own weapons, and wore homemade uniforms sewn by their sisters and wives. Often the government had no direct involvement in their journey to the front, and the soldiers paid for their own train fare or relied on the generosity of other citizens who furnished money, wagons, and animals to units on their way to war. This was a grassroots, do-it-yourself army, which was still very much in the making as it moved to the front.[20]

Frequently, this meant that military units materialized in motion, as men joined their ranks when units passed by. Malachia Reeves remembered arriving in the town of Alto, Texas: "There was a fragment of a company made up for service and they joined us; at Sabinetown another little company joined our ranks, and now we had over one hundred men."[21] Henry Smith, a Texas slave who was forced to join his master when he left for war, remembered getting to the town of Marlin, where "de boys f'om eroun' dar jined up wid 'em."[22] In Green County, east Tennessee, a professor at Tusculum College doubted whether he would have any students left once the local units began their march toward the seat of war. "Two volunteer companies will pass along by here soon and I wouldn't be surprised if the last one of the students don't leave with them."[23]

In Virginia, Robert E. Lee counted on the power of motion to mobilize both bodies and minds as he scrambled to prepare for the Union army's imminent invasion of the state's western region. In May 1861 he wrote a subordinate, "Several companies have been directed to go with the arms from Staunton to Beverly, and to gather strength as they passed along. It is hoped that a considerable force has, by this means, been gathered together."[24] Two months later John B. Floyd, still struggling to muster a sufficient force to defend the Confederacy's vulnerable heartland, detailed an officer from his staff to travel through the counties west of the New River and "raise any and all such men as will consent to march against the enemy now in the Kanawha Valley."[25] Later in the war the Confederate government would turn to conscription and employ thousands of people in a concentrated and systematic effort to enlist virtually every able-bodied man in the service, but in those first few months the nation's emerging army consisted of a host of local units who were expected to round up men as they moved along.

The haphazard nature of mobilization did not result only from the tenuousness of the Confederate state, but also from the disposition of the troops.

Jesse Reid of South Carolina remembered the trip from Columbia to Lees-burg, Virginia, as beating anything he "ever saw for non-discipline and in subordination in soldiers. It seems that every man in the regiment mistook himself for Commander-in-Chief."[26] Texan soldiers, who took the long journey from one end of the Confederacy to the other, left and rejoined their companies at will and stopped to spend time with friends and family who lived along the way. "Who was in command of the Regiment during the time I cannot say," wrote Joseph Polley in hindsight. "The men did pretty much as they pleased visiting the City or country as they preferred getting drunk as often as they chose." Men on the move noted in their diaries such activities as "splurging around Houston until 5 o'clock in the evening," "spending the time until the following day very pleasantly in the agreeable society of some young ladies," or leaving ahead of the main body of the com-pany so "that we might avoid the disagreeableness of traveling with a large company, & thereby enable us to get an egg, a chicken, or pint of milk." Rid-ing on trains through the lush landscape of the Deep South, soldiers "spent all deir time shootin' alligaytors," recalled the ex-slave Henry Smith. "Say dey had ter keep in practice." In Kingsville, South Carolina, Thomas DeLeon spent a night in the company of Georgia troops headed to Richmond. The men entertained themselves by "shooting at a mark, going through squad drill, drinking bad liquor by the canteen and swearing in a way that would have made the 'Army of Flanders' sick with envy."[27]

The record for riotous behavior on the road to Virginia belonged to the New Orleans Zouaves, who left a lasting impression wherever they went. The enlistees, many of whom were recruited from the city's jails, were clad in strikingly colorful uniforms and strange-looking hats. John Henry Cowin, an Alabama soldier who met the Zouaves before they left for Virginia, de-scribed them as a "hard looking set": "Several of them have already been shot by their officers; several have been killed in fights among themselves."[28] The Zouaves began their journey by hijacking their train and leaving the of-ficers' car stuck on the rails. Arriving in Montgomery, Alabama, they em-barked on an orgy of looting, drinking, and destroying civilian property. After having been forced to board the train to Richmond, they went wild in the cars, some riding on the roofs and others between coaches. In the capital the same rampant scenes repeated themselves until officers were finally able to restrain them.[29] By September Louisianans had attained the kind of notoriety that induced civilians to stop them from coming into their homes. "We didn't dare ask for hospitality at a private home as the Louisiana soldiers have gained such a reputation for pilfering and general loutishness that as soon as anyone sees them coming they bolt the doors and windows," wrote the chaplain of a Louisiana regiment. "Usually any affiliation at all with the Louisiana boys is enough to assure one a cold welcome no matter where he shows his face."[30]

The New Orleans Zouaves were a special case, but their style of behavior was not unheard of among other units. The volunteers began their military careers after arriving in Richmond and did not get their first real taste of army life until they participated in battle or endured the rigors of a campaign. For the time being, these companies were mostly groups of young men going on an adventure. And yet in the early days of the sectional conflict this seemed to have mattered very little. As long as the men en route to war performed their role as soldiers, the Confederate citizenry was eager to idolize them as the personification of the South's national ascent. At a moment of grave uncertainty, men and women across the South were willing to forgive transgressions of all kinds as long as the soldiers provided that illusion of military might that made war seem less daunting. In the process of founding a new nation and preparing it for the struggle ahead, the symbolic value of men in uniform matched their importance as actual combatants.

The fresh recruits clearly understood the part they were playing and the expectations placed upon them by the citizenry. Despite the drunkenness and rowdiness that characterized many of the journeys they took, men on the road consciously tried to act out their role as soldiers. Looking back after many years at the first, innocent days of war, one Texan volunteer commented that the soldiers "were continually playing pranks on each other, and on the people who lived on the road along which they traveled; they felt that they were soldiers, and the people with whom they came in contact regarded them as such." Another veteran recalled a young man in his company by the name of Ras Cartwright, who was "a splendid specimen of physical manhood, six feet six inches tall, perfectly erect, and of dignified appearance": "When we stopped at some of the depots, the boys would put the captain's sword on Ras and march around, calling him captain and enjoy the people's admiration of the company's first captain." The fact that Cartwright was not actually an officer was of no significance; what mattered was that he looked like one and that he pleased civilians hungry for images of Southern military prowess.[31]

Far from serving as a passive audience, the men and women who met the soldiers on the road also made a deliberate effort to construct the encounters as demonstrations of Southern military power. Locales that received word of soldiers' arrival often made sure that the neighborhood militia or home guard unit would be present to meet the troops and enhance the martial mood of the event. "In any of the places where volunteer companies existed these turned out to salute us, and to announce that they would be ready to follow us in a few days," remembered a soldier who traveled by steamer from Baton Rouge early in the war. When the Texas Marshall Guards arrived in Shreveport, Louisiana, they "were received by the Shreveport Sentinels, and the three together marched through several of the principal streets, then back to the wharf where several patriotic speeches were made." In Abingdon, Virginia, described Lizzie Hardin, "everyone hurried to the depot" one evening to meet the six o'clock train, which was rumored to be carrying soldiers, "the military being paraded to give a more imposing appearance to the welcome." Movement of men generated complex performances in which the fresh recruits took the role of war heroes while Southern communities masqueraded as belligerent poleis. As men and women, soldiers and civilians, all played their parts in the drama of mobilization, a military ethos began to take shape. In the minds of the thousands who participated in these rites, the inauguration of the Confederacy's fighting force took place not on the battlefield, but on the road.[32]

The calculated attempts to fashion the Confederacy as a society at war were part of a broader phenomenon, defined by the historian Drew Gilpin Faust as a "widespread and self-conscious effort to create an ideology of Confederate nationalism" that pervaded the South during the first months of the nation's life. Both printed media and oral culture were critical to this process of Southern nation building, as newspaper offices, churches, and political meetings became the venues where a new national identity was manufactured. But there was more than just words, spoken or read, involved in this effort. Confederate bodies and their visual impact were equally important. The far-flung train stations and rural crossroads where civilians and soldiers met, danced, and ate became essential sites for the realization of the South as an independent country and for the emergence of a martial spirit that would enable the Confederacy to fight for its existence. The images and rituals produced by these encounters merged with speeches, songs, pamphlets, and other forms of cultural transmission to generate a sense of unity and purpose without which Southerners could not embark on a war against the United States. By incorporating entire communities and bringing a taste of military fanfare to every county in the South, the movement of men to the front lines in 1861 proved indispensable to the project of Confederate nationhood.[33]

Men embarked for war in 1861 from locales as varied and far apart as the Carolina lowlands, the Texas frontier, and the Shenandoah Valley. Among them were slaveholders and nonslaveholders, rich and poor, men who had supported secession for years and those who remained loyal to the Union until the outbreak of hostilities at Fort Sumter. The troops making their way northward represented the different Souths that constituted the Confederate States of America, the fragmented and often incompatible components of a new national entity that spread across nearly one million square miles and incorporated eleven states, some of which had little in common besides the legality of slavery in their territory. Yet while these men departed from every corner of the South and traveled along any number of different routes, their destination, in most cases, was one and the same: Virginia.

Indeed from the moment open hostilities between North and South broke out, there was never any doubt that the military conflict would take place largely on the soil of the Old Dominion. The state's geographic location made it a natural battleground, and the decision to move the Confederate capital to Richmond assured that the Mother of Presidents would be the Union army's first target. Though the government also sent soldiers to Florida, the Carolina seaboard, and the western theater, the great majority of troops in the early months of the war were making their way to the Confederacy's northern front, where battles were expected imminently. In 1861 Virginia was the single most important locus of war in the South, the ultimate prize for tens of thousands of men spoiling for a fight.

The emergence of the Old Dominion as the focal point of the Confederate States of America was in some ways an unlikely development in the annals of the antebellum South. Virginia was the birthplace of American slavery and of the South itself, but over time the state had lost much of its vitality, and by the mid-nineteenth century it had retreated to the background of Southern politics as the more aggressive slave states took the lead in trying to ensure the fate of the peculiar institution and what they termed Southern rights. On the eve of the Civil War the geopolitical center of the section was firmly located in the Deep South. The men who were traversing the region to defend Virginia from enemy invasion were in fact heading toward a border state that until the outbreak of war had enjoyed close connections with Ohio and Pennsylvania and was torn between conflicting loyalties and interests. There was no question that the Old Dominion owned Dixie's past, but the future of the region belonged to the vast territories of the southwestern frontier. Between them lay a century of western expansion, a demographic, political, and economic process of epic proportion that had shaped the antebellum South and the individual lives of its inhabitants.

Everywhere in nineteenth-century America, western migration was a defining feature of life. In the period between the American Revolution and the sectional conflict, more than half of the population moved across state lines, making it an era of unmatched mobility in the nation's history.[34] Though in the popular imagination this phenomenon is usually associated with Northerners migrating to the Midwest, it was equally pervasive below the Mason-Dixon Line; the oldest Southern states lost four times as many people to the western territories as did New England during the great migration of the antebellum era. A total of 700,000 white men and women left Virginia before the Civil War, a third of the people born in the state; the census of 1850 found more than 388,000 native Virginians living in other states, compared with its own population of 949,000. South Carolina sent off almost half of the white people born there after 1800, and Georgia lost a quarter of its free population. Thousands more relocated from the eastern counties of the state to its southwestern corner.[35]

The mobilization of the Confederate army thus meant that for the first time in generations Southern men were heading back to Virginia. Since the mid-eighteenth century, men and women below the Mason-Dixon Line had traveled south and west. With the founding of an independent Southern nation and the necessity of raising an army to defend its northern front, human mobility reversed its course and began to flow in the opposite direction. Soldiers traveling to Virginia from Waco, Texas, Jackson, Mississippi, or Tuscaloosa, Alabama, were taking a journey not only through space, but also through time. Their motion reshaped the spatial and temporal realities that had determined the course of Southern history during the century that preceded the outbreak of civil war.

White Southerners began leaving the Atlantic Seaboard in the late eighteenth century and advanced in a steady flow through the territory that had been opened up by the Louisiana Purchase and the deportation of Native Americans to the Trans-Mississippi West. In the early nineteenth century Kentucky and Georgia absorbed multitudes of migrants, but by the end of the antebellum era these areas had already become exporters of population for more distant destinations. Settlement moved along an east-west axis, with Virginians settling Kentucky, North Carolinians going to Tennessee, and South Carolinians and Georgians striking out for Alabama, Mississippi, and Louisiana. On the eve of the war Southerners were conquering the frontiers of Texas, Arkansas, and central Florida and eyeing the territories of the far west.[36]

Land in the Deep South and Southwest was fertile, abundant, and relatively cheap. Most important, it did not easily cover with frost. This was a critical factor, since two hundred days of frost-free soil were a preliminary condition for growing the crop that made the South not just a section, but a kingdom. While Americans on both sides of the Mason-Dixon Line shared an unbridled enthusiasm for the territories out west, in the South migration was inextricably linked to cotton and to the insatiable hunger the Industrial Revolution generated for the crop. Starting in the 1790s, Southern farmers began growing cotton for international markets, particularly for British textile manufacturers, who preferred the American-grown seed to any other for the mounds of calicoes and muslins they produced in their plants.[37] With the introduction of the cotton gin in the 1790s, which mechanically separated the fiber from the seed, the last obstacle to mass-scale cultivation of cotton was cleared. Tobacco and indigo, the region's traditional staple crops, were quickly abandoned as Southerners plunged into the business of cotton with astounding ferocity; between 1790 and 1800 alone South Carolina's annual cotton exports rose from less than ten thousand pounds to some six million. In the following decades cotton prices fluctuated widely according to trends in the global market, but the demand for the seed continued to expand and to create immense prosperity across the region.[38]

As the attraction of growing cotton increased, so did the compulsion to migrate. The two fed on each other and pushed an ever-increasing number of people to leave the Southeast, where the soil was settled, infertile, or depleted after centuries of cultivation. The new territories, combined with the lure of cotton, provided a ready solution for a rural society that sought to take advantage of the profitability of staple crop agriculture. Going west, migrants brought with them the evolving political economy of cotton and used every suitable acre of land to plant it. Population growth in the Deep South went hand in hand with a rise in the crop's production: in 1819–1829 Alabama, Mississippi, and Louisiana produced roughly 600,000 bales of cotton; by 1859–1860 their output had reached almost three million bales annually. During the same period the population of the three states rose from 400,000 to 2.5 million. In Texas the white population more than quadrupled between 1840 and 1860, and the number of slaveholders grew by 900 percent. This was the cotton revolution at its peak.[39]

Migration fever gripped white Southerners of all kinds, from landless farmers to the wealthiest slaveholders, from those whose families had lived on the same plantation for generations to those who had only recently settled a new plot. Predictably, the poor were the most mobile sector in Southern society, having nothing to lose by moving and being always on the lookout for an opportunity to acquire a vacant patch of land.[40] But in the cotton-crazy antebellum South, even well-to-do men were tempted by the possibility of procuring a larger landholding and increasing their yield. Migration became a popular path to upward mobility among Southern planters, who found in the movement west a way to assert their independence but also to comply with social norms that stressed material success above all other considerations. It was a particularly prevalent trend among young men of the Southern elite, whose opportunities in the east were limited by a shortage of prime agricultural land and by the prospect of sharing their father's inheritance with several siblings. Thousands chose to leave their comfortable lives and move to the unsettled territories lying south and west.[41]

Throughout the Colonial and early national period the expansionist ambitions of Southern men faced fierce military and legal resistance from Native Americans, whose ancestors had inhabited the lands of the Deep South for thousands of years. Yet by 1830 most southern Indians could no longer withstand the combined pressures of individual migrants, land-hungry state governments, and the presidency of Andrew Jackson. Following the passage of the Indian Removal Act, the Federal army forcibly evicted roughly 46,000 Choctaws, Chickasaws, Creeks, Seminoles, and Cherokees, who often left their homes only when put in chains or held at bayonet point.[42]

Southern white men also encountered intense opposition inside their homes. Wives and daughters routinely resisted the decision to move west, which forced them to give up comfortable lives in a familiar environment. Relocation meant an exhausting journey, exposure to deadly diseases, and a great amount of hard work building a home from scratch. Moreover in the homosocial world of the nineteenth century, women's closest companions were female relatives and neighbors. Migration tore them away from this support network and condemned them to long periods of isolation in the wilderness. Nevertheless even the most vehement objections usually had little effect on the family's patriarch as he planned the move that would enable him to buy more land and grow more of the white gold. Even among the most reluctant women, the great majority picked up and moved.[43]

Yet in the antebellum South the goal of getting rich by making cotton was often only a means toward an even larger end: the ownership of slaves. Indeed the institution of slavery shaped western migration in the same way that it shaped every other aspect of Southern life. Owning slaves was the most important marker of success in the Old South, and men of the planter class were perennially preoccupied with increasing the size and quality of their human property. The new territories of the Deep South and Southwest held the promise of unlimited prosperity, where slaveholders and their sons could realize the fantasies that the Southeast no longer seemed to offer. The same drive for slave ownership also fueled the migratory inclinations of small slaveholders who aspired to increase their fortunes and join the ranks of the planter class, and of nonslaveholding yeomen, for whom fresh land was the only hope for accumulating enough cash to buy slaves and achieve the coveted status of master. In its Southern version, movement to the frontier was propelled by both the ideology and the praxis of the slave society, in which ownership of human property defined a white man's identity and social status. Going west, Southern farmers were looking not only for better economic prospects, but also for ways to satisfy their desire for the unfettered power that is the essence of slaveholding.[44]

Trapped in the vortex of Southern expansionism were millions of African Americans, whose bodies and souls paid the price for the abundance of open land and the global popularity of the region's staple crops. The cotton revolution created a gargantuan demand for field labor that could no longer be answered by importing more slaves from Africa, since the Atlantic slave trade had closed in 1808. Slaves in the Southeast, along with those who were still enslaved in the North, remained the only available workforce to fill the needs of cotton growers. As a result, between 1800 and 1860 one million enslaved men and women were forcibly removed from their homes in the older slave states and transported to the new territories of the Deep South and Southwest.[45] The number of enslaved migrants increased with time, starting with some 40,000 to 50,000 in the 1790s, growing to 150,000 by the 1820s, and reaching highs of over 250,000 slaves per decade during the 1830s and 1850s, when the economy was booming and demand for workers in the cotton fields peaked.[46] Roughly 70 percent of the slaves who moved were sold to masters in the Deep South through the internal slave trade, while the rest migrated with their owners.[47]

The mass removal of slaves from east to west developed into nothing less than a second Middle Passage, a vast, transformative, and tragic historical phenomenon that touched on the life of every black Southerner. It tore apart marriages, families, and communities with a brutal finality that for all practical purposes was the equivalent of death. Parents and children, husbands and wives, kith and kin had no hope of ever seeing each other again once separated by the slave trade. In the Upper South, where one in three slave marriages was broken by sale and one in three slave children was taken away from his or her parents, it cast a permanent shadow over black society. No slave was protected from the threat of sale to the Deep South, and few slaves lived without dreading it. In many ways it was the central experience of African Americans in the antebellum period.

Slave coffles on their way to the Deep South were a common spectacle on the roads of the region, especially in the exporting states. Decades after they were freed, former slaves remembered the heartbreaking sight of black men and women being marched off to a new land of slavery. Lorenzo Ivy, who was enslaved in Virginia, told of "droves of Negroes brought in . . . on foot goin' Souf to be sol": "Over de hills dey come in lines reachin' as far as you kin see. Dey walk in double lines chained tergether in twos. Dey walk 'em heah to de railroad an' ship 'em Souf like cattle." Robert Williams recalled, "[I] done see groups of slaves, women, men and children walking down the road . . . all on dey way to de cotton country. Some of dem would hardly have on any clo'es. We lived near de road and dese groups of slaves would come ve'y often when cotton season was in. De white folks would come up from cotton country and buy slaves and carry them back in droves. . . . Dey was just like cattle in a heard."[48]

The slave traders who led the coffles down south were carrying with them not just individuals, but the institution of slavery itself. In 1790, 45 percent of the region's black population lived in Virginia and the state was the geographic center of human bondage in America. On the eve of the Civil War, that rate had dropped to 12 percent and the center of the slave society had moved to western Georgia. While Alabama, Mississippi, Louisiana, and Texas saw their slave populations multiply every few years, the overall number of bondspeople in Virginia increased by a mere 66,000 between 1820 and 1860.[49] The Old Dominion, where American slavery had been born, was no longer the quintessential slave state. Not only was the percentage of slaves within its general population falling consistently as more and more of the enslaved were being sold south, but even those who stayed put were employed in new forms of slavery that sharply diverged from the traditional plantation model. In the last decade before the war, while Lower South farmers were fixated on cotton, rice, and sugar, Virginians were diversifying their agricultural pursuits, hiring out an increasing number of slaves, and indenturing others in the state's burgeoning towns. The institution of slavery was not dying in Virginia, but it was certainly changing as the state moved away from total reliance on staple crop agriculture and into a more diverse and modernizing economy.[50]

The shift in the geographical composition of slavery carried over into Southern politics and had a decisive influence on the course of events that led to the founding of an independent nation below the Mason-Dixon Line. During the months of decision there was a direct correlation between the speed at which Southern states seceded and the predominance of slavery in their territory. The states of the Lower South, in which 47 percent of the population consisted of slaves, left the Union first and with fewer hesitations, while the Upper South, where the enslaved made up only 24 percent of the populace, lingered until Lincoln's call for volunteers to suppress the rebellion.[51] The dynamics of secession threw into sharp relief the transformation that migration, both voluntary and forced, had brought to the region. After decades of mass movement from east to west and from north to south, the political and economic center of the region was now firmly located in the cotton kingdom. The Confederate States of America was the creation of men from the Deep South, whose commitment to slavery and its territorial expansion reflected first and foremost the interests of planters from the cotton states. They founded the nation without bothering to wait for Virginia, North Carolina, and Tennessee to secede from the Union and placed at its forefront men of their own background: a Mississippian, Jefferson Davis, as president of the Confederacy, and Alexander Stephens from Georgia as vice president. In many ways the location of the Confederacy's first capital in Montgomery, Alabama, was more appropriate to the nature and goals of the enterprise than Richmond, an Upper South city that until the outbreak of war was a bastion of political moderation and whose slave market served as a conduit for emptying the region of its black population.[52]

Hence the journey to Virginia drew the volunteers away from the heartland of secession and slavery and into parts of the section that some of them would have barely recognized as Southern. Their movement embodied nothing less than a reconfiguration of Southern space. For nearly two hundred years the section had been expanding by leaps and bounds, reaching farther and farther into the south and west, with no limit in sight. The exigencies of war halted the drive for expansion and instigated a process of concentration. During the first months of the conflict the Confederacy united around Virginia, making its defense against the Yankee invader a common cause and a test for the new nation's resilience. Almost overnight the Old Dominion ceased to be the declining periphery of the cotton kingdom and regained some of its old glory. The white South's mission turned from conquest of the west to a crusade to save the east.

On the road, remembered an army chaplain, the Old Dominion was the "great Mecca" of the soldiers' hopes, and the journey an "onward pilgrimage." All over Dixie, men en route to war were singing tunes like the one Lizzie Hardin heard from a Kentucky unit she escorted to the train station: "No higher honor would I crave / Than to fill a Southern soldier's grave / Who dies for old Virginia." The strong emotional attachment to the cradle of Southern civilization and the deep ties between Virginia and the states spawned by its out-migration were both evident in the response of another

Kentucky unit, who was ordered back to its home state early in the war. "The boys are elated at the prospect of meeting the Yankees upon their own native soil," reported an officer, "but they regret leaving Virginia before having one fight, in order to show the old mother state, that the sons of her sons have not degenerated from the old stock."[53]

Virginia had always been the birthplace of the region, the Mother of Presidents, home to the South's finest families and oldest plantations, a synonym for gentility, refinement, and tradition, an emblem of revolutionary courage and political greatness. Now it had also become the symbol of Confederate independence and of the South's determination to defend its borders from Union invasion. The spatial and temporal dimensions of human mobility merged as soldiers were returning to the origins of the South to fight the battle for the section's destiny. Their movement to the front lines formed a human bridge between the old Atlantic Seaboard and the southwestern frontier, between the past and the future, between the genesis of the Southern way of life and its prospective growth across the continent.

The significance of soldiers' movement from the Deep South back to Virginia was evident to contemporaries, who paid special attention to those men whose travels symbolized the bond between the South's disparate regions. Soldiers from Texas had a particular appeal to begin with, emerging as they did out of a wild and distant frontier where the memory of the Mexican-American War was still fresh and where armed conflict with Native Americans was ongoing. "We were a perfect curiosity on the road," remarked one of the soldiers in a letter home. "The people would come from every direction to see the boys from Texas they had great ideas of the Texans." "Numbers of ladies and gentlemen," reported another soldier, visited the Texans' camp in Richmond and "were astonished at being by the loud Indian War-whoops" the western boys produced.[54] Yet the attraction of Texans did not lie merely in their exoticism or raw masculinity. The very distance they traveled was meaningful. Nicholas Pomeroy, a Texan soldier who had traversed 1,500 miles to get to the capital, remembered fondly how Richmond newspapers fawned over the arrivals from the South's remotest corner, lauding "the men who came all the way from Texas and waded through miles of water in Louisiana etc. to drive out the hateful Yankees from the Sacred soil of old Virginia." Texas and Virginia stood on the opposite ends of the Confederacy's territory and on the two extremities of the South's historical time line. Texans who marched to Virginia personified the unity of the region across time and space and the ideal of an everlasting Southern civilization. Their month-long journeys, which retraced the steps of migrants who had traveled the westward route for generations, brought Southern history full circle. Movement west had created the slave South; now movement east would create an army to defend the nation-state that was founded to secure its future.[55]

Within weeks of the firing at Fort Sumter, Richmond and its surroundings had become a giant military camp where soldiers from every corner of the Confederacy drilled and waited to be sent to the front lines. By late April the governor of Virginia was already warning that the stream of men arriving in the capital independently was growing unmanageable: "Volunteers are simultaneously tendering their services, in person, from all parts of the State, without waiting for orders, as they were required to do by a former proclamation, and are repairing to Richmond, without previous notice, at great expense to the Commonwealth, and before suitable provision has been made for their accommodations and before the services are required."[56] Yet Richmond was about to become much more frenzied as soon as volunteers from other states began pouring in. "Military men are as thick in Richmond as pine trees are in North Carolina," wrote a Georgian to his wife in September. Soldiers were turning up faster than the government could accommodate them, filling the streets, hotels, and private residences. "There is 50,000 troops stationed at Richmond now, and are pouring in by the thousands," wrote an Alabaman who reached the capital in June. The sounds of drum and fife echoed through the city, announcing the arrival of fresh troops. "Nine out of every ten men you see is dressed in military suit," reported the Texan Thomas Gorree. "This is a perfect military camp. Thousands of troops are encamped here. Many are quartered in the different churches, and there are from 2 to 500 arriving daily." The transformation of the city from a quiet Southern town into a bustling wartime capital made a powerful impression on everyone who witnessed it. "Thousands of troops was sent to Richmond from all parts of the South," remembered John M. Washington, a former slave who was hired out in the capital when the war broke out. "So many troops of all discription was landed there that it appeared to be an impossibility, to us, colored people, that they could ever be conquered."[57]

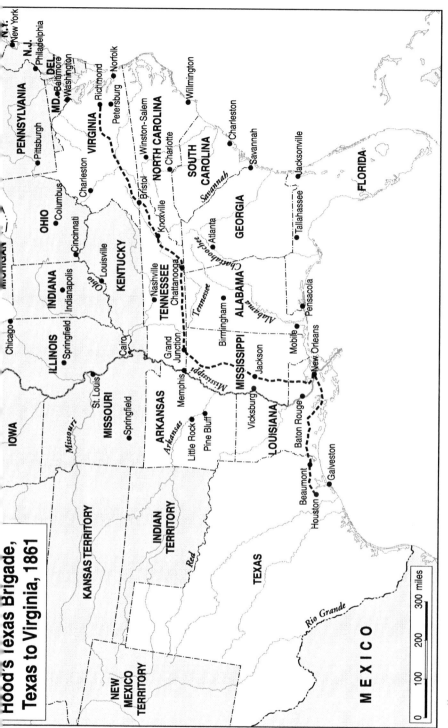

Hood's Texas Brigade,
Texas to Virginia, 1861

Hood's Texas Brigade, Texas to Virginia, 1861

The new arrivals turned the city into a diverse hub where the full spectrum of Southern dialect, dress, and deportment was on vivid display. "Varied, indeed, were the forms one met on every street and road about Richmond," wrote Thomas DeLeon.

> Here the long-haired Texan, sitting on his horse like a centaur. With high-peaked saddle and jingling spurs, dashed by—a pictured *guacho.* There the western mountaineer, with bearskin shirt, fringed leggings, and the long, deadly rifle, carried one back to the days of Boone and the "dark and bloody ground." The dirty gray and tarnished silver of the muddy-complexioned Carolinian; the dingy butternut of the lank, muscular Georgian, with its green trimming and full skirts; and the Alabamians from the coast, nearly all in blue of a cleaner hue and neater cut, while the Louisiana troops were, as a general thing, better equipped and more regularly uniformed than any others in the motley throng.[58]

The fascination ran both ways. Soldiers who arrived in Richmond for the first time were struck by the city's size and grandeur, as well as by its cosmopolitan feel. "This is a beautiful city, by far the most handsome that I have yet seen," wrote a Texan in September 1861. "It is splendidly layed of streets paved, and many superb buildings," reported a North Carolinian to his wife in May. Almost a year later a new arrival from Spotsylvania County, Virginia, was amazed by what had become by then a Southern metropolis, so unlike the farm life he had just left: "There is the greatest combination of people here I ever saw some of all nations Language and tongue I have been steady walking all day and have not seen one fourth of the citty."[59]

Richmondites rejoiced at these visitors from near and far and at their manifest devotion to the defense of Virginia. The *Richmond Enquirer* promised that the "generous brothers of the cotton states," en route to the Old Dominion, "do not intend to lay aside their arms as long as the foot of a sniveling Yankee presses the soil of the South." "The boys say, as they leave, Old Virginia shall be defended, or our bones will bleach on her battlefields." In those early days of war the manpower shortages that would later hinder the Confederate war effort were still far in the future; the stream of men traveling to Virginia seemed so overwhelming that the Richmond press was concerned by the possibility that not all Southern states would get a chance to participate in the noble task of defending the region's mother state. "While, however, there is a rush to the battle field in our older States, which threatens to fill up all the ranks in our army, we must have a thought for the far distant west, and give our young sister States an opportunity to unite their names in the history of our war on the borders of Virginia."[60]

Arriving in town, the volunteers were met by crowds of citizens who waited on the street to hail them as they passed through. Cyrus Jenkins, a Georgian who reached the capital in July, fell into battalion line with the rest of his unit "and march[ed] through the city, with cheers and huzzas for Georgia, by spectators who crowded the walks as [they] passed." The local newspapers followed the gathering of the troops closely, reporting the number of soldiers and their place of origin and noting with satisfaction those units that appeared particularly soldierly. "The New Orleans Washington Artillery, a splendid battalion, numbering three hundred men, reached here yesterday morning," wrote the *Enquirer* in June. "We think we but express the general sentiment, when we say that we have never seen a finer set of citizenry . . . and one of which every state would feel the greatest pride." The paper and its readers were especially interested in units that conveyed a sense of order and competence, like the three companies of cavalry from South Carolina that arrived in July "all admirably mounted": "[They] attracted much attention, from their martial bearing, as they rode through our streets."[61]

After being housed in different camps around town, the Confederacy's evolving army continued to draw multitudes of curious civilians. "We were quartered in the Old Fair Grounds, where our dress parades were attended by large crowds of ladies & men every evening," remembered a South Carolinian. "The Encampments in our vicinity still continue to be the principal attraction, where our citizens repair to spend the afternoons," wrote the *Enquirer*. "Throngs are daily seen at the Central Fair Grounds, at Howards's Grove, and at other points where our soldiers are congregated. Howards's Grove, where besides others, the New Orleans Washington Artillery and the New Orleans Zouaves are stationed, appears, however, to be the favorite resort. There, every evening, one may see thousands of our people witnessing with pleasure their parade." Richmondites who flocked to the camps were undoubtedly attracted by the aesthetic qualities of military parades, but they were also interested in assessing the soldiers' progress in training for a fight. The ladies, continued the *Enquirer*, "take as much delight in the various exercises and evolutions of the soldiers as a veteran General might be supposed to manifest." Acutely aware of the men's lack of experience and of the chaotic nature of mobilization in the Confederacy, civilians sought proof that the volunteers who were supposed to protect them were equal to the task. The public, and its representatives in the press, examined the men and delighted in seeing signs of military bearing and excellent discipline among the newly arrived troops. After receiving them as heroes, Richmondites wanted to make sure that these men could fulfill the hopes of Confederate independence placed upon them. Before major battles gave Southern men the opportunity to prove that they could fight, the instruction camps of the Confederate army functioned as theaters as much as training grounds. Drilling was not only preparation for battle, but also a performance in front of an excited and anxious public.[62]

The soldiers' efforts proved worthwhile. Indeed these afternoon parades in the presence of refined ladies were a far cry from the marching, fighting, and killing that would come to dominate the soldiers' reality later in the war. But as demonstrations of the Confederacy's armed forces they were instrumental; they showed the Richmond citizenry that an army was at work, that the slave states could be counted on to provide a human shield for their most vulnerable sister, that the new nation was neither dream nor delusion but a living, breathing political organism with the ability to wage war. The appearance of the "queerest costumes of the inland corners of Georgia and Tennessee" on the city's streets was a defining moment in the process of creating a nation below the Mason-Dixon Line and in the reinvention of Richmond as the Confederate capital. The arrival of men reified the idea that the South had become a coherent national entity with a capital and an army devoted to defending it. In a region obsessed with states' rights and state pride, the human stream flowing toward Richmond generated a momentum of unity and joined eleven states, hundreds of different counties, and many thousands of people in the effort to mobilize for war. In some ways the Confederacy materialized as a nation on the streets of Richmond, where South Carolina aristocrats and Louisiana convicts mingled while they waited to be sent to the front. For those civilians observing the happenings, the message rang loud and clear: the Confederate States of America was here.[63]

Looking back in hindsight at the first few months of war, Southerners like Cornelia McDonald remembered this period with bitter irony, as a "great gala time," when "young men, friends of the girls and boys . . . were . . . daily visitors and every meal was a festive occasion," when the "parades, galloping back and forth, the music and the stir" aroused civilians' excitement and enlivened Virginia towns. The mobilization of the Confederate army would remain in Southerners' recollections the quintessential symbol of an age of innocence, a deceptive moment of optimism and jubilation that did little to prepare them for the struggle ahead. "Ah! The lovely, joyous, hopeful, patriotic days of the summer of 1861," recalled Fannie Beers, another Virginian. "The Confederate gray was then a thing of beauty—the outer garb of true and loyal souls."[64]

But even if the lighthearted celebrations that accompanied men's departures seemed hopelessly naïve in light of what happened next, at the time they were paramount to the process of forming a nation and enlisting the population in its service. The movement of men to Virginia turned the Confederate States of America from a mere idea into a hard reality and demonstrated to the population that the South had the makings of a sovereign country. At the critical moment of the nation's inception, soldiers in motion created a spectacle of power and unity that engendered confidence and enthusiasm among civilians on the roadsides and among the soldiers themselves. Marching and riding between one locale and the next, the traveling troops incarnated the existence of an independent South, symbolized its capacity for armed resistance, and forged a physical link between the different states that composed the Confederacy. Their moving bodies were both a powerful tool in the service of Southern separatism and its most palpable manifestation. From the ceremonies in their hometowns to their arrival in Richmond, men on the road were the makers of Confederate nationhood.

2

Armies on the March and the Languages of Motion

In the spring of 1862 Fannie Braxton of Orange County, Virginia, was watching the Confederate army make its way to meet the massive Federal force that was preparing to attack Richmond. Though the Civil War had been going on for almost a year, it was her first experience with military movement of this magnitude. On March 22 James Longstreet's Division marched by, a "right formidable looking body of men," she wrote in her diary. "Such a scene I never expected to witness—All seems so strange & unreal." Day after day soldiers passed by, but her excitement did not wane. On April 3 it was Jubal Early's Division that was marching on its way to the beleaguered capital. "Such a mass of *armed* men, I never beheld before! . . . The band played 'Dixie' as they passed the house. They commenced passing about 9 o'clock in the morning, & it was near sunset when the last Regt. filed by."[1]

Living in the very midst of the Civil War's eastern theater, Braxton would soon become all too familiar with military motion. Once war had begun in earnest, the battle zones of the Confederacy were inundated with men on the move. Their marches, straggles, and retreats shaped every aspect of wartime life, from day-to-day realities to politics and culture. Movement of armies incorporated civilians and soldiers, governed bodies and minds, transformed landscapes, and created a visual language all its own. In those areas of the South where the sectional conflict was actually taking place, it became the central feature of the wartime experience.

In 1862 a surge of military activity in Virginia spread from Romney in the west to Norfolk in the east, and from Antietam Creek across the Maryland border to Drewry's Bluff south of Richmond. Confederate soldiers moved from one battlefield to the next, thwarting multiple Union invasions and undertaking aggressive counteroffensives. Over the course of the year, Southern armies fought in Williamsburg and Yorktown, in the Seven Days Battles and in Cedar Mountain, at Fair Oakes and in Harpers Ferry; they returned to Manassas and invaded Maryland, burned dams across the Potomac River and liberated Fredericksburg from Union occupation. In the spring 17,000 men under the command of Major-General Thomas "Stonewall" Jackson executed what was perhaps the Confederacy's most successful campaign of movement. During five weeks of incessant action Jackson's men marched at a pace of twenty miles a day, won five battles, and tied down as many as 60,000 Federal soldiers who otherwise would have been used to reinforce the Union's main effort of conquering Richmond. The Shenandoah Valley campaign earned the men who fought in it the nickname "footcavalry" and demonstrated to both armies the power of motion as a weapon of war. It was a lesson not soon to be forgotten.[2]

Learning how to move the Southern army and how to read the enemy's movements were two of the foremost challenges facing the Confederate military leadership. While some senior officers accumulated substantial experience in the U.S. Army, none had ever commanded forces of this magnitude or directed military actions as complex as those about to take place in Virginia. When active operations resumed in the early spring of 1862, the government and its generals were perplexed by the reports that Union General George B. McClellan was moving his army in the direction of Richmond. Scrambling to get reinforcements to the capital, Robert E. Lee, serving as the military adviser to Jefferson Davis, openly admitted that he had no real idea where the enemy was going and in what force. "Whether it is intended to move against Norfolk or Richmond there is yet nothing to determine," he wrote on March 25 to General Joseph E. Johnston, commander of the Army of Northern Virginia. "But from the accounts received nothing less than 20,000 or 30,000 men will be sufficient, with the troops already in position, successfully to oppose them."[3] As the Union's mammoth army was slowly making its way toward the Virginia Peninsula, the Davis administration had trouble deciding which movement was forming into a real attack and which was merely a feint. "The enemy is pressing us on all sides, and a call for re-enforcements comes from every department. It is impossible to place at every point which is threatened a force which shall prove equal to

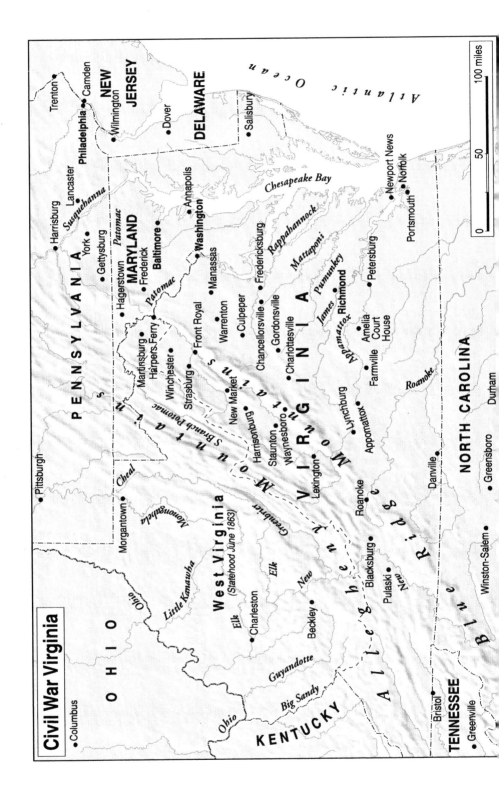

Civil War Virginia

OHIO

PENNSYLVANIA

Pittsburgh

Columbus

Trenton

Camden

NEW JERSEY

Philadelphia

Wilmington

Dover

DELAWARE

Salisbury

Harrisburg

Lancaster

York

Gettysburg

Hagerstown

Susquehanna

Patomac

MARYLAND

Frederick

Baltimore

Annapolis

Washington

Chesapeake Bay

Newport News

Norfolk

Portsmouth

Martinsburg

Harpers Ferry

Winchester

Strasburg

Front Royal

New Market

Manassas

Warrenton

Culpeper

Fredericksburg

Rappahannock

Mattaponi

Petersburg

Morgantown

Cheat

Monongahela

West Virginia

(Statehood June 1863)

Little Kanawha

Elk

Charleston

Beckley

Greenbrier

Chancellorsville

Gordonsville

Charlottesville

Pumunkey

Richmond

James

Appamattox

Amelia Court House

Farmville

Roanoke

VIRGINIA

S. Branch Potomac

Harrisonburg

Staunton

Waynesboro

Lexington

Lynchburg

Appomattox

Roanoke

Danville

NORTH CAROLINA

Greensboro

Durham

Elk

New

Blacksburg

Pulaski

New

Roanoke

Allegheny

Blue Ridge

Guyandotte

Big Sandy

Ohio

KENTUCKY

Bristol

Greenville

TENNESSEE

Winston-Salem

Atlantic Ocean

Mountains

100 miles

50

0

every emergency," wrote Lee to Major-General John B. Magruder, who had sent for additional troops and was unhappy with the administration's response. Magruder was commanding the Confederate forces in the vulnerable port of Yorktown, which actually proved to be one of McClellan's destinations. Yet on March 29 Richmond was reluctant to offer support. "As yet the design of the enemy in your front is somewhat vague and undecided . . . when it is unmistakably ascertained that he shall attempt to force his way up the Peninsula every exertion shall be made to enable you successfully to resist and drive him."[4] Once the Union army actually landed in Virginia's southeastern corner, panic reached new highs. The capture of Richmond and the loss of a considerable part of Virginia had suddenly become a palpable threat. On May 10 Joseph E. Johnston begged that the president order a concentration of all the troops in North Carolina and eastern Virginia so there would still be a chance to hold on to the middle portion of the state. "If we permit ourselves to be driven beyond Richmond we lose the means of maintaining this army," he warned. By the end of the month the government was making preparations to leave the capital if Federal forces continued their advance. Archives were packed and bureau chiefs instructed to prepare to depart at once.[5]

Though McClellan was eventually repulsed and the capital saved, the threat of Union movement continued to loom large. After assuming his post as commander of the Army of Northern Virginia, Lee's principal duty was to drive the Federals from Confederate territory and to prepare for future incursions. Monitoring the enemy's movements and assessing their direction and force became one of his primary concerns, requiring him to sift through "conflicting and exaggerated reports" and to employ spies, scouts, and raiding parties who gathered information behind enemy lines.[6] Lee relied heavily on intelligence brought by J. E. B. Stuart, his resourceful and daring cavalry commander. But he also personally supervised the deployment of scouts from other units. On August 13, while campaigning in central Virginia, he wrote the commander of the department of North Carolina, "Select from the troops under your command some of your most reliable and intelligent men and send them down the south side of James River, to watch the movements of the enemy and ascertain the truthfulness of the report made by the English deserter of the embarkation of a part of McClellan's army. It is of the first importance that I should be advised positively on this point, as our own movements must be in a measure regulated by those of that army."[7] Making sense of enemy movement and mapping out appropriate maneuvers in response were in many ways the essence of Lee's generalship over the course of 1862.

As months sped by, Confederate generals operating in the eastern theater proved they were particularly adroit at moving their armies and relying on mobility to overcome the shortcomings of their small and ill-equipped force. While the very size of the Union army and the heavy wagon trains that followed it around often slowed its pace and transformed every change of position into a cumbersome and conspicuous exercise, Confederate armies could sneak around almost unnoticed. Stonewall Jackson's Shenandoah Valley campaign was the consummate example of how the bold and able use of motion could produce victory against seemingly unbeatable odds. In his famed spring campaign, Jackson raced his soldiers up and down the Valley, descended on Federal forces out of thin air, and escaped their repeated attempts to capture him regardless of the fact that their numbers were nearly four times his. Under the leadership of Jackson, Lee, and others, the use of mobility as a tool of warfare became a hallmark of Confederate military strategy. Using their advantage of interior lines and their deep familiarity with Southern terrain, Rebel officers often succeeded in moving covertly and misleading the enemy as to their real positions. Thus in June, once Jackson had concluded his campaign, Lee asked him to bring his army to the defense of Richmond, but without exposing to the enemy that he had abandoned the Shenandoah Valley. "In moving your troops you could let it be understood that it was to pursue the enemy in your front. Dispose those to hold the valley so as to deceive the enemy, keeping your cavalry well in their front, and at the proper time suddenly descending the Pamunkey. To be efficacious, the movement must be secret."[8]

No less important, the Confederate army learned to move swiftly, with minimum baggage and few stops for rest. In summer, as he prepared to move into northern Virginia, Lee told General James Longstreet, "It is all-important that our movement, in whatever direction it is determined, should be as quick as possible. I fear General Pope can be re-enforced quicker than ourselves; prepare accordingly."[9] Rapid, clandestine mobility, which disguised the army's actual size and goals, was instrumental in facing a larger and better-armed foe. At times it was the Confederacy's only recourse. In

November, when the Union was embarking on another invasion, Lee wrote, "The enemy, apparently, is so strong in numbers that I think it preferable to attempt to baffle his designs by maneuvering, rather than to resist his advance by main force. To accomplish the latter without too much risk and loss would require more than double our present numbers."[10]

Yet as a weapon of war, movement was nimble and versatile enough to serve different strategies. In the course of the lengthy and diffuse struggle over the soil of Virginia, there were instances in which the Confederate leadership tried to use the powerful spectacle of an army on the move to make up for the absence of actual reinforcements. In early June, when Jackson was clamoring for more troops to help him defeat the Union's greatly superior force, both Jefferson Davis and Lee recommended that reserves would be marched up and down the Valley to make it appear as though the army was larger and stronger than was actually the case. Lee contacted the officer commanding forces in the Valley town of Staunton and instructed him "to collect all the troops in that vicinity, raise the community, magnify their numbers, and march down the valley and communicate with Jackson. It will shake Shields and make him pause." "Such a movement may have an effect on the enemy beyond its real value," Davis wrote in a message to Jackson, offering congratulations on his great successes while informing him that no additional troops would be sent.[11]

It was Lee's belief in the ability of his army to march and fight even under the most severe strain that induced him to embark on his invasion of Maryland in September. Leading the Army of Northern Virginia from the outskirts of Richmond to the Potomac River, he sought to move the war into Northern territory and give Virginia and its inhabitants a much-needed break. He also hoped to raise great numbers of fresh recruits in Maryland and to incite the state to secede from the Union. Yet none of these plans panned out. Lee's army reached Maryland on the brink of collapse after months of continuous campaigning. Thousands left the moving columns along the way, and those who stayed underperformed in the pivotal battle of Antietam. Lee retreated across the river without having achieved a meaningful victory or having changed the course of the war. Angry and disappointed with the meager results of his latest endeavor, he blamed the stragglers who had abandoned the army and the officers who could not keep them in line.[12] After months of uninterrupted victories the Maryland campaign brought Lee face to face with the limitations of his own army, which fell apart on the road and proved incapable of executing his plans. Nevertheless the general remained as devoted as ever to the idea that movement was the Confederate army's best hope to win the war. Three days after recrossing the Potomac into Southern territory, his adjutant R. H. Chilton wrote a long letter to Lee's two senior and most trusted subordinates, Stonewall Jackson and James Longstreet. The letter outlined a comprehensive set of new regulations for marching, which were intended to address the myriad flaws in discipline and organization that became all too apparent during the Maryland campaign. The letter ends, however, with Lee's affirmation of what he perceived as the Confederacy's advantages over its mighty foe. If they wanted to climb out of the post-Antietam rut, the generals would have to "impress men and officers with the importance of a change necessary to the preservation of this army and its successful accomplishment of its mission, as its better discipline, greater mobility, and higher inspirations must counterbalance the many advantages over us, both in numbers and material, which the enemy possess."[13] Despite the failure of the Antietam campaign, Lee still counted on his army's powers of movement as one of its primary assets in this prolonged and difficult war.

In the weeks and months that followed, Lee personally oversaw the efforts to rectify the problems in the mechanics of movement that prevented his army from staging a successful invasion of the North. The Maryland campaign exposed a phenomenal shortage of shoes in the Army of Northern Virginia, which hindered the movement of thousands of men. Through the fall the general pressed Richmond to equip his army with footwear, sending detailed reports about the numbers of barefoot men in each division and taking care to divide the shoes that arrived among his different commands.[14] Lee was also engaged with the state of his army's horses, who, like their human counterparts, were greatly weakened after months of intensive labor and insufficient nutrition. By November three-quarters of his cavalry horses had come down with sore tongues, while others were afflicted with the soft foot, a disease "producing lameness, and in some cases loosening the hoof and causing it to slough off."[15] As he was preparing to thwart the North's winter offensive and renew his own operations the following spring, Lee was trying to restore his army's mobility. The use of fast, efficient, and clever military movement was one of the main reasons the Confederacy survived the Union invasions of 1862. As the year drew to a close, he wanted to ensure that this would continue to be the case.

Confederate generals' extensive use of movement made marching an experience as central to the lives of Virginia soldiers as was the ordeal of battle. Men on the move kept meticulous records of the distances they crossed, the roads they had traveled, and the hours they spent on the march. J. William Thomas of the Stonewall Brigade maintained a daily log of his movements and calculated that in his first year of service he had marched 880 miles. Randolph Fairfax figured that in the last leg of the Shenandoah Valley campaign he "marched 240 miles fought one battle and skirmished 2 days. This is almost equal if not fully equal to Napoleon's celebrated march 200 miles in 10 days." The legendary marches of the Napoleonic Wars were a popular image among Virginia troops, who had trouble imagining a more intense experience of wartime mobility than the one they were undergoing. "I have read of Napolian's grand marches in Russia and I always left some doubt for the exaggerating of winter," wrote a member of Hood's Texas Brigade, who was ordered from Fredericksburg to Richmond in early 1863. "But now, with all of its exaggerating doesn't equal the march of Hood's Division from Fredericksburg. It surpasses Napolian's march across the Alps." Marching from Orange County to Yorktown in the previous spring, Thomas Petty felt the same: "At every step the mud hung to our boots most tenaciously, and weightily & every movement with our pack-saddles made our march a real Napoleonic affair."[16]

Even if the distances soldiers traversed in Virginia did not quite amount to the French invasion of Russia, the mobile nature of warfare during 1862 took a considerable toll on the men's bodies and souls. "I have endured & seen others endure that that if a man had told me 12 months ago that men could stand such hardships I would have called him a fool," wrote James Langhorne after his first experience campaigning in Virginia. Langhorne had the bad luck of participating in Stonewall Jackson's first expedition as a Civil War commander, to the village of Romney in northwestern Virginia. Union soldiers had occupied the village in late 1861, and Jackson was determined to drive them out, regardless of the weather, the condition of the roads, or the state of his troops. Leaving Winchester on the first day of 1862, his force was subjected to the worst effects of winter warfare. Temperatures were below freezing, snow and rain fell incessantly, and walking became an excruciating effort. "At one time the road would be covered with hard beaten snow and as slippery as ice as that the horses would flounder about over it continually and slip down," wrote Randolph Fairfax to his mother. "At another time the mud would be so deep & thick that the horses could barely manage to drag the pieces & caissons along." The soldiers ate a meal only occasionally and had no tents to shield them from the blistering cold. Arriving in Romney, "every soldier's clothing was a solid cake of ice and icikles two inches long hanging from the hair and whiskers of every man." Some men died; others became severely ill. "Bob Wood's feet are frost bitten so bad that he will lose his toes if not his feet," wrote another soldier to his family. "Thank God that I am as well as I am for I have been through more than enough to kill a horse in the last two weeks."[17]

The cold subsided with spring, but campaigning continued to bring Confederate soldiers to the brink of collapse. With little food and less sleep, units were rushed between battlefields in forced marches over impassable roads. In the Shenandoah Valley the men of Jackson's army broke down in droves. It was late May, and the soldiers had been in motion for nearly a month. They had marched from Staunton to McDowell and from McDowell to Front Royal, covering a distance of more than 300 miles by relentless marching in pursuit of enemy forces that were about to leave the Valley and join the attack on Richmond. After weeks of unceasing movement and two battles, their bodies could no longer bear the pain. "Whenever the column stopped for a minute, the sleepy officers and men would throw themselves on the ground," recalled Henry Kyd Douglas, a member of Jackson's staff. Robert Barton remembered "moving at a snail's pace and halting, and then moving again and halting again, falling asleep at the halts and being suddenly awakened up when motion was resumed": "We fairly staggered on, worn almost to exhaustion by the weariness of such a march."[18]

Three months later soldiers in the Army of Northern Virginia were pushed to their limits during the Maryland campaign. Tens of thousands were marched from southern Virginia, where they had fought in the Seven Days Battles, to the northern part of the state, and from there across the Potomac River into Maryland. Jackson's men, now serving as part of Lee's army, were once again on the move, covering hundreds of miles on foot and stopping to fight in Cedar Mountain, Grovetown, Second Manassas, Harpers Ferry, and finally Antietam. "No language can describe our fatiguing march and the suffering we endured," wrote Benjamin Farinholt in August, after crossing the Rappahannock River. "Stumbling and falling over rocks and wading through the mud knee deep in some places and having to wade two streams up to our waist both swollen terribly & running like whirlpools . . . our regiment has marched from falling creek to this place one hundred and twenty five miles and we are completely worn out with fatigue."[19] Ten days later a Georgian tried to convey to his wife his state of mind after a month of incessant motion: "I have to take the broiling sun and the drenching rain but I take it all easy and can sleep all night in a wet blanket. I have got so I don't mind it at all, just go ahead like I was a hog and big pig, little pig, root hog or die, I don't care much. We have moved from twice to three times a week ever since the first of August and by the time you were dragged and hauled about like I have been you wouldn't care either."[20] The prospect of invading Maryland aroused great excitement among soldiers who were eager to move the war from Virginia's battered soil and into the North. Yet though spirits were high, the state of the men's worn-out bodies proved to be an impediment to the success of the campaign. Back in Richmond in October, a convalescent soldier summarized his experience during the previous few weeks: "I had quite a bad time; was marched all but to death."[21]

Even high-ranking commanders suffered from the travails of military movement. In May 1862 Major-General Richard Ewell could not contain his frustration at the life he was forced to lead, tossed between different theaters of operation and subject to the whims of superior officers or politicians in Richmond. While leading his men from one battlefield to the next, he privately fumed to his fiancée back home. "I am sick and worn down," he wrote from camp. "I have been keeping one eye on Banks, one on Jackson, all the time jogged up from Richmond, they want me elsewhere and call me off, when at the same time, I am compelled to remain until that enthusiastic fanatic comes to some conclusion. Now I ought to be en route to Gordonsville, at this place, and going to Jackson, all at the same time."[22] Even Colonel Jedediah Hotchkiss, the army's mapmaker, was overcome by Virginia's space and the necessity of navigating through it. Arriving in the Fredericksburg region in December 1862, he wrote his brother, "I pursued the army about 100 miles, in four days, and at last found it here in the low lands, flat lands, swamplands, pine lands, sand lands, endless woodlands of eastern Virginia where, as I supposed, the Gen. wants me to make a map for him, for no one can get along here without some guide. Ask any one the directions to a place and he will tell you two or three ways, any one of which is twice as far as it ought to be."[23] Neither rank nor special skills protected Confederate officers in Virginia from the demands of life on the march.

Nor did it save them from the grueling experience of retreat. In the aftermath of defeat, Confederate armies were force-marched for days, often halting only to skirmish with the advance troops of the enemy. A week after Jackson's force struggled to make its way north across the Shenandoah in pursuit of the enemy, it was once again on the road, fleeing a renewed effort by two Federal armies to end its domination of the Valley. In thirty-six hours of escape from the Union's pincer movement, the army marched fifty-two miles. Henry Kyd Douglas, an officer on Jackson's staff, saw men dropping on the ground "in that desperate state of reckless indifference which it was impossible to describe and which no one can understand who has not traveled in a state of anxiety for days, without sleep, rest or food." A month earlier 55,000 Confederate soldiers retreated from Williamsburg to escape defeat at the hands of the Union army making its way up the Peninsula. A few thousand troops stayed behind and participated in a battle that took place outside of town, at the end of which they continued to retreat toward Richmond. John S. Tucker was among the crowd: "Commenced retreating again this morning at 2 o'clock A.M. the troops nearly all broken down with fatigue, hunger, & want of sleep. . . . Roads awfully muddy & wagons & artillery continually bogging down. The sick & wounded left in Williamsburg at the mercy of the Yankees." Retreating from Maryland after Antietam, Lee's army "marched all night through mud & by very difficult road, crowded by 2 or more brigades abreast, striving for the way & waded the Potomac": "The river banks were very steep & slippery & almost every man fell down they al clung to each other and pulled up by hard labor, our clothes were wet & we exhausted by marching & hunger & loss of sleep."[24]

Yet as arduous and miserable as the Confederate war of motion often was, the men who carried it out knew full well that their ability to move across Virginia's terrain with speed and agility played a crucial role in the South's victories during 1862. Time and again Confederate generals were able to surprise their Federal counterparts by rushing large numbers of soldiers to a battlefield, by evacuating disadvantageous positions stealthily, and by moving armies from one part of the state to the other quickly and efficiently. From the last-minute arrival of troops by train on the battlefield of First Bull Run in July 1861, to the brilliant maneuvers in the battle of Chancellorsville in May 1863, fast-moving feet were often the South's most effective weapon in the face of a much larger and superbly equipped foe. Recounting to his sister the glories of the Shenandoah Valley campaign that had just ended, Randolph Fairfax put his finger on what generations of military historians would later identify as Stonewall Jackson's most remarkable achievement: "Our whole march from Front Royal to Winchester and thence to Charlestown and Harpers Ferry was but a series of success after success and all won more by hard marching than by fighting and bloodshed." Three weeks later the Valley army was already in Richmond, ready to join the fighting in the Seven Days Battles. James Dinwiddie, an artillery officer, was enthralled by the trip as much as he was by the prospect of glory on the battlefield. "I suppose though I have seen none the papers have given a history of our tremendous march from the Valley to Richmond," he wrote his wife. "It was prodigious, and I hope the results may be abundantly great." By mid-1862 the bold and cunning use of motion had made its determining impact on the course of the war. It had become a mainstay of Confederate military strategy and a fundamental component of the soldiers' wartime reality.[25]

Huge detachments marching to and from battlefields constituted the most dramatic form of military motion, but they alone did not account for the profusion of men on the move in the eastern theater. The roads of Virginia were perennially thronged with soldiers who had received a furlough and were going home or with soldiers en route to a hospital. Others were busy moving between units, purchasing supplies, recruiting men, or conveying messages. More often than not, however, soldiers who were not traveling with their units belonged to the ubiquitous population of army stragglers. A straggling soldier is defined as one who has been separated from his unit without authority either during battle or on the line of march.[26] In the Civil War South, stragglers were men who had fled the battlefield in fear, men who had reached the limits of their physical endurance and were too weak to keep up with the rapid pace of the marches, men who were barefoot and could not continue walking until they had obtained new shoes, men who had passed close to their homes and wanted to see their families for a short while, and men who had grown impatient with military life and decided to take some time off to eat better food and get some rest.

Straggling was rampant in every Confederate army and in every period of the war, but in Virginia it reached crisis proportions in 1862.[27] Each time the army got on the road, soldiers who could not or would not keep up with the column dropped out, usually in favor of a hot meal or a clean bed in a local farmhouse. Some rejoined their unit after a few hours; others abstained from service for weeks. One of Lee's aides described central Virginia in September 1862 as a zone teeming with soldiers "scattered . . . unprovided for and uncontrolled, straggling on the road depredating upon the community."[28] Even the famous "footcavalry," Stonewall Jackson's Valley army, suffered from this problem. "Jackson's columns were never the compact surging mass portrayed by his admirers," writes one historian of the Valley campaign. "They tended to be, rather, a weary corps surrounded by hundreds of roving panhandlers."[29]

This state of affairs was clearly visible to anyone traveling along Virginia's roads. When the Confederate army retreated from Yorktown in May, General Joseph E. Johnston noted in an official communiqué, "Several thousand stragglers from this army are in Richmond, or near it, on the way." In June, as Stonewall Jackson's army was fleeing the Yankee pursuit, Watkins Kearns noted, "Innumerable stragglers in the road belonging to our Brigade and others." The summer campaign from Richmond to Maryland produced the same results. "We have a host of stragglers; I find them wherever I go," observed Jedediah Hotchkiss in his journal after the Second Battle of Bull Run. On the way to Fredericksburg in November, Samuel Walkup of the 48th North Carolina Regiment recorded "much falling out, particularly by the barefooted men, about 1/5 of the Regt. one whole company G. Capt. And all fell out except one man and he shoeless."[30]

There were several key reasons for the straggling epidemic of 1862. First was the physical shape the soldiers were in. In the first year of the war many had yet to develop sufficient resilience to the exertions of military life and had trouble keeping up with the pace of their unit's movement. When the army abandoned Manassas in March and moved to meet the enemy south of Richmond, throngs of soldiers were left on the roadsides after collapsing on the move. Albert B. Ross, a captain in the 20th Georgia Regiment, recorded that during a march of "about 11 or 12 miles" most of his unit was "left on the road, broke down and unable to travel." In William Randolph Smith's company, more than half of the men making the same trip were "left along the road having given out." In some regiments the situation improved over time as soldiers got increasingly used to the exigencies of military movement. In others, things remained bleak deep into the campaign season. In June the 5th Texas Regiment was sent to join Stonewall Jackson's army but had trouble keeping up with his pace. "The march was very hard & the day exceedingly hot," reported one private to his sister. "The boys who were continually breaking down & worn out with fatigue would throw themselves out of ranks & their remain till tired nature had restored itself with rest & sleep." This particular soldier dropped out of the column near Charlottesville, while the army continued in haste to the front lines below Richmond. He stayed in the countryside for several days and heard about the Seven Days Battles after they ended.[31]

The tendency to straggle was also largely the result of the acute food shortages in the Confederate army. Despite the abundance of supplies in the South during the early years of the war, hunger was a constant reality for soldiers on the move. "We haveint very good times now for we dont git mutch to eat now for we move about so mutch," complained a soldier who had relocated six times in the course of June 1862.[32] Generals leading the war of motion instructed their commands to pack light, often leaving behind cooking utensils in the wagon train or sending them ahead by railroad to the nearest depot. "The road to glory cannot be followed with much baggage," declared Major-General Richard Ewell, as his command was preparing to leave camp and pursue the Union army. Upon leaving for another hurried march, Stonewall Jackson directed his men "to carry no baggage but their blankets, and no wagons except ammunition wagons and ambulances."[33] While men could carry only the minimal amount of provisions, the commissary departments that were supposed to feed them failed to meet the logistical challenge of providing for an army whose men moved too fast or over terrain too rugged for wagons to pass. While Confederate officers displayed considerable competence at using railroads to move soldiers between battlefields, they were unable to harness their era's most advanced technology to better provide for the men in the ranks. As soldiers crisscrossed Virginia on foot, the wagons carrying their rations were habitually lost, delayed, or far ahead of the column. As one soldier summed up the reality of army life in Virginia, "When we get stationary for a week or so we can get what we want from the sutlers' wagons, but when we are moving about everything is scarce."[34]

Southern soldiers campaigning in the eastern theater subsisted for days on end on what they had managed to take in their knapsacks or what they could pick from trees and fields along the way. Often that did not amount to very much. "All we live on is roasted corn, gathered green out of the fields, as our Commissary wagons have not gotten up," wrote a bitter Benjamin Farinholt during the Second Bull Run campaign. Henry Talley described to his mother the lack of food on the retreat from Yorktown: "We com very nearly starving on the way. We went 3 days and nights without eny thing to eat but a little parched corn so you may [see] we was hungry." Falling back from Williamsburg, an exhausted and defeated William Randolph Smith had nothing to eat for forty-eight hours "except what we could get along the road and that was next to nothing, for the country is very poor and had been overrun by the front of the army." Soldiers who refused to bear the hunger any longer or had grown too weak fell by the roadside.[35]

Another problem that plagued the Confederate army's war of motion was the scarcity of shoes. Within a year of the war's outbreak, thousands of Confederate soldiers were marching barefoot, after having used up their old shoes and been unable to obtain new ones. The limited industrial infrastructure of the slave states could not keep up with the mass demand for footwear, and the Northern naval blockade made importation increasingly difficult. The quartermasters of the army were helpless in the face of the shoe shortage, despite making honest attempts to solve the problem by withdrawing all shoemakers from the ranks so they could work at their craft or by purchasing the precious items in large quantities whenever those were available. Some officers estimated the number of barefoot men in their ranks at 30 percent; others complained that a full 50 percent of their units were in the same condition.[36]

Confederate soldiers walked shoeless on snow and ice in the dead of winter and slipped in the treacherous Virginia mud in spring. During the summer, when war making was at its peak, there was nothing to separate their feet from the scorching ground. Feet became calloused, blistered, and covered in blood, often making it impossible for men to keep marching. "We are now station near Culpeper C.H.," wrote Henry Talley to his mother in November 1862. "We was 4 days marching from Winchester to this place distance 80 miles it was a very hard march indeed we come all throu the mountains and a good many of our boys was barefooted and the wether was very cool all the time we was on the march I am barefooted myself and no way to git any shoes so you know we see a hard time of it." A month later William Cowan McClellan wrote his father asking that a pair of boots be sent to him from home as soon as possible: "I am now completely barefooted. The snow two inches deep raw hides have been issued to the troops to make masking which last about a weak or ten days." McClellan stayed in the ranks despite the absence of shoes. Other soldiers who suffered from the same predicament did not.[37]

Straggling was endemic in Virginia also because this densely settled and prosperous state provided men a plethora of safe havens where they could stay. Soldiers who drifted away from the main body of the army melted into the civilian population and enjoyed generous hospitality in farmhouses, plantations, and towns across the state. Some went so far as to effectively transform military movement into tourism by checking into taverns or hotels. As night fell on units moving through thickly populated areas, officers found it virtually impossible to keep the would-be stragglers in the ranks. Shielded by darkness, shoals of hungry, barefoot, and exhausted men stepped off the road and began knocking on doors.[38]

While material conditions were crucial to the upsurge of straggling, so were some deeply entrenched cultural mores. As white men operating in a society based on dependency and hierarchy, Confederate soldiers were accustomed to a great measure of personal freedom and did not adjust easily to the idea that another man had a right to prevent them from doing as they saw fit. Many soldiers were decidedly unapologetic about their inability to stay in the ranks. "It was nothing uncommon to see a soldier lying on the road side completely worn down from carrying his knapsack," wrote Thomas Selman in March as Hood's Texas Brigade was marching to the Peninsula. "And right here I will say that no one knows how hard a soldiers life is until he marches in the night over a muddy road with a heavy knapsack on his back. I felt tired myself and disobeyed orders several times by stopping." The soldiers of the 9th Alabama Regiment found the movement to Yorktown

similarly onerous and were as unabashed about their failure to obey marching orders. The Alabamans were transported from Richmond by boat, dis-
embarking at a place called Grovestown Wharf on a rainy night in late
March. While the distance they were asked to cover was only ten miles, the
soldiers refused to go on. "We could not see our hands before us and then I
would fall into a mud hole up to my knees," wrote William Cowan McClellan to his sister. "I lugged on about five miles the Reg. being scattered all
over the country." Finally McClellan decided that he had had enough. Seeing a light some distance from the road, he and two of his comrades left the
column. "We found a good clever fellow, hot supper on tables. We dryed our
clothes & blankets spred down the carpet & had a glorious nights rest." The
next morning they caught up with the regiment, finding it "composed of the
Col., drummer, and 10 privates." The rest of the unit had vanished during
the night. Characteristically no punishments were meted out. At that early
stage of war the army's policies toward stragglers were exceedingly lenient,
and offenders were punished lightly or escaped with no penalties at all. Officers struggling to keep their units together found it easier to turn a blind
eye to the men's transgressions and simply accept them back into the ranks
when they chose to return.[39]

Yet at the same time it was becoming increasingly clear that straggling
was severely undermining the Confederate army's ability to fight. At the
battle of Kernstown in March, 1,500 men, almost one-third of Stonewall
Jackson's force, were absent from a fight against 9,000 Federal soldiers. By
September, when the Army of Northern Virginia invaded Maryland, the
problem had reached unprecedented proportions. Thousands of men left the
ranks daily and caused irreparable damage to the Confederate effort to move
the war north. Lee began the campaign with 55,000 soldiers, but only 37,000
actually participated in the battle of Antietam, a far cry from the Union's
75,000 effectives.[40] Lee reported to Jefferson Davis that on the morning of
the battle one of his brigades consisted of a mere 120 men, and another had
no more than 100. The army's efficiency, he warned, "is greatly paralyzed by
the loss to its ranks of the numerous stragglers. . . . A great many men belonging to the army never entered Maryland at all; many returned after getting there, while others who crossed the river kept aloof."[41]

The destructive impact of straggling was as clear to the men in the ranks
as it was to the generals in charge. "It is undoubtedly unfortunate that we

could not continue active operations but it was impossible to proceed with the army in such a state as it was," wrote Randolph Fairfax to his mother two weeks after the battle. "The men ragged and barefooted and the ranks reduced to such an extent by straggling that we could not have brought half our force into a fight. It is really shamefull how some of our men have behaved. There was not half of our army I am confident engaged in the battle of Sharpsburg, the rest were straggling about the country along our line of march through Va." "The system of straggling is a most abominable one, and has lost to us in more than one fight the services of 15 or 20,000 men," wrote another officer to his mother. "There are cases of men who are really sick and barefooted, who cannot keep up with their commands and of course ought to be excused, but the regular genuine system—ought to be severely punished." In the wake of the failure in Maryland, soldiers supported dealing out the harshest of punishments to stragglers. "The common people do not know what the army is composed of," wrote an infantry captain to his wife. "Thare are men here who can put the devil to shame in the conception and execution of wickedness. Genl. Jackson has ordered the file closers to shoot on the spot any man who leaves ranks on the march. . . . I expect a good many executions will take place in this army soon."[42]

The calls within the army for strong measures against stragglers resulted from the failure of more lenient means. For months officers commanding the Virginia armies had made earnest attempts to stem the tide and force their men to stay in the ranks. Stonewall Jackson published new marching orders for his army in May, stipulating that soldiers would march fifty minutes out of every hour, with one hour allotted for lunch. At no other time would men be allowed to leave the ranks. He further ordered that "proper distances must be preserved, as far as practicable, thus converting a march, as it should be, into an important drill, that of habituating the men to keep in ranks." In September Jackson filed charges against one of his subordinates, Brigadier-General A. P. Hill, for permitting men to straggle from the line of march on two different occasions without trying to stop them.[43]

Lee was similarly aware of the problem as his army embarked on its invasion of Maryland. In a letter to Jefferson Davis he referred to straggling as "one of the greatest evils, from which many minor ones proceed" and admitted, "It has become a habit difficult to correct." Addressing his army as it left Virginia for Maryland, he referred to stragglers sternly as "those who desert their commands in peril" and warned, "Such characters are better absent from the army on such momentous occasions as those about to be entered upon." Lee was constantly preoccupied with the problem of straggling throughout the campaign and took proactive measures to prevent his army from falling apart in motion. He expanded the provost guard and ordered brigade commanders to appoint officers as guards to stop soldiers from leaving the moving columns. Furthermore he suggested that a military commission would accompany the army to punish men caught leaving the ranks.[44] Yet even these firm actions proved mostly futile in controlling the Confederate army on the move. Reporting to President Davis after the battle, the general admitted that his efforts to check the problem had failed. "I have taken every means in my power from the beginning to correct this evil, which has increased instead of diminished," he wrote. "The stream has not lessened since crossing the Potomac, though the cavalry has been constantly employed in endeavoring to arrest it."[45] In hindsight Antietam proved to be a turning point in the campaign against straggling. The disappointing results of Lee's much-anticipated invasion of Maryland revealed that stragglers were more than just another wartime nuisance and that the inability to control soldiers' movement was costing the Confederacy crucial victories. In the wake of the campaign the army and the government embarked on a concentrated effort to reorganize the troops and improve discipline, eventually succeeding in making some headway against the problem. The following summer, when the Army of Northern Virginia once again set out north, this time into Pennsylvania, straggling was no longer an issue. At least for a while soldiers had grown used to staying in the ranks.

Marching, retreating, and straggling, Confederate soldiers serving in the Old Dominion were constantly on the move. As the war expanded and intensified during 1862, the pathways of Virginia were filled with hundreds of thousands of men, animals, and vehicles, the machinery of a nineteenth-century army at war. Entire divisions marched to battle while multitudes of individuals straggled away from the army in search of a brief respite. Others traveled to hospitals or used their furloughs to go home. Horses, oxen, wagons, and carts were constantly on the move as commissary officers attempted to supply the nation's expanding military force. Railway stations were packed with men going from one battle zone to the other and from one threatened city to the next. The wounded and the dead were carried to the rear while raw recruits were transported to the front. A year into the Civil War, Virginia had become a world dominated by military motion.

Nowhere was this transformation more evident than in the towns and cities located on the main roads or near major battlefields. Almost overnight the small and quiet locales of the antebellum era metamorphosed into transportation hubs, supply depots, and hospital centers that catered to thousands of travelers. In Staunton, reported one soldier, "little is to be seen but moving masses of soldiers, ambulances, transport wagons, floating officers of all grades, men and women in search of sick or wounded relatives, etc." One hundred miles to the north soldiers found the town of Winchester a "small and crowded village crowded with sick and wounded officers and soldiers." A Georgian woman who accompanied her husband to Gordonsville, an important junction in central Virginia, encountered "so many soldiers, such immense trains of ammunition and cannon, etc.": "Troops are pouring in by carloads." The state's transportation facilities caved under the pressure of the army's peripatetic activity. Traveling from Petersburg to Smithfield in the spring, Sara Pryor "found the country literally alive with troops": "The train on which I traveled was switched off again and again to allow them to pass." The same scenes recurred anywhere in the South where armies were active. In Jackson, Mississippi, the British businessman William Corsan met a "shouting, hustling, dusty, perspiring mass of 'butternuts,' niggers, rifles, bayonets, blankets, cannon and ammunition wagons, tents, cavalry horses, hacks, ambulances, omnibuses, and all the heterogeneous accompaniments of an army on the move." In neither of these places, reported travelers, was it possible to get a meal or find an empty bed. Southern communities of every size were overwhelmed by human beings on the go.[46]

This was particularly true in Richmond, which emerged as the epicenter of movement of both Virginia and the Confederacy as a whole. Once chosen as the Southern seat of government, the genteel town was reinvented as a capital city at war, home to the nation's administrative center and army headquarters as well as to major factories, hospitals, and a central rail station. From the outbreak of hostilities to its evacuation in April 1865, it was swamped with refugees, government workers, and soldiers in every capacity, who increased its population from 38,000 to 120,000.[47] Thomas DeLeon landed in the capital in the early days of 1862 and found "a stir and bustle new to quiet Richmond." On the streets he met throngs of attachés, hangers-on, and "crowds of officers from all quarters" who had come in to spend their furloughs. Arriving in Richmond in December, William Corsan encountered a city whose "streets and hotels were literally crammed with soldiers, officers, and civilians, of all ranks, connected with Government business. Trains of quartermasters' wagons, bodies of Federal prisoners, ambulances with sick and wounded, mounted aides-de-camp, or masses of determined, though rough-looking Confederate troops, trailed through the streets incessantly."[48]

Yet beyond a national capital, Richmond was also the focal point of the military contest in the eastern United States. The Union's attempts in mid-1862 to capture the city turned its environs into a giant battlefield and its streets into pathways for the passage of whole armies. "Richmond is all hurly burly now, and thousands of soldiers are passing through," wrote James Dinwiddie to his wife on April 14. "A division of ten thousand men passed down main st. yesterday evening on their way to the peninsula." Over the course of the war the same scene was repeated every time the Union army came near the capital. In July 1864 the refugee Judith McGuire reported in her diary, "Troops are constantly passing to and fro; army wagons, ambulances, etc., rattle by, morning, noon, and night."[49]

In the aftermath of battle many of the same men returned to the city in ambulances and on crutches, desperate to reach a hospital or a place of rest. Gruesome processions of wounded men became a trademark of urban life in Civil War Virginia, giving civilians a firsthand look at the horrors of war and placing on the population the burden of caring for thousands of incapacitated men. "All day the wounded here were borne past our boarding-house in Third Street, to the general hospital," wrote John B. Jones, a clerk in the Confederate War Department, after the battle of Seven Pines in June. "Hundreds, with shattered arms and slight wounds, came in on foot." The retreat from Williamsburg brought into Richmond "squads of convalescent sick, barely able to march, who had been sent ahead to save the ambulances for those worse than they. It was a black Sunday afternoon, when those wan and hollow-eyed men limped painfully through the streets on their weary way to Camp Winder Hospital." In the wake of the battle of Cedar Mountain in August, the town of Staunton received train after train of "men without arms and legs and shot in the head, body, etc." These sights, wrote the local journalist Joseph Waddell, "give us a horrid view of war." A few weeks later, when the Confederate army returned from the bloody battle of Antietam, the picture grew gloomier still. Thousands of wounded men overran the Shenandoah Valley in every condition of laceration and dismemberment. "This has been the most awful day we have ever spent," wrote Laura Lee in Winchester. "Directly after breakfast the lines of ambulances began to come in, and since then it has been an incessant stream. 3000 wounded men have been brought in. Everyplace is crowded with them." "If we were not so used to it, the sight of multitudes of wounded and suffering soldiers constantly arriving, would be shocking," remarked the jaded Waddell in his diary.[50]

Following the wounded were their family members. Despite the reigning confusion in the wake of large engagements, civilians in Virginia knew enough about the whereabouts of their relatives in uniform to go and look for them in towns near battlefields. In mid-October John Sale, a forty-three-year-old father serving in Richmond's defenses, found out that his son, also a soldier, was sick and had been brought to the capital. "I have just received a note from Johnnie," he wrote his daughter in Norfolk. "He is in Richmond in the hospital. I am going to see him in the morning but I will run the risk of being court martialled by doing so, as we are forbid going to town without permits, but I would go if I thought I would be cashiered for it." After the brutal Seven Days Battles, which took place right outside of Richmond, the city swarmed with "thousands of fathers, brothers, mothers, and sisters of the wounded," who had arrived "to attend their suffering relations, and to recover the remains of those who were slain." So great was the demand for vehicles, recorded John B. Jones, "that the brother of a North Carolina major, reportedly mortally wounded, paid $100 for a hack to bring his brother to the city."[51] Often even the most attentive care accomplished little. Thousands of wounded men perished either on the battlefield or in their hospital bed, and the city was soon overrun by funeral processions. "I was sorry to see how frequent the hearses were through the streets," commented an officer.[52]

In the countryside the movement of armies shaped lives and landscapes to an equally dramatic effect. Farmers residing in areas of intense military activity experienced the conflict through the comings and goings of individual soldiers and entire divisions, distinguished officers and broken-down stragglers, hurried messengers and snail-paced wagon trains. As fighting between North and South escalated during 1862, armies on the move became part of daily life on the farms and plantations across Virginia. Even the most stationary civilians were incorporated into wartime mobility when men in uniform camped in their homes, crowded their fields, and consumed their provisions.

Indeed more often than not the interaction between soldiers and civilians revolved around nutrition. The inability of the Confederate army to feed its mobile units meant that the only hope for a proper meal on the road depended on the generosity of civilians with well-stocked smokehouses and barns. Soldiers seemed to take for granted the willingness of the population to feed and house them; after all, these were the people they were fighting to defend. Yet at a time when provisions were becoming alarmingly scarce and expensive, every soldier knocking on a farmhouse door was a liability. Throughout 1862 Sigismunda Stribling Kimball of Shenandoah County recorded in her diary a stream of Confederate and Union soldiers who stopped by her house asking for food or threatened to confiscate what was not given voluntarily. "Soldiers here all the time for something to eat," she commented wearily in October, when the Confederate army passed by her house en masse. In Orange County, Fannie Braxton's home turned into a soup kitchen every time the Confederate army changed positions across the state. Men were "crowding in & out begging for something to eat," forcing the family in some cases to feed dozens of soldiers a day.[53]

Often hungry men did much more than simply ask farmers for food. Soldiers regularly stole villagers' hogs and poultry, consumed the vegetables in their gardens, and tore down rail fences for firewood. When thousands of troops moved from the Rappahannock lines to the Peninsula in the spring, Fannie Braxton's aunt gave "doleful accounts of damage done them by Tomb's Brigade—not an enclosure left." In the summer, as soldiers were moving back north on their way to the battles of Second Bull Run and Antietam, the same scenes were replayed, with "much mischief" done in the village and the farms. The experience of Orange County was typical of other areas in the Confederacy where armies operated on a large scale. In November 1862 the Mississippi planter Hugh Terrance was on his way to Salem, North Carolina, where he hoped to place his daughters for the duration of the war. He got as far as Jackson but was forced to turn back after receiving word that the Confederate army was about to retreat along the same path. "I always dreaded the falling back of our army as much as I did the coming in of the Yankees," he wrote his sister. "Our army was scattered for twenty or more miles wide and committing depredations wherever they went. It is truly disgraceful to the Confederate Army I have not space to go into particulars—suffice it to say they desolated the country. There is no such thing as a friendly army on a retreat."[54]

The growing friction between the civilian population and the soldiers who moved in its midst was epitomized in the changing attitudes toward Hood's Texas Brigade. Early in the war the Texans received a hero's welcome as they made their way from the Lone Star State to Virginia. As time went by, however, civilians' enthusiasm was replaced with open hostility. The roughness and virility that used to seem so attractive as symbols of the Southern martial spirit were no longer assets when the same men were roaming Virginia searching for food. By 1862 Hood's men had become blatantly aggressive in their quest for supplies, and the civilian population had learned to fear them. "Hunger compelled us this evening to kill another hog," recorded Thomas Selman of the 4th Texas Infantry as he and several of his comrades were tramping across the Shenandoah Valley in September. The men he was with also stole a bee gun from an old lady who was kind enough to lend them a skillet to cook their meat; Selman disapproved of the theft and considered going back to let her know that he had not been involved in it. Yet in the end he thought the better of it. "We did not go to the house to tell the old lady that we were innocent of stealing her honey for we knew she would not believe soldiers," he noted in his diary. By 1863 the Texans' exploits in Virginia were present even in the mind of Robert E. Lee. When ordering General James Longstreet to move the unit to a new base of operations in February, he emphasized the importance of choosing a location where the soldiers would not be "liable to prove injurious to the agricultural interests of the country." This effort enjoyed only limited success, according to H. Carrington Watkins, a Virginia planter. "Hood's Division is encamped all around us and you can form but a poor idea of the annoyances of having thieving rascals strolling about your premises all day," he wrote a friend in March 1863. "Nothing escapes them and with a strong guard around my house, they now turn to rob my garden. . . . I am afraid to leave my premises for a moment lest every thing should be overrun." Gone were the days when feeding soldiers was a patriotic duty. Confederate armies moving across the land wreaked havoc on fields, pastures, and pantries, leaving the citizenry bitter and helpless in their wake.[55]

As time went by, Virginians also began to lose patience with the sick and wounded populating their towns. In September, Winchester was flooded with soldiers who were left behind as the army invaded Maryland, as well as with men who were wounded during the campaign. "Our town is now suffering intolerably from the army under your command," wrote Robert Young Conrad, a prominent citizen, to Stonewall Jackson on September 15. "Some seven or eight thousand sick & straggling soldiers are now in town, and the roads to town are filled with more approaching. Four or five buildings are filled with the sick, and our streets are thronged with others. No adequate arrangements appear yet to have been made . . . either for medical attendance or food, and not the least attempt at police or cleanliness." If something was not done soon to remove the soldiers from town, Conrad warned, disease would spread and supplies would be exhausted. A few days later some of the men had left Winchester and appeared up the turnpike in Staunton, where they were received with similar antipathy by people like Joseph Waddell, who wrote, "The town is full of them. Many look very forlorn, hands and arms hurt, faces bound up, badly clad, bare-footed and dirty. We are afraid to offer them shelter lest they fill the houses with vermin."[56]

If the sick and wounded were becoming a burden by late 1862, straggling soldiers were fast attaining the status of public enemy. Though men in the ranks were often hungry, they still had access to army rations, and their officers were at least nominally responsible for feeding them. Stragglers, however, were entirely dependent on the civilian population for food and shelter. "Stragglers are pouring in—some of them very insolent—& they are literally stripping the country," wrote Fanny Braxton as she watched the army march toward the battlefield of Bull Run in August. When Benjamin Farinholt was allowed to leave his unit and go into the country to recover from an illness, he found that civilians living by the road would not take him in after having been treated badly by other soldiers. Farinholt went from one residence to the other until he found a welcoming couple in a "kind of out of the way place."[57]

Fully aware of stragglers' damaging effect, the army's high command competed with civilians in expressing vitriol toward the men who were ambling around Virginia. A few days after Antietam, Lee wrote Jefferson Davis, stating, "A great deal of damage to citizens is done by stragglers, who consume all they can get from the charitable and all they can take from the defenseless."[58] The following day he instructed his chief of artillery to send out armed detachments: "Rid the country of this annoyance of stragglers, using the most stringent measures, punishing them as severely as you choose, handing them over to your men, to do your pleasure on them."[59] By late 1863, despite certain success in containing the problem, stragglers had acquired such a reputation that officers were referring to them as criminals. "I am painfully aware of the annoyance to which the people of Winchester & vicinity are subjected by skulking soldiers & by rowdies & cut throats who wear the uniform of soldiers, but do not belong to the army," wrote Brigadier General John Daniel Imboden, commander of the Valley District, to Robert Young Conrad in November. "I have issued an order to my command to arrest all such stragglers & vagabonds on sight & if they run or resist to shoot them." While stragglers were rarely shot in Winchester or elsewhere, their presence had become a great burden on the careworn citizenry of the Confederate home front. This would remain the case for the rest of the war.[60]

As 1862 wore on, military motion came to have an effect on the home front not very different from the one it had on the men in the ranks. Civilians lived in the shadow of the columns marching in their midst and the host of stragglers who trailed behind them. They coped with the constant stream of wounded, hungry, and barefoot men, who relied on their patience and generosity to survive the hardships of armed service. Movement blurred the line between battlefield and home front, bringing the war to any locale the army passed through and enlisting civilians as an auxiliary force in military operations. Virginians did not have to leave their homes or don uniforms to take part in the hostilities of the sectional conflict. All they had to do was live along the routes of war.

The extent of military operations in the Old Dominion and the growing presence of men on the move in communities across the state transformed Virginians into astute and careful onlookers of armies' mobility. Most of the time they did not have much choice. The fog of war and the inscrutability of battlefield news left little to rely on besides what they actually saw with their own eyes. As troops swept through the Old Dominion in 1862, numerous civilians spent their days watching every horse rider dashing into town and every wounded soldier going to the hospital; they monitored every wagon train on the move and noticed every unusual sign of action in camp; they detected every development at the railroad station and followed every straggling soldier trudging along the way. They learned to read sounds and sights of movement, from the shouting of soldiers retreating in a rush to the clouds of dust that preceded an army on the march. Virginians followed the progress of the war by observing its motion, turning the marches and retreats into identifiable symbols that offered some legibility in a world that often made little sense. As time went by, movement increasingly took on meanings that went far beyond carnal concerns and shaped the citizenry's understanding of war.

One area where civilians were particularly attuned to the comings and goings of men in uniform was the Shenandoah Valley. Running southwest along 160 miles between the Blue Ridge Mountains on the east and the Allegheny Mountains on the west, the Valley was a region of vital strategic importance to both sides. In 1862 the Shenandoah was the scene of more military movement than practically any other area in the Confederacy. From the early invasions of the Union army in late winter, through Stonewall Jackson's spring campaign, to the retreat from Maryland in the fall, soldiers in the Valley were constantly in transit. Wherever they went, the citizenry was there to watch, chronicle, and make sense of their movements.

On June 2, 1862, John Peyton Clark of Winchester recapped in his diary the events of the previous three days. These were exciting times in the lower Shenandoah Valley. Jackson's army had arrived on May 25 after a series of victories and liberated the town from Union occupation. But within five days the Confederate army started to retreat south as news arrived that the Federal army was returning. Clark understood this immediately: "Upon Friday it was evident that the movement backward had begun by immense wagon trains passing through the town over the Valley Turnpike and upon Saturday and Saturday night the whole of the army passed through." Like Clark, numerous Valley denizens had spent the previous months sitting by their front windows or standing by the roadsides, observing the movements of the armies and contemplating their implications. On March 11 Mary Lee of Winchester followed the Confederate army as it was evacuating her town: "They took leave of us, & we stood on the porch watching for, we knew not

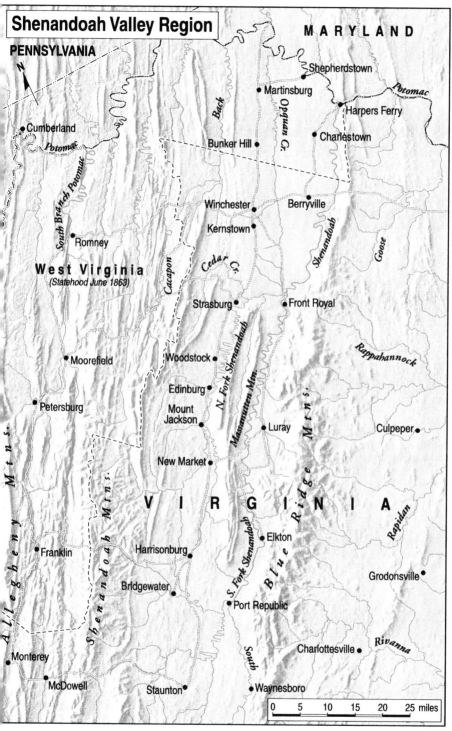

Shenandoah Valley Region

what; all the gentlemen we saw were prepared for a battle—the cavalry dashed by our door cheering . . . then a full battery; then two very large guns." In Staunton, Joseph Waddell went out on May 7 to watch the army as it began its march into the Allegheny Mountains. "We are all at a loss to know the destination of the army, but presume it will soon turn and move down the Valley." Similarly perplexing was the departure of the troops east on June 18. "To the surprise of everybody, the troops near town began to move off in the direction of Waynesboro this morning," he recorded in his diary. "General Jackson was in town nearly all day; but no one found out the purpose or cause of these movements."[61]

Knowing the whereabouts of the Confederate army and where it was going next was critical for men and women living in a region that had become a full-fledged war zone and constantly changed hands. Civilians watched closely the Southern soldiers stationed in their locales and trembled with every sign of withdrawal. In November Lucy Buck of Front Royal heard the brigade that had been camped outside her house leaving: "Ah me what a thrill the sound of those passing footsteps sends through my heart, like the heavy lingering tread of departing hosts, for surely after they leave our day of grace will have ended and we be delivered up to the Philistines again." "I saw the last cavalry picket ride off sadly enough, for I knew that with the morning might come our enemies," wrote Cornelia McDonald in December when soldiers left Winchester to join the rest of the army in Fredericksburg. Both women had good reason to be afraid, as the experience of the past year had indeed taught them that every departure of Confederate soldiers presaged the return of Federal forces and the reoccupation of their town. The movement of Southern soldiers was a sinister and somber spectacle that foretold the humiliation and hardship of life under enemy rule.[62]

This was the case even though Northern occupation in 1862 could barely be considered brutal and would pale in comparison to the hard war policies the Union army would implement later in the war. Yet Confederates were nevertheless shocked by their initial encounter with an occupying army. "The Yankees are behaving outrageously," wrote one of Jackson's aides to his father shortly after the Federal army entered the Valley. Soldiers were "imprisoning men & trying to force them with their service—stealing everything—horses, cattle, negroes, corn, wheat, flour wherever they find them." Major-General Richard Ewell reported in disgust that the "stupid, ignorant Dutch" were "ill-treating the people, robbing and stealing and wantonly killing all the stock."[63] Union troops in the Shenandoah did not commit rape or murder, and they generally showed considerable respect for private property and gender norms. But the demands created by the need to sustain an army away from its own supply base, combined with growing acknowledgment that the Southern citizenry was supporting the rebellion, had tangible results. Federal soldiers regularly occupied civilian homes, confiscated mules and horses, emptied smokehouses, and consumed the corn, coffee, and sugar the citizenry struggled to amass in the crumbling Confederate economy. Soldiers tore down fences, trampled on fields, and ruined carefully cultivated gardens. Some towns were sealed and the civilians' freedom of movement greatly curtailed. Men who had not been recruited into the army were often arrested or expelled; others were forced to take the oath of allegiance to the United States. The institution of slavery suffered a particularly devastating blow with the arrival of Union forces, as those men and women who had been kept in bondage all their life could flee to the relative safety of Federal outposts, never to be seen again by their masters. The sound of Confederate soldiers leaving prefigured these actions and many more that the Union army would never commit but that Confederates would never stop dreading.[64]

As the realities of Union occupation set in, Confederates in the Valley became accustomed to watching, deciphering, and recording the movements of enemy forces in their midst. On the eve of the first battle of Winchester, Mary Lee noticed "great excitement" in town: "Wagons are coming in; cavalry dashing & we have put out our lights to reconnoiter." On the following day the Federal soldiers were defeated and chased out of town by Stonewall Jackson's army. Five days later, however, they were back. "The hills seemed to be overcast with dark clouds of the enemy's columns," wrote Lucy Buck. "They poured in from every direction, infantry, artillery, and cavalry, through the waving wheat trampling it under foot." In Clarke County, Matthella Page Harrison received news of the Yankees' return before breakfast. After sending her brothers into hiding, she concealed everything she thought "northern thieves might take fancy to," and stood by the window. "We could see them racing over the fields. Soon we saw the White Post road darkening with them. Thinking one company might be scouring the country I began counting them, but they came so fast and were so numerous I soon gave up in despair. They had five baggage trains."[65]

Few particulars of military motion escaped the eyes of Valley citizens. In Winchester, Laura Lee knew precisely how many infantry, cavalry, and artillery units passed by her house when the Union army made its way to the battle of Kernstown on March 23. A few days later and a few miles up the Valley turnpike, Sigismunda Stribling Kimball was also keeping a close watch on the Union forces operating by her house: "There is a Regt. at Berryville but they are crossing at Castlemans's Ferry—this evening we could see long trains of wagons, crossing the mountains." In Staunton townspeople were equally rigorous in their monitoring of train movements. On May 4 the Confederate army was returning to the Valley after having feigned a movement east to mislead the enemy. Despite the secrecy that shrouded all of Stonewall Jackson's operations, Joseph Waddell knew that something was afoot and ran out of his house at every suspicious sound. "A little after 3 o'clock there was another whistle, and I went to Judge T's gate to see the train. It was a long train, drawn by two engines, and was full of soldiers!" Waddell was not the only one tracking the army's surprising return. "A number of ladies were on the hill, to see what was to be seen."[66]

Watching and recording the movements of armies served Shenandoah residents as a powerful tool in their ongoing struggle against the uncertainty of wartime. While the home front was never entirely cut off from news sources, transmission of information was uneven and easily interrupted by battles, enemy occupation, and the general disorder caused by war. Letters from the army were habitually lost or slow to reach their destinations, causing endless anxiety among families at home. Newspapers arrived irregularly, and even when they did they could hardly be relied on to convey the truth. War correspondents and their editors often knew very little about the actual progress of the war and were reduced to filling their columns with rumors, guesswork, and information obtained from the most questionable sources. Often they were unable to say with certainty which army had prevailed in a given battle or how many soldiers were wounded and killed. Valley residents faced a constant deluge of news that was eventually revealed to be entirely false. Promising victories turned out to have been humiliating defeats, generals who were reported killed were found alive and well, and confident predictions that the European powers were about to recognize the Confederacy proved time and again to have been wrong. In the Shenandoah Valley people read the newspapers avidly but knew that they could not believe the stories they told.[67]

In the absence of reliable news, Valley towns were awash in rumors. On May 1, after Stonewall Jackson's army disappeared into the Blue Ridge Mountains, Joseph Waddell was out and about in Staunton, gathering news. "The first rumor this morning was that Jackson's army was on the way to Winchester," he recorded in his diary that night. "The next, and apparently more reliable, that Jackson was marching into the Valley to meet the enemy at McGaheysville, while Ewell was moving to meet a Federal force in Page county; the third, that Jackson was at Port Republic last night, and Ewell in the camp at Swift Run Gap; and the last, that Jackson was at Harrisonburg. Coming home before night, I met the Express boy who was said to have brought the *third* report. He contradicted it entirely." Despite Waddell's considerable successes in obtaining information about the movements of armies throughout the war, he was constantly frustrated by the profusion of contradictory reports and false news. "I often mention rumors which turn out to be untrue, and many details are incorrect as stated—but I do not generally correct such ones, principally because of the impossibility of obtaining perfectly reliable intelligence," he apologized in his journal. Other Valley residents shared the sentiment. "I often feel at a loss to know what to write, when I take up my pen at night," confessed Mary Lee to her diary. "Were I to write all the rumors of each day, it would take all my time to contradict them, the next; & by the time the truth is ascertained, more startling occurrences have rendered them flat, stale & unprofitable."[68]

Information of a personal nature was similarly malleable and ambiguous. The aftermath of battles brought outpourings of rumors about the fate of local men, who were often reported to have been killed, wounded, or taken prisoner without there being any firm basis for the news. On October 1 Cornelia McDonald recorded in her diary, "Some days ago there was a cavalry skirmish near town, and Edward and Holmes McGuire were reported killed or captured. We were nearly distracted at hearing it, but about nine o'clock Edward rode up safe and sound." A month earlier Mary Lee was trying to rekindle doubts as to the reported death of her friend, Colonel William Baylor, commander of the 5th Virginia Regiment: "There is a faint hope that the report of his death is not true; I have heard it contradicted from two sources; a man has come who says he saw him yesterday; God grant it may be true." Yet whoever the man saw, it was not Colonel Baylor, since he had indeed died in the Second Battle of Bull Run on August 30.[69]

After the bloody Battles of the Seven Days in July, John Peyton Clark accidentally discovered his brother-in-law in a list of mortally wounded soldiers published in a Maryland newspaper. "The shock to me of this intelligence was beyond description," he wrote in his diary. Yet he refused to accept the news as final, since there was still a chance that "the newspaper account might be exaggerated, as frequently is the case." The following day, Clark wrote, "current rumors came to me to the effect that Mr. Jones was certainly dead, which though I could trace to no perfectly reliable source, yet had such an air of authority about them that they left me in little doubt of the fact." On the other hand, there were reasons to remain cautiously optimistic. "Hope was again slightly revived by information that an acquaintance of Frank Clark's had arrived in town last night and reports that Frank told him upon Saturday morning at Harrisonburg that Mr. Jones had had his leg amputated but was doing well. Upon this slender thread of hope I have been resting all day." Doubt remained for two more days, until Clark finally received "direct and positive intelligence of poor Frank's death."[70]

In this climate of perennial skepticism, movement of soldiers in all its shapes and forms had the potential of providing the rare commodity of solid information about what the armies were actually doing. Civilians who monitored every sign of military motion were trying to deduce whether a battle was about to take place and which units would participate in it. They tried to predict which army was most likely to occupy the locale they resided in and whether they should expect their stores to be raided and their slaves to run away. They wanted to know if husbands, fathers, and sons serving in the Confederate army were in danger or when they might be coming home. By watching the movement of soldiers and animals, wagons and cars, cannons and caissons, Valley denizens hoped to find answers to these questions and to many more.

No less important, the observation of movement provided an illusion of certainty for civilians caught in the vortex of war. The men and women who stood by the roadside did not always understand the implications of the movement they witnessed, nor were they always right in guessing where the soldiers were headed or why. Yet even when they were entirely in the dark, following military motion gave civilians a sense of control over their own lives and over the events taking place around them. If they could not obtain reliable information about the progress of the war and the well-being of their men, Valley denizens could at least monitor the armies moving among them. In the war-stricken Shenandoah Valley, that was, more often than not, as much comfort as could be had.

Even when the close observation of military movement did not yield the answers civilians were hoping for, the habit of watching soldiers traveling along Virginia roads produced far-reaching consequences of a different kind. The men and women standing on the roadsides did not simply look at the armies passing by. Rather they drew strong impressions and extracted profound meaning from any and every feature of wartime mobility, such as the appearance of soldiers, the shape of their column, the pace of their movement, the strength of their animals, and the condition of their vehicles. Through this ongoing process of scrutiny and interpretation, the motion of armies evolved from a physical reality into a visual language of powerful effect. Images of advances and retreats, of running and straggling, of marching and fleeing, signified the strength of the army and the state of the cause. The very essence of war, victory and defeat, was embodied in the motion of the soldiers going by.

There were few experiences in the day-to-day lives of Southerners that matched the thrill of watching an army on the march. The sight of a large body of Southern men moving briskly in tight formation fulfilled the citizenry's expectations of what a military force should look like and spelled success on the battlefield. "Had a grand time this morning watching 'Rhodes's Brigade,' as it passed," wrote Fanny Braxton when the army marched by her house en route to the Peninsula. "I never saw as large a body of military together, they made quite a glittering appearance, with their bayonets gleaming in the sun." A few months later, when the Confederate army was marching to Maryland, the visual effect created by thousands of bodies in motion was augmented by the exchange of shouts and cheers between civilians on the roadsides and men in the ranks. Passing through Leesburg in northern Virginia on a moon-lit evening in September, John Tucker met "ladies & citizens crowded through the side walks cheering us up & seeming perfectly delighted to see us—which was duely appreciated judging from the deafening yells that went up from each regt. as they filed by." Individually the men who made up the marching columns were exhausted, hungry, and ill-clad; yet their movement en masse was the vision of triumph itself.[71]

The spectacle of a Confederate army marching confidently to battle had a particularly potent effect when the threat of enemy occupation seemed imminent. Such was the case in Richmond during the spring of 1862, as news of the Union's advance from the Peninsula swept through the capital. Civilians knew that their army had abandoned the front lines in northern Virginia and was making its way south to face the invasion, but for a while the men were nowhere to be seen. "Absolutely in the dark as to the actual movement and its consequences . . . hearing only the gloomiest echoes from the Peninsular advance . . . it was but natural that a gloomy sense of insecurity should have settled down upon the masses, like a pall," wrote Thomas De-Leon. "But gradually, the army that had been manœuvering about the Rappahannock began to arrive," an endless stream of muddy men pouring down Main Street. The soldiers, who arrived after months of uninterrupted service, looked terrible. "Smeared with the clay of their camp, unwashed, unkempt, unfed; many ragged and some shoeless. But they tramped through Richmond—after their forced march—with cheery aspect that put to flight the doubts and fears of her people. Their bearing electrified the citizens." Men and women filled the streets of the capital, cheering the troops vociferously and showering them with the usual combination of flowers, food, and kisses. "The reception given us in the city was a brilliant affair—a complete ovation," recorded a soldier in one of the marching columns. "The ladies thronged the doors, windows, balconies, and streets and cheered us on with smiles of welcome and words of kindly encouragement."[72]

Excitement turned into frantic joy when the movement of soldiers heralded liberation from enemy rule. Stonewall Jackson's army reappeared along the Shenandoah Valley turnpike in late May, after months of absence during which the area was occupied by the Federal army. On May 23 Confederate soldiers showed up in Front Royal, surprising and defeating the Union garrison and sending it on a panicked rout toward the Potomac. Pursuing the enemy on the Valley's main road, the soldiers met a citizenry overcome by relief and delight. "The villages along the road were illuminated & the ladies wild with excitement waving their handkerchiefs," wrote an officer to his wife. Passing through Middletown, another soldier recalled, "We marched with our colors all uncovered, and the band of every regiment going at full blast, each probably playing a different tune. . . . Everything in town turned out to greet us, men, women, girls, children, dogs, cats, and chickens." Continuing north for five miles, the soldiers drove off the enemy's rear guard from Newtown and marched through its main street "amidst the most violent demonstration of joy on the part of the ladies of the beautiful town."[73]

The same night Jackson's men marched to Winchester, and early the next morning they crushed the Union army in a battle on the outskirts of town, prompting the Federals once again to take to the road. As they entered Winchester on the heels of the fleeing army, the Rebels encountered another exhilarated citizenry awaiting them on the roadsides. "We all rushed out & the streets resounded with our shouts & cheers as soldier after solider, our own men, came rushing by," recounted Mary Lee. "Our passage through Winchester was perfectly glorious—the pavements were crowded with women & children & old men waving their handkerchiefs and weeping for joy and shouting at us as we passed by," wrote Randolph Fairfax two days later. Victorian manners were set aside as the town's Confederate population celebrated the return of its army. "We went through Winchester such holowing I never heard," wrote another soldier. "The ladies was out from one end of town to the other waving their handkerchiefs and flags and holowing and cheering us on our way. We was four in a breast for one mile you could see and all yelling at once." The victorious return of the Confederate army was a rare moment of ecstasy for civilians who were increasingly encumbered by the mounting physical and mental pressures of war. The food shortages, bereavement, and spiraling inflation were momentarily forgotten when columns of triumphant men in gray entered town. This was military movement in its most thrilling form.[74]

As for the soldiers, they did not always need an admiring audience to enjoy the sight of their own mobility. Despite their hunger, fatigue, and sore feet, the men in the ranks were frequently awed by the powerful image of an army on the move. "There is something grand and imposing in the march of an army as it winds down the hills or stretches across the valleys," wrote William Randolph Smith after the first time he participated in a regular march. "To a person standing and looking at an army pass it seems as if there is a never ending string of men, horses, wagons, and artillery." Joseph Polley of Hood's Texas Brigade experienced the same sensation when his unit left its camp on the Rappahannock and began its journey south: "Last nights march beggars description. The moon was shining brightly through the cold still and bracing air. The Regt. formed a line nearly two miles in length I would frequently get ahead and sitting down watch the dusky forms of men as in panoramic succession and with all their baggage." Even when the circumstances surrounding an army's march were less than auspicious, the sights could still be formidable. In the midst of the Confederate retreat from Williamsburg in May, the Alabaman John Tucker stopped to describe the view of the army as it made its way on a muddy night's march: "The country surrounding for miles being all cleared up rendered the view magnificently beautiful—the whole plane being covd. With Troops, artillery, cavalry, wagons, ambulances & c all moving in the same direction extending as far as the eye could see."[75]

On sunny days or when troops were marching through Virginia's majestic scenery, the wonders of nature merged with the aesthetics of the march to create magnificent landscapes of motion. Robert Barton remembered crossing the Massanutten Mountain in the central Shenandoah Valley: "The rising sun greeted us as we reached the top of the mountain, whence looking back down its western slope a long line of rifles on the winding road glistening in its rays. The army in the far off curves of the road looked like a great snake with a shining back twisting along its sinuous path." On their way to Maryland in early September, Confederate soldiers were stirred and empowered by the sight of their army making its way along northern Virginia's beautiful terrain. William Pegram tried to convey the image to his mother: "How grand a spectacle presented itself when our army was crossing the Potomac—There was the river several hundreds yards in width, the mountain scenery around, the troops up to their waists in water, the setting sun and the bands playing Dixie and 'My Maryland.'" So striking was the view of the troops marching en masse that another soldier was convinced that the army was ten times larger than its actual size: "Our line when marching is over fifty miles in length with not less than five thousand wagons & c. Our line of artillery is over five miles in length while moving. You can come as near the number of men as I can. I dont think there is less than 500,000 men in all this crowd."[76]

Unfortunately for Confederate sympathizers, the Union army made for an equally impressive spectacle while wending its way across the South. When Federal soldiers first entered Winchester in early March, John Peyton Clark could not help feeling a sense of awe and intimidation at the sight of the enemy filing by: "About ten o'clock the panorama commenced, melancholy and distressing enough to all good citizens. Regiment after regiment filed by, each preceded by a band of music discoursing 'Hail Columbia, Happy Land.' . . . The troops were evidently dressed in their best, and every effort was made to produce the greatest display and impression possible." Watching the Union army move during the battle of South Mountain on September 14, George Neese, a Confederate artillerist, stopped to admire the sights of motion even when his own men had been defeated and were on a retreat: "Before I left I stood for a while and gazed at the magnificent splendor of martial array that was slowly and steadily moving toward us across the plain below like a living panorama, the sheen of the glittering side-arms and thousands of bright, shiny musket barrels looking like a silver spangled sea rippling and flashing in the light of a midday sun."[77]

Armies on the march came to epitomize bravery, virility, and triumph because the harsh realities of nineteenth-century warfare created little else in the way of uplifting or inspiring images. Civil War battles were ghastly affairs, which left their participants terrified and exhausted. Often it was not entirely clear which side had actually won a battle and what the implications of that victory would be. Furthermore the high rates of casualties on both sides in some engagements meant that even the winning side was hardly in the mood to gloat. The series of six brutal conflicts in the vicinity of Richmond that came to be known as the Seven Days Battles exemplifies this point particularly well. While the Confederacy achieved a crucial victory by thwarting the Union invasion, it lost more than 20,000 in killed, wounded, and missing, compared to the Union's roughly 16,000 casualties. In the Seven Days Battles as in other engagements, the pride soldiers felt at their hard-won victory was overshadowed by the impact of the sights they saw and the sounds they heard. In this state of mind, a feeling of elation was often inappropriate, if not impossible.[78]

The aftermath of battle was in some respects even worse. After the guns fell silent, combat zones were left densely covered by dead bodies and dying men, who lay on the ground groaning from pain and begging for help. Jedediah Hotchkiss arrived on the battlefield of Cedar Mountain to find "the ghastly horrors of the day after the battle": "God save me from such spectacles, the dead, the dying, the mangled, the screaming, the blackened living and dead humanities." "I rode over and looked at the battlefield at night," wrote James Dinwiddie to his wife during the Seven Days Battles. "Heard the slowly rolling ambulances driven about, while all over the field small dim lights flickered in the hands of hundreds of men, looking for their comrades in arms. It was a solemn and painful scene, and can only be witnessed but neither described nor imagined." Soldiers gazed at piles of human beings with heads and arms shot off; they stepped over disemboweled horses and tripped into pools of blood. "The field smells so bad I don't know how we will live if we stay here longer," wrote another soldier.[79]

The carnage remained visible for a long while after a big battle, reminding soldiers what fighting actually meant. A week after the Seven Days a South Carolinian whose unit was camped near the battlefield was still under the spell of the dead bodies lying around him: "There has been such noise and confusion of late that the stillness reminds me of a cotton factory when it suddenly shuts down. Still, still as death. The weight of the dreadful silence is almost as terrorizing as the battle itself." Arriving on the battlefield of Second Bull Run five days after it took place, Isaac Hirsh stumbled upon corpses of Union soldiers that had "turned perfectly black from laying so long exposed to the sun." A field of ten acres was entirely covered with dead bodies, "black as crows and swelled up to twice their natural size." The Confederacy prevailed in the battle and routed the Union army in the most humiliating manner, yet the spectacle on the field was anything but uplifting. "Such a sight I never saw nor never want to see again," he testified in his diary. Battlefields provided soldiers with a plethora of static, horrifying images; victory was easier to associate with the vision of an army marching cheerfully in the sun.[80]

Bodies in motion were as central in shaping images of failure as they were in evoking images of success. The quintessential symbol of defeat in 1862 Virginia was the stampede, a military force fleeing in fear of a pursuing enemy. Stampedes erased the formidable impressions created by marches, transforming armies from well-disciplined, awe-inspiring formations into packs of frightened men running to avoid death or imprisonment. Confederates derived immense satisfaction from watching Union routs, which exposed their powerful foes at their weakest, most vulnerable moments. Soldiers and civilians diligently recorded the details of enemy flight and were happy to retell them whenever the opportunity arose. When Stonewall Jackson's men arrived in the village of Romney in January 1862 they discovered that the Union garrison stationed there had evacuated upon receiving news that a Confederate force was on its way. Richard Waldrop, a soldier, reveled in stories civilians told of the enemy's hurried escape: "The people about here say they never saw such a frightened set of men in their lives. The miserable wretches hearing that Jackson and Ashby . . . were coming, actually *cried* & the cavalry were so much alarmed that they didn't take time to untie their horses but *cut* the halters & ran off." Waldrop had suffered greatly during the march, but the tall tales he heard about the enemy's departure made the effort seem worthwhile. "I suppose they would have destroyed Romney when they left if they hadn't been in such a hurry."[81]

The Union exodus from Romney would pale in comparison to the spectacles of flight that took place later that year across Virginia. The most striking episode was the retreat of the Federal army from the Shenandoah Valley in May, when Stonewall Jackson's army resurfaced in Front Royal and chased the entire Union force from Confederate soil. At that point Confederates in the northern Valley had been living under occupation for more than two months, and there could hardly be a more enjoyable sight than their enemies running scared toward the Potomac. In Winchester, Mary Lee reported feeling "intense joy at seeing the Yankees running out of town." Cornelia McDonald similarly rejoiced at the sight of great numbers of men fleeing "down the hill side to swell the stream of humanity that flowed through every street and by way, through gardens and over fences, toward the Martinsburg turnpike, a confused mob of trembling, fainting objects that kept on their mad flight till they were lost in the clouds of dust their hurrying feet had raised. Nothing could be distinguished, nothing but a huge moving mass of blue, rolling along like a cloud in the distance." Joseph Shaner participated in the battle that took place on the outskirts of town, and then went on to chase the flying bluecoats: "They run like dogs and run on through Winchester at a double quick and we after. I never have seen such a grand sight in my life . . . as they passed through Winchester the citizens fired on them with pistols and shot guns." Watching the events from her farmhouse outside town, Matthella Page Harrison shared the sentiment: "The Yankees ran like greyhounds, throwing away their clothing as it became cumbrous." The image of helpless animals also came to mind as Southerners watched the Federal army leave Front Royal. "Every man for himself they scampered out of town like a flock of sheep," wrote Lucy Buck. "Such an undignified exodus was never witnessed before." The spectacle of flight compromised the virility of Union soldiers, reducing them from honorable men to pitiful creatures. In the eyes of those watching them, there could be no greater degradation.[82]

Civilians and soldiers studied not only the contours of the bodies that made up a stampede, but also the array of material possessions the runaways left behind them. In 1862 the Union army was the best-equipped military organization in history, and its soldiers invaded the South accompanied by large caravans of wagons loaded with all the comforts that nineteenth-century modernity could offer. Union soldiers in Virginia ate well, wore warm coats, and walked in good shoes. But while the commissary's wealth eased the hardships of the service as long as the army was stationary, at times of speedy retreat it was a great encumbrance. Federal armies on the run could not carry everything with them and were forced to leave behind vast quantities of weapons, animals, equipment, and stores. Southern roads strewn with Union valuables augmented the chaotic impression of the stampede, emerging as another potent symbol of a humiliating defeat. "The scene on the other side of Newtown baffles description," wrote Watkins Kearns in his diary, as he was pursuing the Federal army down the Valley turnpike in May. "The road is lined with wagons, ladies with the valuable stores of the Yankees all of which fall into our hands." Galloping over the same road, Henry Kyd Douglas saw "wagons broken down, overturned, some with their contents scattered, some sound and untouched, some with good teams, some horseless, sutlers' stores, officers' luggage, knapsacks, bibles, cards, photographs, songbooks, and cooking utensils—a general wreck of military matter."[83]

A few weeks later the same sights were on display near Richmond, in the wake of the Federal army's failure to conquer the Confederate capital. Andrew Gillett described what he saw: "The Yankey in retreating mad Bridge through the swamps of nap sacks and overcoats and put dirt on them for the wagons and horses to go over on. I seen miles covered with shoes overcoats nap sacks canteen, guns, and a great many other things. They burnt hundreds of comisorie stores and tuns of powder." "You can form no idea of the amount of property destroyed & left by the Yankees in their retreat," wrote John Thornton of the 3rd Virginia Cavalry to his wife. Thornton had been to the Union's abandoned camps the day before, where he saw not only blankets and clothes, but the kind of military equipage Confederate soldiers could only dream of: portable ovens, solid tents, bedding, and the finest medical supplies. In the wake of the brutal fighting during the Seven Days Battles and the enormous casualties the Union army was able to inflict on the Confederacy before it retreated in haste, there was little cause for celebration. Nevertheless the great tract of land covered with valuables bespoke the fear and desperation of the Union soldiers as they were pushed back to the coast. The Union army was only barely defeated at Seven Days, but its disordered departure from the scene of battle left a vivid reminder of the Confederacy's ultimate triumph.[84]

Adding to the solemn spectacle of retreat were the thousands of dead and wounded who were often left behind as the army made its way to the safety of its gunboats or its own territory. "During the night the enemy run off leaving thousands of their unburied dead and unattended wounded in our hands together with some three or four thousand prisoners," wrote Benjamin Farinholt after the Second Battle of Bull Run. Abandoning comrades, whether dead or alive, was an unmistakable marker of weakness that Confederate soldiers rarely failed to note. This was the case in engagements both large and small and among soldiers of every rank in the army. J. E. B. Stuart, the Confederacy's famed cavalry commander, gleefully reported his accomplishments in a small skirmish near Williamsburg in early May: "The enemy's cavalry after repeated charges were entirely routed, and betook themselves to the shelter of artillery and infantry posted further on; leaving eight dead on the road besides the many wounded and riderless horses following in their wake." Stuart's own men, according to his narrative, behaved admirably. "They captured the enemy's flag and withdrew bringing every wounded man (4) in a very orderly manner."[85]

Stuart's attention to the way his own troops departed from the battlefield in this minor engagement demonstrates the extent to which Confederates were concerned with the image of their own retreats, and not only with the impression of Federal flight. Losing in battle was unfortunate but forgivable; leaving a battlefield in frenzy was a disgrace. In those instances when Southern soldiers were on the losing side and were forced to withdraw, they noticed and recorded the speed, formation, and general mood of their columns as they got away from a superior foe. In the Shenandoah Valley soldiers took particular pride in the dignified manner of their departure after the battle of Kernstown. Jackson's 4,500 men attacked a Federal division numbering 9,000, could not hold their line, and were forced to withdraw. Even so the soldiers were proud that their defeat did not end up in an embarrassing rout. Jedediah Hotchkiss noted that the battle was bloody and resulted "disastrously" for the army, but added, "Our retreat was conducted in good order—& our front only fell back a few miles." Frank Buckner Jones, a private, concurred. "When having exhausted the supply of ammunition we were ordered to retire," he recorded in his diary. "The men retired in good order, as there was no panic and no running, although they were scattered." Two months later, on May 30, Lucy Buck was watching the Confederate army fall back toward the southern Valley, as news arrived that large Union forces were coming back. This was a week after she saw her enemies leaving town sheep-like, and she was pleased at the realization that Southern soldiers "did not go 'hurry-scurry' like the Yankees but marched out with becoming dignity." Nothing could change the fact that it would only be a matter of hours before she would be back living under Federal occupation, but in the meanwhile she could at least embrace the positive impression her own army made as it was falling back.[86]

Antietam was another instance in which Confederate soldiers felt a sense of achievement about their dignified withdrawal even though they had failed to win the battle. "Just after midnight our forces began to retreat," James Boulware, a doctor in the Confederate army, recorded in his diary. "No one can imagine the crowd and pressure on such occasions unless he has been present in such a time, but no confusion." Writing his wife, Jedediah Hotchkiss portrayed the safe and quiet fording of the Potomac River by "our immense train and large body of troops" with "McClellan's vast army close behind & watching our movements" as a military achievement in and of itself. "The movement was equal to a great victory & left us free for new plans." Hotchkiss was no doubt trying to console both himself and his wife for the disappointing outcome of the Maryland campaign. Yet his glowing depiction of the army's retreat from Union soil demonstrates how Confederate officers perceived the significance of a well-managed, orderly retreat to the morale of the army and to its self-image as a capable military force.[87]

If a frenzied retreat was commensurate with dishonor, it was only natural that Southern soldiers, ever sensitive to their public reputation as honorable men, would be acutely aware of the images conveyed by motion. In July 1862 William Roane Aylett, an officer in the 53rd Virginia Infantry Regiment, set out to discover who had spread rumors that his unit had fled from the battle of Seven Pines, in which the Confederate army was defeated. The first letter he sent was directed to E. C. Hill, an adjutant. "I understood that you wrote to some one in the county of King W. shortly after the battle of 'Seven Pines,' a letter, in which I am told you stated that in that action my company 'was the first to run' and that I 'led them' or was the 'second to follow the first man who ran' or something to that effect," Aylett wrote. "Will you simply say whether my information is correct or not—and whether you have written or spoken in any manner reflecting injuriously upon the behavior of my company or of myself in battle?" Next he wrote to Charles Hill Ryland: "I have just learned from a reliable source, that shortly after the battle of 'Seven Pines' you wrote and sent home a letter reflecting upon the conduct of my company in that action—that upon the *outside* of the envelope of this letter was written this, or some tantamount expression—'the Taylor Grays in the fight at Seven Pines ran like dogs.'" Accusing a military unit of behaving like a set of frightened animals was the surest way of undermining its reputation. In a culture that valued honor beyond any other character trait, this was more than Aylett was willing to tolerate.[88]

Yet as time went by, there were also instances in which Confederate soldiers readily admitted that their units had escaped the enemy in a manner so denigrating it was hard to see how they would ever fight again. This was increasingly the case toward the end of the war, when the Rebel army was cracking under the pressure of Union attacks. In the fall of 1864 the Shenandoah was once again the setting for several dramatic stampedes, yet this time the soldiers on the run were Southern. In September and October the Confederate army lost a series of battles along the Valley turnpike, and its terrorized soldiers fled. "Sunday was another day of defeat and disaster for us," wrote a scandalized Richard Waldrop to his father. The enemy had swept "like an avalanche" along the Confederate fortifications at Fisher's Hill and "drove everything before them & scattered our troops in every direction, capturing a great many." Thomas Greene described the retreat of the Confederate army from Winchester in September as "the most disgraceful stampede any southern army ever suffered." For Charles McVicar, the Confederate departure from the battlefield on Rude's Hill in October was the "first stam-

pede I ever saw." McVicar had been in the service for three years and had
experienced many of the war's horrors, but he was not prepared for this one.
"I never was so mortified in my life," he wrote in his diary, "never witnessed
such a day." In 1864, just as in 1862, the panicked motion of demoralized
and defeated men epitomized the ultimate downfall of a military force.[89]

No less than soldiers on retreat, Confederate stragglers provided the army
and the home front a host of unwelcome images that caused considerable em-
barrassment and raised serious questions about the ability of the South to
carry out its war for independence. Civilians in the eastern theater no doubt
had plenty of reasons to resent stragglers regardless; their rowdiness and
incessant demands for food and shelter alienated entire communities and
tested the patriotism of the most devoted Confederates. Yet what was at issue
between the stragglers and the citizenry went far beyond material considerations. Men and women on the roadsides were deeply offended by the images
of tired, hungry, and barefoot men trudging wearily along the way. Everything about the stragglers' appearance disgusted this highly attentive and
abundantly critical audience: the state of their apparel, the slow pace of their
motion, the weary looks on their faces. Even when the Rebel army was on a
winning streak, the stragglers who followed it incarnated the poverty of the
Confederacy and the weakness of its war effort. They made for a spectacle of
exhaustion and submission that no Confederate citizen was happy to watch.
    Yet watch them they did. Stragglers turned up in every city and every
town and were an inescapable presence on country roads. During the retreat
from Yorktown to Richmond in April, the civilian population easily followed
the transformation of the army from a fighting force into a mass of worn-
out stragglers. "It was impossible to keep the weary and half-starved men to
regular routine," wrote a sympathetic Thomas DeLeon from the capital.
"They straggled into Richmond muddy-dispirited-exhausted; and throwing
themselves on cellar doors and sidewalks, slept heavily, regardless of curious starers that collected around them." Other civilians were less forgiving
toward soldiers who had dropped out of the ranks and wandered into their
towns. When 5,000 stragglers reached Winchester in November, Mary Lee
admitted that she "had rather have the advance than the refuse of our
army." Lee, an astute and dedicated observer of wartime motion, wanted to

see the head of the marching column because that is where soldiers looked their best. She wanted to see movement that carried the promise of victory and symbolized the martial spirit of the Confederacy. Five thousand idlers straggling along were hardly what she had in mind.[90]

Civilians were frustrated by the scene of stragglers trailing behind the main force regardless of how well the rest of the army was performing. On June 6, as Stonewall Jackson's victorious men were racing up the Valley and preparing for another showdown with Union troops, Joseph Waddell was disgruntled at the sight of the army's tail end arriving in Staunton, referring to them as "our own sick, wounded and broken down men . . . a miserable, woebegone dirty-looking set." Throughout the war Waddell made few distinctions between the wounded and the stragglers; worn-out soldiers irritated him even if they had extenuating circumstances for looking the way they did. After Antietam, when Staunton absorbed its share of casualties in need of care, Waddell was openly contemptuous of those soldiers who could not carry themselves with dignity. "All the wounded men who can walk have been creeping up from Winchester, trying to get to their respective homes," he wrote. The fact that these men were forced to march for nearly 100 miles after having been wounded in battle because their government could not provide them with transportation obviously meant little to this particular witness of wartime motion.[91]

Waddell was equally unmerciful toward soldiers who were reduced to straggling because they had no shoes. While some civilians felt sorry for the barefoot men, others like Waddell displayed severe antagonism toward soldiers suffering from lack of footwear. "A large number of soldiers had arrived on the train, principally such as were more or less broken down by their march of yesterday," he wrote on May 4. "Many of them are badly clothed and almost destitute of shoes. Altogether their appearance was rather tattered." The following day he again lamented the state of some regiments who passed through town. "Train after train has arrived to-day, being various regiments . . . all of which have been through this place once or twice before. But how different their appearance since last summer? Many of the men are ragged, and quite a number entirely without shoes. They also look dirty, and sickly." A few weeks later, however, Waddell discovered some encouraging information about the sights of raggedness that had so bothered him: "The destitution of clothing, shoes +c in our army, when it passed through Staunton, was merely because the men had been on the march, more or less remote from the depots of supplies, and not because the articles could not be furnished." It was a relief to find out that there was an explanation for the soldiers looking the way they did.[92]

While Waddell and others were perturbed by many aspects of the soldiers' appearance, they often found bare feet to be the most critical flaw. Soldiers could fight unshowered, in shabby clothing, and even covered with vermin. Marching and fighting without shoes was another matter. Waddell understood full well that the absence of sufficient footwear in the army was a serious concern that indicated a larger problem of supply and organization. If the Confederacy could not provide its soldiers with shoes, it was hard to expect that it would hold steadfast in the face of the Union's mighty force. Bare feet not only made individual soldiers seem pathetically ill-suited for battle; they made the entire Southern war effort seem improbable. The image of the shoeless soldier was the epitome of everything that was wrong with the Confederacy, everything that civilians preferred not to see.

By the end of the year some soldiers openly acknowledged the damage their bare feet and unkempt appearance had caused to their image in the minds of people on the home front. Following the South's smashing victory in the battle of Fredericksburg in December 1862, John Sale wrote his aunt describing the events. The battle had been a particularly gruesome affair, as one wave of Union soldiers after another was sent to attack an uphill stone wall, behind which stood Confederate soldiers who shot at the Federals mercilessly. "Our men were behind a stone fence and they charged it, but it was no go. Old, dirty, barefoot rebel was not going to run so fast—it hurt sore feet to run on them." Sale's sarcastic tone reveals just how central bare feet had become in white Southerners' perceptions of the army and how bitter some soldiers had grown about being seen as weak, impoverished and helpless. "Our army is not the naked rabble that it is represented to be," he added.[93]

Like marching and retreating, straggling evolved into much more than a form of soldiers' mobility. Stragglers came to embody defeat and demoralization, and they were treated accordingly by the civilian population. Even when they had legitimate reasons to be away from their unit and even when their sluggish and unsteady movement was the result of a serious injury or the absence of shoes, the sight they presented men and women on the roadsides earned them a cold welcome. Civilians like Joseph Waddell and Mary

Lee were annoyed with stragglers no matter how well they behaved or how great the suffering they had endured, since stragglers forced them to acknowledge the poverty of the nation and the vulnerability of the army. Stragglers created a distressing image of weakness that demoralized the citizenry and called into question the comforting delusion of Southern men's unassailable physical vigor and indefatigable commitment to the cause. Often that was a worse offense than abstaining from a battlefield.

In many different ways military movement formed the essence of the war experience in 1862 Virginia. This was true for soldiers who were marching, retreating, and straggling across the land, as well as for civilians who lived in the shadow of the armies' mobility. The peripatetic nature of warfare dictated the physical realities of armed service and the rhythm of life in towns, farms, and villages across the battered piece of land where North and South fought the Civil War. Motion incorporated combatants as well as noncombatants, penetrating every aspect of Confederates' wartime existence. It linked peaceful locales and blood-soaked battlefields into a single domain predominated by the comings and goings of generals and privates, infantry and cavalry, wagons and trains. Movement, more so than violence, created the eastern theater of war and defined its boundaries.

As the war grew longer and harsher, and as more civilians were caught in its path, the centrality of military motion seeped from the realm of the corporeal to the cultural and symbolic. The movement of men in uniform emerged as a language that epitomized concepts of courage and cowardice, strength and weakness, honor and shame. Both soldiers and civilians read closely into its visual vocabulary and ascribed complex and shifting meanings to the speed, posture, and formation of the troops as well as to the state of their footwear, uniform, accoutrements, and vehicles. No aspect of military motion escaped the close scrutiny and creative interpretation of men and women seeking to decipher the dangerous and confusing world of wartime. Their evolving perceptions of how war was fought and what armies were made of were based on the abundance of images created by the straggling, marching, and fleeing of the men in the ranks.

Americans living outside the main theaters of operation often heard of military movement only as rumor, a line in a newspaper report, a passing reference in a letter from a husband or son. But for the men and women who lived, traveled, and fought in Virginia during the campaigns of 1862, motion was a defining element of the Civil War. Undoubtedly this was because the conflict actually took place on Virginia territory, because the entire state was effectively turned into one great battleground. In other parts of the South men and women did not encounter movement on this scale, nor did they react to movement in such powerful and complicated ways. But in the Old Dominion, where two determined armies fought for four long years, where war was an everyday occurrence of tremendous significance and effect, the motion of armies penetrated deeply into the human experience of Southerners in every capacity and place. As fuel for the Confederate war machine and as a crucial influence on Southerners' imaginations, bodies on the move were the sum and substance of life across the Confederacy's most contested terrain.

3

Southerners on the Run

Decades after she became a free woman, eighty-seven-year-old Sarah Poindexter reminisced about how she learned of emancipation. "I sho' recall de
excitement in de neighborhood when roving crowds of niggers come 'long
de big road, shoutin' and singin' dat all niggers am free. Snow was on de
ground, but de spirits of de niggers was sho' plenty hot." The roving crowds
were Africans Americans exploiting their first opportunity to move freely
beyond their places of bondage and to bring word of freedom to their fellow
slaves. To those observing them along the way, their motion on the snow-
covered road signaled that emancipation had finally arrived.[1]

Like Sarah Poindexter, numerous slaves experienced the demise of the
peculiar institution through human mobility. Slavery in the American South
collapsed on the road, as hundreds of thousands of men and women escaped
their bondage and embarked on a new life of freedom under the protection
of the Union army. Their flight sent shock waves of change across the Confederacy, destabilizing slave communities from Virginia to Texas and usher-
ing in the end of the old regime. American slaves did not rise in rebellion
against their masters, and only rarely did they use violence to throw off the
shackles of bondage. Instead they ran. Liberation in the South materialized
through the movement of black bodies and its irrevocable impact on those
who stayed behind.

Black flight during the Civil War catapulted America into the age of emancipation and remains one of the most significant events in the nation's past.
In our historical imagination it rightfully stands out as a unique symbol of
African American heroism, perseverance, and hope, a rare moment of victory for the oppressed. Yet at the time, the flight of bondspeople from the
farms and plantations was also part of a larger wartime experience that cut

through race, gender, and class lines. Blacks were not the only ones running away. Throughout the Civil War fugitive slaves shared the pathways of the South with hundreds of thousands of deserters, stragglers, and skulkers who had absconded from the Confederate army as well as with roughly one-quarter million white refugees who escaped from their homes in the face of Union invasion. The Confederate States of America was a world of departures and captures, where runaways of all hues used motion to obtain freedom and resisted the authorities that tried to restrict them. The conflicts that ensued between slaves and masters, soldiers and officers, husbands and wives posed profound challenges to the power structures of Southern society. Flight, of both blacks and whites, gnawed away at the social order of the Confederacy until it finally came tumbling down.

One of the hallmarks of American slavery in the generations preceding the Civil War was the ruthless and effective system devised by the white South to prevent the escape of its enslaved workforce. Slave movement was limited, monitored, and penalized more than other unlawful slave activities such as trading, learning to read, consuming alcohol, or even plotting rebellions. Slaves were required to carry a written pass every time they left their place of bondage, and slave patrols roamed the pathways of the region, searching for runaways and punishing bondspeople who were caught without proper documentation.[2] Well into the twentieth century, former slaves remembered in detail the horrors they suffered at the hands of the armed gangs who worked to police them. "When de patrollers caught you from home after dark without a pass, you were stripped and beaten on de spot dat you were caught on," recalled a woman who was enslaved in North Carolina. "Some slaves have never recovered from some of dese severe whippin's." "These patrollers took two of my brothers, one seven years old and the other one five years old, and I have never seen either since," recollected another ex-slave. "Where they were carried, none of our family has ever been able to find out."[3] Entire white communities joined together in a collective effort to keep bondspeople in their place, inflicting the worst violence on delinquents and making sure others were kept in a perennial state of fear. "Paddyrollers won't no name fur dem debils," was a common opinion among those who survived bondage and lived to tell the tale.[4]

As a result escape into freedom was extremely difficult in the Upper South and almost impossible in the cotton states. Approximately 500,000 slaves lived in the border state of Virginia, and in 1860 only 117 successfully fled to the North. During the previous decade no more than a thousand bonds-people ran away every year from all the slave states combined. Even slaves who were determined to free themselves could rarely overcome the combination of patrols, a dense white settlement, a treacherous natural landscape, and their own limited geographical knowledge. Many escaped for brief periods to the woods and swamps in their neighborhoods, but very few had the resources that enabled long-distance travel.[5]

The outbreak of the Civil War changed this situation dramatically and permanently. While circumstances varied greatly from one locale to the other, for the first time since the American Revolution large-scale escape became possible.[6] The departure of the male masters for the army and the arrival of Union forces opened possibilities hitherto unimaginable. Slaves enthusiastically grasped the opportunity to flee their bondage; by the end of the war at least 500,000 would end up under Union rule, and in areas close to Union military presence entire slave populations would leave their masters behind. Before any official proclamation was issued, the upheaval of war opened the way for slaves to assume control over their bodies and to flee into the camps of the Union army. In the aftermath of war the idea of freedom would expand to include a wide range of concepts, such as compensation for labor, legalization of black marriage, and education for black children. But while the conflict was raging on, freedom translated first and foremost into a novel ability to move at will.[7]

The process of wartime emancipation began on the night of May 23, 1861, in Hampton, Virginia. Three male slaves paddled their way to Fortress Monroe, a strategic naval gateway to Virginia that Union forces occupied as soon as hostilities between the sections broke out. The slaves asked for refuge, explaining that their masters intended to remove them to North Carolina, where they would be beyond the reach of Northern soldiers. The Federal commander, General Benjamin Butler, agreed to take them in. The following morning, when requested by his Confederate counterpart to return the fugitives, he refused, arguing that the slaves had been employed building fortifications for the Confederacy and were thus considered enemy property that might be used against the Union. By declaring the slaves "contraband

of war" Butler set a vital precedent that would have immediate consequences. The Union army had begun to cooperate with fugitive slaves.[8]

Word of Federal receptiveness to escaping bondsmen spread like wild-
fire. Two days after the first slaves were admitted into Union lines, the village of Hampton was abandoned by its white inhabitants, who fled into
Confederate lines. In the confusion of evacuation, their slaves stayed behind
in the woods. Eight bondsmen arrived that day in Fortress Monroe, and
forty-seven followed within the next twenty-four hours. By July nine hundred slaves from the area had found protection around the fortress.[9] During the next four years similar patterns would materialize in every single
Confederate state. While some areas stayed out of Union control until the
end of the war, by 1865 most Southern communities had had some form of
contact with the invading army and had experienced its impact on the slave
population.[10]

Everywhere in the South the arrival of the Union army instigated massive
departures of slaves who fled into enemy lines. In November 1861 the Union
navy landed on the Sea Islands of South Carolina. Approximately 7,000
enslaved men and women resisted their masters' attempts to remove them
and remained. By the summer of 1862 they were joined by 3,000 more, and
at the end of the war the number of fugitive slaves on the islands reached
30,000.[11] "Everywhere the blacks hurry in droves to our lines," wrote a Northerner from Hilton Head Island in 1861. "They crowd in small boats around
our ships; they swarm upon our decks; they hurry to our officers, from the
cotton houses of their masters, in an hour or two after our guns are fired."[12]
In March 1862 Federal forces occupied New Bern, North Carolina, and were
immediately confronted with masses of fleeing slaves from the countryside.
General Ambrose Burnside, commander of the force, reported to his superiors, "The city is being overrun with fugitives from surrounding towns and
plantations . . . it would be utterly impossible if we were disposed to keep
them outside of our lines as they find their way to us through woods &
swamps from every side." In August a Confederate general in North Carolina estimated that one million dollars' worth of slave property was fleeing
to the Yankees every week.[13]

In Virginia the permanent Union presence and incessant military activity facilitated large-scale escape and hindered most efforts to stop it.
Following the Union occupation of Winchester in July 1862, John Peyton

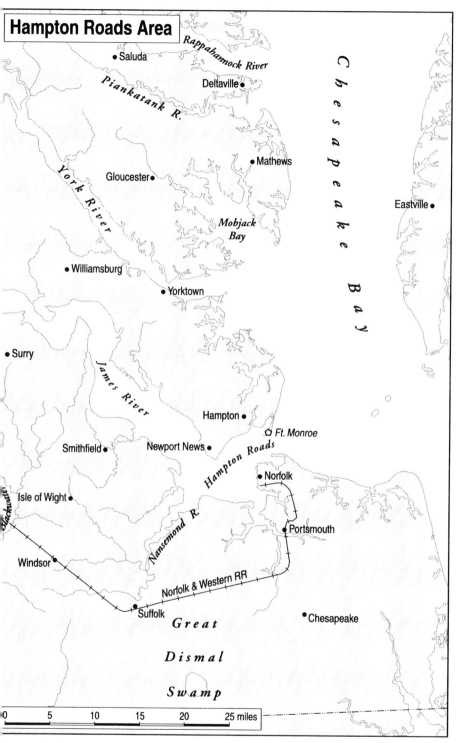

Hampton Roads Area

Clark, a Confederate civilian, recorded in his journal, "The whole town is infested by these negro dens containing runaway negroes from the surrounding country."[14] Roughly at the same time, the renowned fire-eater Edmund Ruffin wrote that not a single male slave was left at Beechwood, his Virginia plantation. At Shirley Plantation on the James River, slaves absconded every time Union forces were near enough, until the entire population of the place was gone.[15] At Glen Roy, William Patterson Smith stood helpless as his workforce was melting away. By August 1862 fifty-five of his slaves had left, constituting "a large portion of the most valuable negroes" belonging to him. Unable to locate them on his own, he asked his nephew in Richmond to inquire as to their whereabouts among the slaves of his neighbors who had been caught and arrested. The response he received was not hopeful:

> I endeavored to ascertain the fate of your runaway negroes & induced the Provost Marshal to publish a list of those in confinement at this place—of course you know that few are returned—but you may not know that few have been recovered although the newspapers publish frequent accounts of captures made by this that & the other general— I have no idea that negroes will be saved in any part of Virginia hereafter except under military surveillance—those who hold them would do well to remove them beyond the future incursions of the Yankees.[16]

The arrival of Union forces in the lower Mississippi Valley set in motion thousands of slaves from the great cotton and sugar plantations of the region, which were home to 700,000 black people. In March 1863 Kate Stone recorded from her Louisiana plantation, "All the Negroes are running away now," and in March 1864 the newly arrived Northerner Isaac Shoemaker reported that 5,000 former slaves had left their masters and arrived in Vicksburg under the custody of black Union soldiers.[17] The march to the sea of General William Tecumseh Sherman in 1864–1865 sealed the fate of slavery in many locales that had remained stable for the better part of the war. Between 20,000 and 25,000 slaves joined Sherman's army as it made its way through Georgia and the Carolinas, which increased the overall number of fugitive slaves in that department to 95,000. In the final months of the war, when Union forces penetrated deeper and deeper into the Confederate

South, the exodus of African Americans from farms and plantations increased rapidly and heralded the final demise of the old order.[18]

While the arrival of the Federal army in slave territory provided bondspeople with the initial opportunity to leave, there were other factors encouraging their flight. The first and most critical threat to their fragile existence was compulsory removal in an attempt to prevent either their confiscation by the soldiers or their own escape. "Dey shifted niggers from place to place to keep de Yankees from takin' 'em," recalled Dilley Yellady, who was enslaved in North Carolina. "When dere got to be too many Yankees in a place de slaves wus sent out to keep 'em from bein' set free." By the second half of 1863 this practice, which contemporaries named "refugeeing," had become commonplace in plantations along the coastline from Virginia to Florida and in the Mississippi Valley.[19]

Blacks dreaded and despised these forced relocations that stripped them of any stability and comfort they had achieved. Refugeeing meant disintegration of families and communities, as well as abandonment of the little property accumulated in their cabins and of carefully cultivated plots. It also meant a harsh journey, harder labor, and scarcity of food. A former Louisiana slave who was compelled to leave his home remembered the journey as "the awfullest trip any man ever make": "We had to hide from everybody until we find out if dey Yankees or Secesh, and we go along little old back roads and up one mountain and down another, through de woods all de way."[20] Texas was a popular destination for the relocation of slaves, as few believed that the Union army would ever reach so far. According to one estimate, in the year following the occupation of Vicksburg, slaveholders in the Mississippi Valley removed no fewer than 150,000 black men and women to the Lone Star State.[21] "By and by people got so thick on the big road that they was somebody in sight all the time. They jest keep a dust kicked up all day and all night," recalled Mary Lindsay, a former Texas bondwoman. "They was whole families of them, with they children and they slaves along, and they was coming in from every place because the Yankees was gitting in their part of their country, they say."[22] Many slaves underwent not one but several dislocations, as their masters tried to get away from the widening perimeter of war. Lize Smith, a Richmond slave, was removed to Waco, Texas, and then to Pine Bluff, Arkansas, but her master did not stop there. "I was at Pine Bluff when de Yankees was shooting all over de place. De fighting got so hot we all had to leave; dat's the way it was all de time for us during de War—running way to some place or de next place."[23]

The intention of an owner to remove his slaves precipitated immediate attempts at escape. "Mamma will have the Negro men taken to the back country tomorrow, if she can get them to go," wrote Kate Stone in July 1862. "Generally when told to run away from the soldiers, they go right to them." If the Union army was not close enough, slaves fled to the woods, swamps, and forests and awaited developments there. A Northern Quaker living in a camp of fugitive slaves in South Carolina recounted the escape of one black woman: "One morning her master ordered all the house servants to the field, a not uncommon custom in busy times, but, when he ordered them into a wagon, she hid away, and saw all the others driven Southward."[24] Many who did not have a chance to run before they were forced to relocate did so along the way, taking advantage of the confusion on the road.[25]

The frenzied flight of masters in the face of an advancing Union army allowed slaves the freedom to make choices like never before. When Fanny Braxton and her family left their Virginia plantation, they realized that while their slaves "seemed loath to give us up," none of them "wanted to come with us." A family that fled from Mississippi sent one member back to try to bring the "deserters" who had stayed behind: "We fear he has had a great deal of trouble, and is perhaps unable to *persuade* any of the 'contrabands' to accompany him to Georgia." As both masters and slaves were turned into refugees, the seemingly unshakable balance of power between the races was beginning to shift.[26]

The war created still more circumstances that pushed enslaved Southerners off the plantations. The escape of some slaves exposed those left behind to a harsher regime of labor and to the masters' frustration and rage. As the war lingered, supplies of food and clothing ran out all over the South, and some owners could not or did not bother to maintain a reasonable level of subsistence for their slaves. Large numbers of black men also fled the prospect of impressment. Being put to work for the Confederate army promised the worst form of slavery in the American South: a combination of backbreaking labor, scarce provisions, separation from family, and brutal supervision by army overseers. Those who could not help being drafted often took advantage of the proximity between Confederate and Union posts and fled their enslavement in the trenches for service in the Federal army.[27]

At first those who escaped were mostly young men who were physically fit, had fewer family obligations, and were more familiar with the terrain from previous experiences visiting wives and running errands for masters. But later in the war women and children joined them in great numbers. In Union-occupied territory the roads were packed with black escapees of every age and description. When John Peyton Clark looked out the window of his Winchester home in August 1862, he saw "a wagon drawn by four horses filled with negro women and children, two or three of them being infants at the breast. On the pavement and in the road following the wagon in truth there was a 'black cloud,' a large number of negro boys, women, and men, the men being with one or two exceptions very old, as was the case with some four or five exceptions with the women."[28] In March 1863 a Union commander in Lagrange, Tennessee, complained of the large number of contrabands finding their way into army camps, consisting of whole families "stampeding and leaving their masters."[29] The population of two fugitive slave camps near Memphis contained at that time 52 percent children, 25 percent adult females, and 23 percent adult males.[30]

Wartime conditions made escape possible, but they did not make it easy. Martha Harper Robinson was six years old in 1862 when she ran with her uncle from a Virginia farm to Richmond. As the white folks were distracted by a local wedding, the two started moving. Within four hours of traveling they could hear the bloodhounds on their tracks. "My poor heart started jumping as the sound neared and neared," she remembered. "I just knew every minute that we would be caught and carried back." But her uncle persisted, and they got across the Pamunkey River, avoiding their pursuers. "I remember every detail of that trip as if it was yesterday. We hid in the woods all day and traveled only at night. I would get hungry and cry, and one night I remember my uncle held my mouth until I got quiet."[31]

Runaways needed to overcome tremendous obstacles on their way to Union lines. Even slaves who knew the terrain of their neighborhood well were often at a loss as they got farther and farther from home. "The slaves didn't know how to travel," remembered Daniel Williams, who had seen many of his fellow bondsmen get caught on the run. "The way would be marked when they'd start North, but somehow they'd get lost, 'cause they didn't know one direction from another."[32] Yet even successful attempts were terrifying and punishing experiences. Slaves left the plantations at night, hid in swamps and woods during the day, and slowly made their way to the nearest Union post. Some managed to obtain rafts or carts, but most had to swim substantial distances or walk many miles without proper shoes. Some smeared their feet in turpentine or onions to eliminate their smell and confuse the blood-hounds. They undertook the journey over rugged terrain without provisions and had to rely on whatever food they could obtain along the way. More often than not, they did not eat for days at a time.[33]

Even if the Union army was relatively close, attempting to reach it entailed a great deal of courage. The massive departure of white men for the army and the general undermining of slavery in areas close to Union forces did not imply that the white South was willing to give up its unpaid workforce without a fight. Owners showed remarkable determination to keep their slaves in check, especially once they realized that any slave who reached Union lines was lost to them for good. All the usual means were put in action, with greater ferocity than ever. Planters who did not remove their slaves altogether watched their human property closely. In one Virginia plantation, an alcoholic master "used to set in his big chair on de porch wid a jug of whiskey by his side drinkin' an' watchin' de quarters to see that didn't none of his slaves start slippin' away."[34] Other owners revoked passes to visit families or chained their slaves at night.[35]

Slave patrols, manned by every available white male and accompanied by packs of bloodhounds, stepped up their efforts and exerted unprecedented violence against slaves who were caught moving about without permission. The patrols were joined by Confederate pickets, guerrilla forces, and provost guard units who hunted down runaways and made up nothing short of lynch mobs.[36] In a sharp departure from antebellum practices, some runaways were summarily executed, often in the presence of the entire community; others were shot on the spot, run over by the patrol's horses, or dragged on the ground to the nearest jailhouse.[37] When Jack Frowers tried to escape in the direction of the Union army from the inland village to which he was removed, twelve men and sixteen bloodhounds went out after him. When caught, his master first set the dogs on him, and then took him to the blacksmith, "who put a ring around my ankle, bending the ends when it was red hot . . . and then a heavey timber chain was wound twice around my waist, and locked. The chain weighed as much as fifty pounds, and was put next to my skin, and I wore both these darbies four weeks, and got a hard flogging every day beside."[38] Prince Bee remembered what happened to his brother after he was caught trying to escape: "The old Master whipped him 'til the blood spurted all over his body, the bull whip cutting in deeper all the time. He finish up the whipping with a wet coarse towel and the end got my brother in the eye. He was blinded in the one eye but the other eye is good enough he can see they ain't no use trying to run away no more."[39]

Evacuation in the face of Federal invasion triggered some particularly horrifying scenes as whites tried to prevent their property from passing into Union lines. On the South Carolina coast, slaveholders on the run from approaching gunboats burned down the slave quarters, destroyed the bondspeople's provisions, and killed slaves who were reluctant to leave with them.[40] The commander of the USS *Pawnee,* who landed on Hutchinson Island on December 5, 1861, found that "two days before, all the negro-houses, overseer's house, and out-buildings, together with the picked cotton, had been burned. The attempt had at the same time been made to drive off the negroes, but many had escaped, although some of their number, they said, had been shot in attempting to do so. The scene was one of complete desolation." Intense fear of the masters prevailed even after they were gone. A slave who managed to stay behind on the Islands told an interviewer, "If Massa Elliott Garrard catch me, might as well be dead—he kill me, certain."[41]

The ordeal of flight often continued after the escapees had arrived in Union camps. Even when greeted by sympathetic soldiers, fugitive slaves were still exposed to capture, punishment, and reenslavement. This was especially true in the border states, since slaveholders who had remained loyal to the Union were exempt from the military policy of slave confiscation and later from Lincoln's Emancipation Proclamation. Men and women who had escaped bondage in Kentucky and Tennessee could easily be taken back to their masters, as soldiers had no authority to shield them and officers were often determined to remain on good terms with the white population, whose loyalty was deemed essential to the Union cause. A hospital steward in an Illinois regiment, writing to Lincoln in September 1862, complained about the capture of a former slave by the name of Bob who had been employed as a cook until forcibly returned to his owner. "Such transactions are common here, and are susseptible of the plainest and most posative proof," he added. "And negro hunters, too, are searching, sometimes in gangs, almost daily our camp for fugetive Slaves in persuence of written permits from aforesaid Genl."[42]

Elsewhere in the Confederacy black escapees were always vulnerable to Confederate raids on Union camps and to the prospect of Union retreat from occupied territory. John M. Washington, a former slave who had joined the Union army, remembered "hundreds of colored men, women, and children" who followed the Federal forces on foot as they left Warrenton, Virginia: "Poor mothers with their Babys at their breasts, Fathers with a few cloths in Bundles or larger children accompanying them followed close in the foot steps of the soilders."[43] The town of Winchester changed hands dozens of times during the course of the war, and each time the Federal army evacuated in the face of Confederate advance, slaves who had fled their masters were forced to leave with the army. On May 25, 1862, as Stonewall Jackson's troops were making their way back to Winchester, black men and women stampeded out of town to the manifest pleasure of the white inhabitants. "The Yankees had told them," recorded Mary Lee,

that "Mr." Jackson would kill them all, men, women & children & they believed their dear friends, & flew out of town when they found Jackson was near. . . . Children were picked up dead on the road, over-run by the retreating army; it is said 250 were drowned in attempting to cross the Shenandoah; the free servants have been afraid to come back . . . women were going about crying looking for their husbands & children; & children were picked up on the road having lost their friends. Some of the slaves have returned voluntarily; some, were picked up by our cavalry & returned to their owners & there are numbers in the jail in Charlestown & Martinsburg; they are not allowed to cross the river.[44]

The Union army itself was frequently far from a safe haven for black people trying to escape their bondage. White Northern soldiers were steeped in the typical racial prejudices of their time, and many expressed deep antagonism toward the dark-skinned, destitute people arriving in their midst. A sympathetic Northerner who was familiar with the situation in Fortress Monroe blamed the failure of plans to better the situation of the fugitives on the extreme "proslavery hostility" among Northern officials, who disobeyed orders and did everything in their power to create "cruel delays" in the way of assistance. The commander of the Federal barracks in Louisville, Kentucky, on the other hand, complained that the city was full of "roving worthless negroes" and added that he was "ashamed to find so many officers disposed to debase the noble principle for which we are battleing and degenerate it into a mere negro freeing machine."[45]

Many soldiers in Sherman's army openly tried to rid the march of the slaves who had joined it, and the general's famous order no. 15, which allocated forty acres of confiscated land to every black family, was also intended to be a convenient solution for the thousands following his soldiers.[46] Male fugitives could earn a measure of respect and recognition by serving as laborers and later as soldiers, but women and children were commonly seen as nothing more than a nuisance, even when they were in fact the families of men fighting for the Union cause and valuable workers in their own right. The refugee camps that sprang up around Federal military bases were crowded, unhealthy environments, where women, children, and the infirm lived in shanties and scraped together a living either by doing work for the army or by receiving some form of charity. White Southerners indulged in stories about the misery of those slaves who dared to leave their masters and ended up in the contraband camps on the roads of the South. A white refugee from Tennessee wrote from Louisville, Kentucky, in October 1862, "I tell you those poor darkys that are running off are seeing sights, they are on the road side begging persons for mercys sake to take them & feed them & they will work for them while they live & in many places they are starving to death. I see every day accounts of the sufferings of those poor runaway slaves."[47] This particular slaveholder, like so many members of her class, surely had a vested interest in portraying fugitive slaves as dying a slow and painful death, yet in this case she was not entirely wrong. As Thavolia Glymph has put it, the world of contrabands in the Civil War South was "as dangerous and dehumanizing as the one they had left behind."[48]

Yet in the face of myriad dangers and obstacles, hundreds of thousands seized the day of freedom and fled. The official tally of slaves who attained their freedom during the war is roughly 500,000, but that figure does not account for the untold number of unsuccessful attempts slaves made to escape from bondage. Former slaves' testimonies abound with stories of intrepid efforts to reach Union lines that foundered in the face of unbeatable odds. "My uncle Ed Miles run away to the North and joined with Yankees during the War," recounted Mattie Logan, who was enslaved in Mississippi. "He was lucky to get away, for lots of them who tried it was ketched up the patrollers. I seen some of them once. They had chains fastened around their legs, fastened short, too, just long enough to take a short step. No more running away with them chains anchoring the feets!"[49] The number of men and women who made it into Union lines during the war belies the full scale of black flight and its consequences. Any account of slavery's collapse must take into consideration the thousands of bondspeople whose attempts at fleeing did not bear fruit but whose defiance of the system was immensely harmful to the white endeavor of keeping slavery intact.

Successful or not, these departures shook the system to its core. While most slaves stayed put, the disappearance of a minority was enough to make clear that a different era had begun and that what once seemed inconceivable was now coming to pass. Slaveholders were not wrong to panic in the face of slave flight, for once it began it could not be stopped. The effect of the runaways was felt immediately among those who stayed behind. Information about the widespread disorder trickled back into slave communities that had remained stable and caused substantial changes in the pace of work and the overall demeanor of those still enslaved. Even when most or all the slaves on a particular plantation remained and continued to work, whites reported insolence, laziness, and general "demoralization," a code word for any aberrant slave behavior.[50] As early as January 1862 planters were complaining about their slaves being in a "high state of insubordination" and bidding "open defiance" to the authority of overseers.[51] By June a somber Mary Lee had come to terms with the new status quo in her household: "We are all being led by paths we know not of; I am sure Billy will go; Sarah is sick in her room, nearly all the time, & Emily devotes most of her time to her baby, but we scuffle from day to day, the best way we can."[52] Even when slaves continued to work obediently, their frame of mind had been altered by the knowledge that escape might be possible, that one way or another, freedom might soon be theirs.

Paranoid as always, the owners worried that running away was only a harbinger of much worse things. As Leon Litwack has written, "To many whites, in fact, there was little to distinguish the runaway from the rebel; both threatened to bring down the system, and reports of new desertions invariably fueled talk of subversion, insurrection, and the very death of slavery." The nightmare of a murderous slave insurrection would remain a figment of the white imagination, but in the war-stricken areas of the South what did materialize was the gradual disintegration of a system that for hundreds of years had been based on the enforced immovability of blacks. Wartime escapes had a crushing impact on slavery precisely because long-distance flight had been so unusual before the war. Even when slaves were defeated by the hardships on the road and came back to their owners, things would never be the same. Motion meant freedom; once enough human chattel had obtained the ability to move at will, their owners could not bring them back to the life and labor of the antebellum era. There was no need for violence. Slavery had begun to wither away.[53]

At the same time that slave flight was evolving into a mass phenomenon, another group of human beings on the run was making its way along the roads of the Confederacy. In some respects these men must have resembled the fleeing slaves. They too were hungry, often shoeless, dressed in shabby clothes, and determined to avoid their pursuers. They too took advantage of wartime chaos and of the shortage of manpower for conducting effective pursuits; they too wished to escape physical pain and forced labor; and they too wanted their freedom and were willing to take risks for it. Yet there was one major difference: these fugitives were white, and their ragged outfits were the gray uniforms of the Confederate States of America. In the wartime South black and white were both on the road, fleeing authority and conquering distance.

The official number of deserters from the Confederate army is 103,400, yet this figure vastly underestimates the number of men who actually left the service against orders.[54] It does not include thousands and thousands of soldiers who abandoned their units for varying periods of time but were not considered to have committed desertion. These men were regularly listed by their officers as "absent without leave," and they often returned to the service before their unauthorized leaves were reported as permanent. It is thus virtually impossible to reach a precise estimate of how many soldiers absconded from the army, how long they were gone, and how many of those first recorded as merely absent ended up leaving the service for good. However, even if a definite number is hard to come by, evidence from virtually every unit in the Confederate army suggests the prevalence of absenteeism. Morning reports from companies and regiments, correspondence between officers, and statements by members of the army's high command all attest to the fact that men in the Confederate army were routinely away from their units, even if only temporarily and even if they had every intention to return. Furthermore the highly conservative figure of 103,400 is inconsistent with other estimates by senior Confederate functionaries. In November 1863 Secretary of War James A. Seddon noted in an official communiqué that absentees from the army made up over one-third of its overall numbers. By the end of the war the Confederate army listed half of all soldiers—200,000 men—as absent without leave.[55]

Confederate soldiers could hardly be blamed for their desire to get away. Service during the Civil War was a grueling physical and mental experience, subjecting men to a long list of afflictions that often made life difficult to bear. Hunger, cold, heat, exhaustion, and disease wore out their bodies, while boredom, fear, demoralization, and homesickness took a heavy toll on their souls. Moreover the hardships of the service were often compounded by gnawing doubts about the Confederate cause. Many soldiers went into the army with little faith to begin with, whereas others lost their initial enthusiasm when they realized what being a soldier actually meant. Some gave up hope that the war could ever be won, while others remained deeply committed to Southern independence but were even more determined to provide for their starving families back home. For any and all of these reasons, Confederate soldiers left the army in droves. Some men abandoned their units for only a day or two, to visit relatives in a nearby farm or to look for some decent food in town. Others withdrew for several weeks, going home to plant a crop or to rebuild a house that had fallen prey to Union troops. Still more left the service altogether and spent the rest of the war in Union-occupied territory or hiding in their neighborhoods. From the beginning of the conflict to its very end, Southern roads teemed with men in uniform who were absent without leave. Whether they were defined as deserters or skulkers, stragglers or absentees, Confederate soldiers habitually used their legs to express their discontent with the service or to fulfill their commitment to dependents who needed them at home. Regardless of their reasons for going off, it was movement, rather than mutiny, that functioned as soldiers' most common form of resistance in the South's armed force.

Absenteeism bedeviled every Confederate unit, from the most seasoned fighting forces serving in the front lines to regiments stationed in areas of the South where the war was only barely felt. It cut across class, age, and rank, encompassing disenchanted dirt farmers from Alabama, who deserted in opposition to secession and a slaveholders' war, as well as men from the best families of Virginia, who were deeply invested in the Confederate cause yet chose to take some time off from the service when the opportunity arose. Violation of movement regulations was not unique to any particular class or group in the Confederate army. Its different forms and configurations appeared among rich and poor, young and old, conscripts and volunteers, in the western Confederacy and in the east.[56] The depth and breadth of the problem is most evident in the fact that at certain moments the military even had trouble controlling its officer corps. In September 1862, as the Army of Northern Virginia was struggling to regroup after the failure of its invasion into Maryland, a brigadier general charged with collecting absentees in the town of Winchester reported, "The number of officers back here was most astonishing."[57] The level of desertion in the officer corps during the campaign prompted Robert E. Lee to suggest that Congress pass a law vesting the president or the War Department with the power to strip officers of their positions "upon clear proof of bad conduct in the presence of the enemy, leaving their posts in time of battle, and deserting their command or the army in the march or in camp." He continued, "There is great dereliction of duty among the regimental and company officers, particularly the latter, and unless something is done the army will melt away. You will see by the field return this day sent to General Cooper the woeful diminution of the present for duty of this army. The absent are scattered broadcast over the land."[58]

While September 1862 was certainly a low point in the army's four-year struggle to control its manpower, the presence of officers among the crowds of absentees attests to the potential for disorder in the Confederate ranks. Granted, discipline greatly improved during 1863 and enabled the South to continue fighting effectively through 1864. But as the Confederacy's prospects began to darken in the fall of that year, the failure to control desertion and absenteeism in all their shapes and forms returned with a vengeance. In

the last months of the war it reached massive proportions and had a determining influence on the South's military fate.

Men started leaving the army without authorization almost as soon as
they joined it. James Powell recalled the summer of 1861, when the soldiers
in his Virginia company realized that fighting for the South would take
them far from their homes. After only a couple of months in the service,
they already "became very homesick and tired of the war, and began to fall
off and go back home." Powell confessed, "I too, became tired of this sort of
work, tramping through the mud under privations that affected the health,
spirits, and strength."[59] In January 1862 a group of soldiers from the 44th
Virginia Infantry apologized for having left camp to go home the previous
month without permission. "We were under the impression," they wrote in
their petition, "that all volunteers were entitled to forty days in the course
of twelve months, and if they could not get furloughs, they had a right to go
without." In those early days of war, offenders were treated leniently, and
many soldiers wandered away from the service without suffering serious
consequences.[60]

Virginians who were serving close to home did not see a reason to stay in
camp between battles if their families needed them, especially during plant-
ing and harvest times. Regiments stationed in or passing through populated
areas intermingled with civilians freely, and soldiers were often lured by the
amenities of cities or the comforts of country homes. As he was marching up
and down the Shenandoah Valley in 1862, Watkins Kearns, a soldier in the
27th Virginia Infantry, routinely left his command with other men after deciding to "take it on [their] responsibility for the day." They slept in private
homes and dined in local hotels and reported having had "a good time general." On returning to his unit from one of his excursions he learned, "The
whole company including myself... were under arrest. Slept very soundly
nonetheless." On a day in July 1862 James Bradfield of the 17th Virginia Regiment recorded his activities: "Go down to the run take a good wash fix up
and then run the blockade to Richmond." In the capital he ate dinner, drank
whiskey, and spent a pleasant night at the Exchange Hotel. Like Kearns and
Bradfield, tens of thousands straggled behind the armies and stayed away
from their units for days or weeks.[61]

A year after the beginning of the war, the problem of absenteeism had
become so widespread that the government and the army took emergency

measures. The provost guard was expanded, all nonmedical furloughs were revoked, and conscription was enacted by Congress. Absenteeism did not stop, but the general effort to keep men in the service proved at least partly effective, and by the spring of 1863 the number of soldiers in the Confederate army had increased. Yet in the summer, following the defeats at Gettysburg and Vicksburg, the movement away from the army resumed. Virginians re- treating from Pennsylvania took unauthorized leaves to visit home, while others gave up altogether. R. H. Depriest wrote his wife in August 1863, "Thare is some runing of narely evry night thay have more guard round the camp than was to keep them in and stricter orders too." A conscription of- ficer in South Carolina reported to his superior, "It is not uncommon for squads of ten or fifteen to come in from the army, having made their way across the country on foot, and generally bringing their arms."[62]

The increase in unauthorized leaves was also the result of the situation on the home front. Two years into the war the living conditions of soldiers' families were deteriorating rapidly, and thousands of women were sending letters to their husbands, begging them to come home. "They say the yan- kees ar runing a way by rigament and our army isant mutch beter thay ar runing a way by company and ar talking about runing away by the riga- ment," commented Michael Freeze on the state of affairs in his unit. "[Wives writing from North Carolina] say that they ar starving and cant hold out more then too month longer and I hard a heap of men sware that if their families would sufer that they would stack armes and go hoom." Confeder- ates, both male and female, were unwilling to accept the fact that by joining the army, white men had lost their power to care for their families. Soldiers emphasized over and over in their applications for leave the absence of "male assistance" or "any white male relative" in their crumbling households as a reason for the army to grant them a few days of freedom.[63] The men aggressively pleaded with their officers for furloughs, recounting the misery of dying wives, starving mothers, and sick children. "I appeal to you . . . to try & do something for me as I heve a large and helpless family to take care of . . . & corn is 60 dollars," wrote one soldier, while another implored, "I have not been home in over one year . . . my wife & children have no one to do any thing for them. . . . Justice to my family demands that I go." Captain James H. Skinner of the 52nd Virginia was declined a furlough by Gen- eral Edward Johnson several times but insisted on trying again. "I am thus importunate," he explained, "from an *imperative* sense of duty: the exigencies of the service are severe indeed, if in addition to the toils, privations & discomfort of the soldier's life must be superadded a denial to him . . . of all opportunity of taking care of & providing for the comfort of those, whose well being is his chief concern and most sacred trust."[64]

Requests for furloughs also came directly from wives and mothers, who stated their circumstances to their husbands' superiors. Eliza Minnally from Lunenburg County, Virginia, wrote to the general in charge of the 59th Virginia Infantry asking that her husband be allowed to come home as she was now "left without anyone to make arrangements for providing" her "with another year's provisions." Mrs. Frankling Brickle directed her letter to General Henry Wise, with even more details about her delicate situation: "Janel Wise Sir I weill stat my case to you I am in a bad fix I have three litly children and no body to stay with me and I am a lukin to be confine the last of this month and I want you if you plese to grant my husband a farlaw for 10 or 12 days wile I am in beed so plese give him a farlaw."[65]

The reality in the Confederate army was that when a furlough was denied a soldier would in many cases set out on his own. The determination to reach home at all costs stemmed from the deepening despair of families in distress and of men who felt their responsibilities to their loved ones trumped their obligation to the army. Others were also helped in their decision to desert by their dwindling faith in the Confederate cause and by a growing sense that the army was fighting a misguided or unwinnable war. Yet the fact that so many took the liberty of going home against orders was also the result of the soldiers' deep-seated habit of controlling their bodies' physical movement. In the antebellum period mobility was an essential right of white men. Along with voting, owning property, and bearing arms, it defined their status as a privileged class and set them apart from slaves and white women, who were barred by law or custom from moving as they saw fit. The mobilization of the region's ruling caste for service in the Confederate army entailed forcing its members to give up this privilege and to adhere to a strict regime of military discipline. This proved to be a difficult if not impossible task. Some soldiers openly warned that if they were not permitted to leave they would do so illegally. The men in Hood's Texas Brigade wrote President Jefferson Davis to protest not having received furloughs like other units, though they had been fighting gallantly for years.

"All that we asked of him," wrote one soldier, "was to put us on an equality with the rest of the troops and if he did not we would put ourselves on an equality and that was as good as to sa that we would go home any hour."[66] The imprint of social domination was too strong and could not be erased even by a fierce commitment to secession or by a genuine dedication to comrades. As free men in a society based on dependency, they believed in their right to control their own mobility and exercised it liberally. Going home to see one's family, even when an application for leave of absence had been unequivocally denied, epitomized the white man's refusal to accept that service in the armed forces meant loss of agency over one's own body and its motion.[67]

In the summer of 1863 absenteeism was becoming so widespread that soldiers in some units were required to declare in their applications for furloughs that they had not been absent without leave from the army during the previous sixty days. Demanding from soldiers a record of good behavior for such a short period of time exemplifies how low the standards of discipline in the Confederate army had dropped and how prevalent the abuse of regulations regarding movement was becoming.[68] And yet things were about to get worse. As 1864 wore on, defeat struck everywhere. Soldiers were exhausted and families grew increasingly helpless in the face of spiraling inflation and diminishing food supplies. The increasing presence of the Union army and its policy of forgiveness toward Confederate deserters also tempted many who had grown tired of the war and no longer saw a purpose in fighting for a lost cause. As the year drew to a close the reelection of Abraham Lincoln, Sherman's march, and Grant's renewed offensives in Virginia caused widespread despair followed by mass desertions. In September a soldier serving in the Shenandoah Valley watched his unit dissipate within a matter of days: "There are only about 400 men left in our brigade which a week ago numbered upwards of 1200 a great many men took to the mountain & escaped & will be coming in from time to time."[69] The Confederate War Department estimated that in the four months between October 1, 1864, and February 4, 1865, nearly 72,000 men deserted from the armies east of the Mississippi.[70] Samuel Walkup, colonel of the 48th North Carolina Infantry, stood by helpless as his soldiers left the service. "We have been decimated and more than decimated by desertions," he wrote in his diary on March 4, 1865. Robert E. Lee shared the sentiment: "Hundreds of men are deserting nightly and I cannot keep the army together unless examples are made of such cases."[71]

Men who wanted to break away from the Confederate army had no shortage of opportunities to do so as military units were large, scattered, and often on the move. Soldiers easily snuck out of camp at night or stayed behind when their regiments were on the march. "Our Confederacy has dwindled down mightily," wrote John Sale to his mother in October 1862. "As you know, a great many deserted when we left camp, and some since."[72] Soldiers serving close to home or on their way from one theater of operations to another often jumped off trains or simply strayed from the line of march when they passed by their neighborhood. A Confederate official described what happened to the soldiers of the 16th South Carolina Regiment when they were ordered on short notice from Charleston to Jackson, Mississippi:

> They had been nearly two years away from home; had but recently closed an arduous campaign in North Carolina; were ordered to Charleston, where they hoped to remain. The order to go forward to the west was the signal for a general desertion. They took their arms with them, intending, as I am satisfied, to return to their commands after a hurried visit to their families. But finding among their friends and through the country a change of tone, a weariness with the war, a readiness to counsel and encourage desertion, they have but with few exceptions remained at home.[73]

The aftermath of a substantial battle left many units particularly disorganized and easy to abandon. A few days after Gettysburg an officer reported that the state of affairs in Pittsylvania Court House was "really deplorable": "There are any number of persons that have returned here since the last battle that have no authority for being here."[74]

While every soldier traveling in the Confederacy was required to carry a pass, men proved remarkably apt at forging travel documents and proceeding undisturbed. The provost marshal of Richmond testified in 1863, "Many well-born and bred, who would once have shrunk from the least moral delinquency, boldly barter all in the alteration or forgery of an official paper to get away from the army." Soldiers writing home confirmed this observation. Watson Dugat Williams, an officer with the 5th Texas Regiment, reported to his fiancée from a camp near Richmond that the army's efforts to seal all entrances into town and to make sure every soldier on the move was carrying a pass resulted not in men giving up their cause of slipping into the city illegally, but rather in a thriving industry of counterfeit paperwork: "The only way to get there now except by legal passes is to forge passes and the most extensive forgeries are carried on in this respect you ever heard of."[75]

Another popular avenue of escape was medical leave. An absolute majority of soldiers in the Confederate army needed some form of medical attention during the war due to either battle injuries or disease, and in most cases it required them to leave their units. Going to a hospital provided a rare opportunity to travel legally over long distances, and thousands used it to go home. Moreover soldiers who were granted a furlough by a hospital surgeon were entitled to free transportation and were exempt from the obligation to travel with a passport.[76] Accordingly, some soldiers never made it to the hospital, others walked out of the wards, and still others waited until they were discharged and then went home instead of back to camp. While there are no definitive statistics on this phenomenon, partial figures are sufficient to indicate its extent. Nearly 6,000 soldiers deserted from Virginia hospitals between September 1862 and August 1864; in one instance in Georgia, 135 men out of 330 who were transferred from one hospital to another never got there, though the distance between the two places was only twenty miles. Confederate officials estimated that two-thirds of the soldiers furloughed from hospitals never returned to duty.[77]

Officers railed against the abuse of sick leaves and tried various means to stop it, usually with meager success. Following the retreat from Yorktown in May 1862, General D. H. Hill wrote the secretary of war with "deep mortification" to report, "Several thousand soldiers and many individuals with commissions have fled to Richmond under pretext of sickness. They have thrown away their arms that their flight not be impeded. . . . Do make General Winder hunt up all who have not surgeons' certificates." Two months later the provost marshal of Charleston assigned guards to accompany the sick and wounded on their way to the hospital because he was concerned that they would disappear. In August Brigadier General Henry Wise detailed an officer to examine the hospitals in Richmond to find out how many of his men were actually there. His subordinate reported that most of the corps's sick soldiers had been transferred to other hospitals, "taking care to select

those nearest their homes and in a great many cases they have never reported
to the hospitals they were ordered to but went direct to their homes and are
now skulking duty. . . . I am satisfied that at least two thirds of the absent sick
are fit for duty." A week later one of the missing soldiers wrote Wise admit-
ting that he was indeed at home, since he assumed that having been sick and
unfit for duty "it would be just as well for me to come home and there receive
the attention of Dr. Peachy as to go to the Hospital."[78] Even doctors candidly
admitted that their patients were using sickness as an excuse for skulking.
One doctor serving with an Alabama regiment wrote his father in May 1862,
"Send word to all my sick men at home that they must come on immediately
or I will have to send for them and punish them as deserters. There are several at home on furlow that can come & must come."[79]

Yet while some officers were trying to stem the tide, others copied their
soldiers' behavior and readily abused medical leaves. In February 1865 General Fitz Lee was asking for the whereabouts of a cavalry captain who had
gone missing from his post. His subordinates established that the man had
received a certificate of leave and was sent to a hospital in Charlottesville,
yet chose instead to convalesce at his home in Fauquier County. It was a case,
wrote one officer, showing "a loop hole that ought to be closed up." Yet at that
point it was much too late, as soldiers of all ranks had become accustomed
to misuse a doctor's permission to leave camp. Even high-ranking officers
were not immune to the temptation of medical furloughs. In February 1862
Colonel William C. Scott, commander of the 44th Virginia Infantry, was in
Richmond, spending time away from his unit. Writing his superior, General
Edward Johnson, he announced, "I want a General Court Martial for the
three or such of my officers as have been away without permission or who
have overstayed their time." Yet even as he was purporting to impose strict
discipline on his delinquent subordinates, Scott's own situation was somewhat ambiguous. He had left camp and arrived in Richmond to receive
medical treatment at a hospital, where a local surgeon provided a certificate
allowing him to remain for an additional twenty-five days. Yet Scott had
other ideas for how to use his sick leave. When writing to his superior he was
actually no longer in the hospital, but rather visiting his "old mother," who
"has been very ill & is still ill, though better." Sensing that the general might
not be thrilled with his conduct, he added that he intended to return to his
regiment as soon as she was well, assuring him that he "would prefer being

at camp than away."[80] The fact that even a colonel was not above violating the terms of his leave goes to show just how pervasive this mode of conduct had become.

Ordinary furloughs were considerably less common than medical ones, but when granted, they too provided openings for soldiers to stay home. When Edwin Penick, a soldier in the 38th Virginia, made a gentle inquiry about a leave of absence, "the old doctor told me God sake not to say any thing about it at present as the General was mighty freted about the men staying away so whenever they had furlows or sent away on sick list." Officers who did endorse applications for furloughs acknowledged this problem implicitly in statements such as "My men heretofore furloughed have returned"; "they are both good & reliable men & will no doubt return promptly to the time if permitted to go on leave of absence"; and "I have the utmost confidence in these men & believe that they will certainly return to duty at the expiration of their furloughs."[81]

The irony of furloughs in the Confederate army was that they were simultaneously a channel of desertion and a means of preventing it. Authorization of regular furloughs officially ended in March 1862, when it became evident that something had to be done to check the uncontrolled movement of men in and out of the military.[82] Yet despite the written regulations, and despite widespread absenteeism and desertion, soldiers continued to receive furloughs until the very end of the war. Officers, particularly junior ones, attempted to halt the surge of unauthorized leaves and increase their personal popularity by giving their soldiers permission to go home legally.[83] One soldier commented in August 1863, "I am in hopes they will continue to give furloughs this fall and winter and I think they will to keep the men from runing a way so much." Alexander Haskell Brown, the provost marshal of Charleston, issued officers a warning after "a great many leaves of absence and furloughs having been granted by officers not authorized to grant them, and a great many informal leaves of absence and furloughs having prosecuted at these Head Quarters."[84]

In many cases officers approved requests for furloughs even when the circumstances were far less tragic than death or starvation of soldiers' families. In November 1863 Captain N. B. Street of the 26th Virginia explained why he was asking that one of his soldiers be granted twenty days of leave: "His wife has taken up with another man, has treated his child very cruelly and is converting his property into money evidently making her arrangements to leave with this man." One deserter who was actually caught at home was allowed a few more days of leave because his sister had just died. The cavalry unit that was supposed to bring him back to the army was satisfied with a "positive promise from him that he would report in a few days." Other soldiers were granted furloughs to take care of "important business" or to get married. In the last months of the war even Robert E. Lee gave in and authorized furloughs liberally to keep his men from continuing to leave in great numbers.[85]

The practice of granting leaves of absence was motivated not only by pragmatic considerations of maintaining morale and giving men hope that they would be able to reach their homes without committing a treasonable offense. Equally important was the basic assumption that soldiers could not be altogether stripped of their rights as free men and that their commitment to their private affairs could not be ignored. The Confederate army was an organization of white men fighting for what they perceived as white men's rights. As such it was based on a delicate balancing act between consideration and compulsion, agency and obedience, accommodation and resistance. The idea that even the lowliest private was a master with both privileges and responsibilities was deeply ingrained in both soldiers and officers and had a crucial impact on the management of enlisted men's movements. Officers acknowledged the fact that their soldiers were free men who had left helpless families at home, and soldiers were unabashed in asserting that they had other obligations. In a rural society it was impossible to care for a family without being physically present on a farm, and thus the mobility of men in the army was the key to their ability to sustain hegemonic positions within their households as well as to enjoy some measure of control over their own bodies. Furloughs were both a sign of respect for the soldiers' traditional privileges and a way of keeping them in the army. Officers could only hope that those who were allowed to leave would choose to return.[86]

But even in the Confederate army toleration had its limits, and once absenteeism had become a mass phenomenon with disastrous implications, a wide variety of harsher means was devised to bring men into the army and prevent the rest from running off. For the first time in the history of the American South, large numbers of white men experienced a measure of the violent hounding their slaves had been subjected to during 250 years of bondage. The same culture of mastery that bred consideration for the white man's freedom of movement also furnished Confederate authorities with the techniques to deal with those whose transgressions were no longer tolerable. Generations' worth of experience in hunting down runaway slaves was put into use chasing members of the region's ruling caste, whose unauthorized movements now jeopardized the very existence of the Confederacy. Even as the social system of slavery was disintegrating, familiar scenes from antebellum manhunts were reenacted all over the South, this time with an all-white cast. Although white men would never employ the same inhuman cruelty toward those whom they perceived as their social equals, the quest for ways to control the mobility of soldiers inevitably invoked the most obvious frame of reference for coping with human beings on the run.

The Confederate army began hunting down its absentee soldiers before the first battle of the war was fought. By June 1861 officers were running ads in local newspapers urging men to return to the service and requesting the assistance of Home Guard units in apprehending them. One type of advertisement pertained to specific absentees and included a detailed description of age, height, weight, complexion, color of eyes, and scars. A reward of thirty dollars was typically offered for bringing a deserter to an officer, fifteen dollars for placing the culprit in a jailhouse. A second type of ad called all deserters from a particular unit to return to the service immediately. Officers continued to publish these notices until the summer of 1863, largely to no avail. Such ads had been a useful tool in catching fugitive slaves, but when the escapees were white men, they proved to be remarkably ineffective.[87]

As the months went by it became evident that local law enforcement authorities were also incapable of dealing with the growing number of men who had become tired of army life and were making their way home. Starting in the spring of 1862 the Confederate government stepped in and tried to stem the tide of desertion from its armies. The national military police was put in charge of tracking deserters and bringing them back to the service; provost marshal units were expanded to the division and corps levels; conscription officers were authorized to arrest deserters, and railroad conductors were instructed to scrutinize all passports, which were required of every soldier on the move. By the fall of 1862 provost forces were monitoring every road and railway where armies were camped. Starting in 1863 entire regiments were taken from the front lines for weeks at a time and detailed to

go after deserters in their home counties. In 1864 the writ of habeas corpus
was suspended for all desertion cases, and the Confederate Congress passed
a law that made helping deserters an offense punishable by a fine of up to
$1,000 or by a prison sentence of up to two years.[88]

The manhunt after the South's white runaways engulfed every state of the
Confederacy and took place everywhere from the front lines in Virginia to
the frontier settlements in Texas and Florida. Over the course of the war
thousands of men were employed by local, state, and national authorities in
finding and arresting soldiers who were absent from the army without permission. "I 'members when de war commence, Jeff Davis called for volunteers," recounted Tom McAlpin, who was enslaved in Alabama, "den a little
later when de south needed mo' mens to fight, Jeff Davis' officers would go
th'ough de streets, an' grab up de white mens an' put ropes 'round dere
wrists lak dey was takin' dem off to jail. An' all de while dey was jus' takin' 'em
off to de war. Dey made all de white mens go." "It has bin a sight to see and
hear tell of how they have bin a runing a way," wrote William Tesh to his
family from Virginia in August 1863. "They have got guards all a long the
mountains and all through the country a takeing them up."[89]

The streets of Richmond were the scene of a perennial cat-and-mouse
chase between men who were eligible for service and the city's military police. The provost guard, wrote an officer to his wife in July 1862, "walk the
streets day and night and arrest evrybody who do not have papers or some
showing from the proper authority." The previous evening they had taken
under custody 113 officers and soldiers who were caught without passes in the
Exchange Hotel, one of the capital's premiere attractions.[90] This was hardly
the only group of detainees to include officers among its members. Indeed
the capital witnessed frequent arrests of officers who were staying in town
illegally, avoiding the travails of the service and enjoying the pleasures of
bars, hotels, and fine company. In April 1863 the provost marshal of Richmond embarked on an operation to locate and register all officers staying
in town without proper documentation, at the end of which a force "over-
hauled officers and hastened their return to their respective posts of duty."
A year later the enrolling officer of the surrounding Henrico County published the names of ten officers who had been absent without leave for so
long they were erased from the rolls of the Confederate army.[91] By the last
few months of the war provost marshals were combing Richmond for bu-

reaucrats and others who had previously been exempt from service but were now needed in the army. "The 'dog catchers' are out again," reported the war clerk John B. Jones in October 1864, "arresting able bodied men (and sometimes others) in the streets, and locking them up until they can be sent to the front."[92]

In the rural South provost guards, local militia forces, conscription officers, and detailed troops spent months sweeping counties from one corner to another, using the best of slave patrol methods, including bloodhounds and gunfire.[93] "There is a squad of forty men sent out in this country to gather wandering conscripts," wrote John Lowery to his mother from North Carolina. "I hear that they run like turkeys our men fire on them but have not heard of them killing any one yet."[94] Charles Hutson was one of the soldiers who was detailed for a deserter-hunting expedition the next fall. "We have been steady at the work ever since our arrival, moving from place to place and 'skirmishing' the mountains as we go along," he wrote his family from a bivouac. "We may continue at this task for a long time & travel far southward the mountains are covered with these rascals."[95]

Indeed some of the fiercest confrontations between men who had left the army and those who were sent after them took place in the mountainous regions of North Carolina, Virginia, Georgia, and Alabama, which were home to many of the men who had actually committed desertion and did not intend to return. Attempts to make arrests in this region often ended in shootings when deserters refused to surrender. In the Blue Ridge Mountains the leader of a deserter gang shot a scouting party that came after him and remained in hiding for another month before being arrested. "He is a desperate character & will try to escape if the least opportunity is afforded," warned the officer who made the arrest. General Gideon Pillow, the superintendent of the volunteer and conscript bureau in Alabama, testified in July 1863 that there were between 8,000 and 10,000 deserters hiding in the mountains, many of whom had deserted a second, third, and fourth time. "They cannot be kept in the army so near their homes," he wrote the authorities in Richmond. "As fast as I can catch them and send them to the army they desert and bring off their arms and steal all the ammunition of their comrades they can bring away.... They have killed a number of my officers and in several instances have driven small bodies of cavalry."[96] Two brothers reported from Davidson County in North Carolina, "Thare is so many deserters here that the home guard is a feared to go without a heape of them or some of us." As the war continued, the conflict between deserters and their hunters escalated steadily. The rates of absenteeism and the desperate need of generals for manpower forced Confederate authorities to allocate greater resources and adopt harsher means in an attempt to replenish dwindling regiments. At the same time the suffering of families on the home front and recurring defeats on the battlefield made thousands more determined than ever to stay out of the service.[97]

Thus two years into the Civil War the pathways of the South were occupied by runaways of both races, who had previously stood on two sides of a rigid racial divide but were now struggling with analogous threats and obstacles on their way to freedom. Like the black flight from plantations, white flight from the army evolved from an individual enterprise into a group activity. Civilians grew used to contingents of men moving together, avoiding their pursuers. "It is nothing strange to see from 8 to 10 in gangs going on making for different parts of Virginia and North Carolina," wrote Mary Davis on deserters in southern Virginia.[98] "A bold case of desertion took place in the 12th Alabama Regt. last night," recorded Samuel Pickens in his diary in August 1863. "Out of a co. of 32 men 21 went off, with arms and accoutrements. Two squads went in pursuit of them with instructions to take them dead or alive if possible."[99]

Fleeing the army also forced deserters away from the roads, the domain of masters, and into the South's alternative geography.[100] "De woods wus full of Rebs what had deserted," remembered a former North Carolina slave.[101] A white North Carolinian reported from Montgomery County, "The woods is fool of conscripts and deserters and they are doing mis chief and threatning to hell or destroy the property of any of them neighbours that speeks aganste them."[102] White men who had served in the antebellum slave patrols were hiding in the same lush, barely passable forests and marshes that gave refuge to their slaves. "It is almost impossible to get the men out and into our army," reported Gideon Pillow on the state of affairs in Mississippi and Tennessee. "They hide and dodge in the thickets and swamps and mountains, and when hard pressed they run into the enemy's lines to elude capture by my officers."[103] The fugitives were also using the same techniques Southern slaves had perfected over centuries of resistance. "Dey would hide out in day time an' sneak at night," remembered Jim Allen, a former Alabama slave.[104] "The only prac-

tical way of hunting them will be dogs and mounted men under the command of an experienced woodsman who is familiar with the country," declared a Confederate officer who was in charge of the manhunt in Taylor and
Lafayette counties in Florida.[105] Years later Abram Sells, a former Texas slave,
perceptively summed up what had happened to the white men in his neighborhood over the course of the Civil War: "I 'member how some 'r' march off
in her uniforms, lookin' so gran' 'n' den how some 'r' dem hide out in de
wood' to keep from lookin' so gran'."[106]

Confederate soldiers who were caught in areas of Union occupation and
were trying to return to their units also entered the same geography in their
flight from the enemy. In May 1864 Charles McVicar registered in his diary
such a journey, which consisted of "traveling through fields, swamps, marshes,
woods and thickets, rolling into the ditches, falling over stone piles, under
cover of the night." Joseph LeConte, a professor of chemistry and geology at
the South Carolina College, set out from Columbia a few months later in an
attempt to get to Liberty County, Georgia. Traveling through the woods to
avoid Sherman's march, he encountered both soldiers and civilians transformed into runaways and relying on African Americans for survival. "I had
formerly known him as the pink of gentility, neatness, and propriety," he
wrote of an acquaintance he had met in the thicket, accompanied by two black
men. "He was now roughly and shabbily dressed, very much sunburned and
very dirty. He was, moreover, literally armed to the teeth with two navy re-
volvers and a huge bowie-knife in his belt and a double-barrelled gun on his
shoulder. He was the most dangerous and ruffianly-looking I ever saw." Caroline Hunter, who was fourteen when the war broke out, recalled both her
owner's relegation to a fugitive and the burden it cast on his slaves: "While de
war was going on my massa had to stay in de woods. De Yankees have 'cused
him of spying on 'em he knowed if dey caught dey would kill him. Many
a night when it was late an' ve'y dark my mamma had to get up an' go in de
woods to see if massa had enough kiver an' food."[107]

In areas under Confederate control, sharing the geography of flight eventually led to the formation of interracial groups of runaways who moved together and put up a joint fight against Confederate authority. In July 1864 the
colonel commanding the mountain region around Asheville, North Carolina,
reported the escape of a delinquent by the name of Kirk, who had crossed into
Tennessee with "a small band of Indians, Negroes, and deserters . . . traveling

in the night and avoiding all roads." In the very last weeks of the war, a North Carolinian refugee recounted a story about a band of deserters who had raided a neighboring home, taking jewelry, silver, watches, pistols, and more. When local citizens organized to exact revenge, they discovered four African Americans among the white robbers. A Mississippian remembered a man who left his company lawfully and went home but soon relocated to an island opposite the town of Bolivar, where he "gathered around him a gang of desperadoes, negroes, and whites, and began systematically to prey upon the people on the mainland, who finally organized a force, and after capturing him, brought him over and shot him to death in a cane brake."[108]

Confederate troops were sometimes ordered to conduct pursuits that combined the duties of the slave patrol and the provost guard by capturing both runaway slaves and men who were avoiding military service. The provost marshal of Charleston ordered his guards in July 1862 to "examine carefully every vehicle capable of concealing a person and to arrest every one not having the proper passport," as it was reported that "soldiers without passports and negroes" were sneaking past the sentries on the bridges. In April 1863 John Robert Bagby, an officer in the 4th Virginia Heavy Artillery Regiment, was ordered to enter the town of Williamsburg with no less a force than five companies of infantry and two hundred cavalry and "arrest all persons liable to conscription" as well as "all the runaway negroes to be found."[109]

The simultaneous and often interlocking hunts after deserters and fugitive slaves were related not only in execution but also in purpose. In both cases the pursuers were after the most precious commodity in the Confederate South, the labor of men.[110] The Confederacy suffered from a critical shortage in manpower that encompassed every aspect of the war effort. There were not enough men to fight battles, build cannons, repair fortifications, or grow crops. Throughout the war the demand for slave labor was a source of severe conflict among owners, state authorities, and the Confederate government. Early in the conflict slaveholders were reasonably cooperative and agreed to hire out some of their workforce to public authorities. But as the need for laborers on the home front increased, and as a growing number of slaves fled the public works into the camps of the Union army, owners began to openly defy impressment regulations. In many cases they actively assisted their slaves in running away, back to the plantations.[111] In some areas runaway slaves who had been recaptured by Confederate authorities were placed in depots that were established in military camps of instruction, where the army also rounded up its conscripts. White and black men were thus housed in the same facilities before being sent to perform their involuntary service.[112] On the eve of defeat, the white South brought this point to its logical conclusion when it resorted to arming slaves and turning them from laborers into soldiers. Male bodies, whether covered in black or white skin, were the key to keeping the Confederacy alive, and controlling their physical motion was instrumental for the authorities seeking to extract their labor.

This was hardly surprising, since the inextricable link between labor and movement was a fixture of life in the nineteenth-century South. In the antebellum period, planters used slave patrols, passes, and severe punishments to keep bondspeople in their place and to bring back those who had dared to leave. During Reconstruction white employers would create a binding labor system and enforce brutal vagrancy laws to control the mobility of the former slaves and to coerce them into providing their toil.[113] The war incorporated white men into this order as it transformed them from independent farmers into workers in a mass-scale organization. Success on the battlefield, as in the cotton field, depended on the ability to direct large numbers of human beings in performing synchronized actions. Even if soldiers in the Confederate army maintained a fair measure of freedom in their movements, the demand for their services exposed them to some of the same concepts of controlling labor that were ingrained in a society that was based on its ability to effectively rule millions of involuntary workers. From the runaway ads for fugitive soldiers to the all-encompassing requirement to travel with a pass and the pursuits of the deserter hunters, white men were learning what it meant to be a Southern worker.[114]

Soldiers in the service fully realized that losing control over their physical mobility meant that they had been relegated to the position of unfree laborers. Even an esteemed and high-ranking officer like the topographer Jedediah Hotchkiss resented his situation. Lying sick at home in November 1862, he knew that he had no choice but to return to duty. "Am getting ready to go back next Monday," he wrote in his diary. "War is a hard thing, every man a slave to power and can have no will of his own." When Randolph Fairfax was camped with his unit outside Winchester, he was frustrated by the strict limitations on visits to town imposed by Stonewall Jackson. Only five men from each company received a special pass to go each day, and only for a few hours. "Every obstacle is thrown in the way of the enjoyment of the poor private," he wrote his mother. "I am sure there is no field negro that has not more liberty than we have." Certainly, military service was never as coercive and dehumanizing as chattel slavery, and soldiers who had spent their entire lives in the slave South understood full well the difference between their circumstances and those of actual human property. But for most white men army life was a new and entirely unwelcome experience of powerlessness in the face of authority and an infringement on their sacred rights as masters. As the war became harder and families got increasingly desperate, some soldiers grew to see the service as their own version of human bondage.[115]

The slave society also had an important influence on shaping the punishment of deserters. The Confederate army had no uniform policy for dealing with desertion, and generals regularly shifted between ordering harsh sentences and employing lenient, even forgiving policies. Lighter forms of punishment included head shaving and solitary confinement. Crueler means were often reminiscent of the measures taken against runaway slaves on the home front. Men were branded, sent to hard labor with a ball and chain, or sentenced to bucking and gagging.[116] Some endured whipping, the most emblematic punishment of slavery. Offenders were tied to a tree with their back bare and often received thirty-nine lashes, a number of Old Testament origins that was habitually used in the South to discipline slaves.[117] Using the lash as a punitive measure was by no means unique to the Confederate army. Whippings were regularly administered in the U.S. military both before and during the Civil War. Yet in the context of a slave society, whipping a soldier was particularly degrading, as it brought members of the master class eerily close to the position of slaves. As a result there was considerable antagonism toward this practice both within and outside of the army, and in April 1863 the Confederate Congress proscribed it. Nevertheless records indicate that it remained in use for the duration of the war, and even when not actually utilized it was consistently present in the rhetoric commanders used to govern their soldiers. When Eldred J. Simkins returned from an extended furlough that included an unauthorized detour through his family's home in Florida, his commander threatened that "If he finds out I ran off—he will give me a licking."[118]

Generals reverted to execution of deserters only rarely, and death sentences, even for recurring offenders, were usually commuted to whipping. But in those cases when all appeals for amnesty were denied and a soldier was sent to be shot or hanged, entire regiments were brought out to watch and learn. In March 1863 Michael Reed observed the "ignominious death" of a deserter, which he described as "a horroable thing to stand by an witness although it is right an just that it should be done." A squad of deserter hunters in troublesome Montgomery County, North Carolina, threatened to "appoint a day for their execution" and to summon the inhabitants of every neighborhood where the men were hiding to "see them whoop them deserters to death."[119] In the volatile climate of the wartime South, public executions of runaways served as a powerful tool for the intimidation of both whites and blacks. When six fugitive slaves were caught in Henry Middleton's South Carolina neighborhood by the local patrol, three were returned to their masters and three were hanged. "The blacks were encouraged to be present," Middleton reported. "The effect will not be soon forgotten."[120]

Yet even as they faced the prospect of summary execution, neither blacks nor whites were deterred. The flight from plantations and army camps continued unabated despite all attempts to stop it. Fugitive slaves exploited the gradual disappearance of their masters from the plantations and the sweeping advance of the Union army into Confederate territory. Fugitive soldiers took advantage of the bureaucratic anarchy that characterized the operations of the Confederacy and the difficulty of conducting pursuits over the great expanses of Southern land. In April 1863 John Robert Lowery spent three weeks in the mountains of North Carolina "hunting up deserters and conscripts." Though his unit had conducted a spirited chase and sometimes marched up to twenty miles a day, the expedition was a failure. He reported, "I think we are doing nothing and we never will catch them, for there are too many hiding places in these mountains." Eldred J. Simkins was sent to collect deserters in South Carolina but was equally overwhelmed by the number of absentees and by having "a small number of men about 20 & hav[ing] to operate over the whole state."[121] Confederate authorities on all levels constantly ran into insurmountable obstacles in managing hundreds of thousands of soldiers who moved between battlefields, hospitals, prisoner-of-war camps, and training facilities. Some officers spent a great amount of time trying to track down their missing soldiers, even when they could guess where they had gone. In January 1863 Colonel Edward S. Willis, commander of the 12th Georgia Volunteers, tried to bring back to camp "certain men who have foiled me in every effort I have made." The two soldiers in question, according to Willis, had disappeared after battle by faking injuries and exploiting the chaotic system of prisoner exchange. Back in their home state of Georgia, they reported to the local camps of instruction, which Willis described as "dens of skulking" where "worthless soldiers" were shielded from their officers. Ironically the two were detailed to "collect stragglers" and remained safely removed from the front lines in Virginia. By that point they had been missing from their unit for eight months, and Willis could only beg that something would be done to "bring back all who are able to perform *any duty* in camp."[122]

Despite local successes in capturing men and sending them back to their masters, the techniques of dealing with fugitives developed during slavery did not withstand the test of war. The determination of slaves to free themselves and the crushing power of the Union army hindered even the most vicious efforts of slave patrols and home guard units. The soldiers' sense of personal freedom, combined with the structure of the army and the magnitude of the geographic spaces in which it operated stood in the way of the forces that functioned as military police. Yet desertion and emancipation were not merely similar phenomena. The profusion of runaways on the roads of the Confederacy embodied two fundamental changes that took place during the Civil War: the ascent of black freedom and the descent, if only temporary, of white freedom. The pathways of the South served as a point of convergence for these parallel but inverted processes. While African Americans were winning their freedom through movement away from the plantations, white men who joined the army were forced to relinquish their right to move at will. While the pass system for blacks was compromised and slave patrols were losing their effectiveness, whites were pleading for travel documents and encountering an expanding police operation that attempted to restrict their motion. The concurrent manhunts that took place across the Confederacy were an intersection between the slaves' new ability to act, resist, and liberate themselves through movement, and soldiers' new subjugation to army discipline and its coercive powers. Though they had emerged from two diametrically opposed points of departure, the circumstances of war threw blacks and whites into similar and interlocking conflicts over freedom of motion, an essential right without which any broader idea of liberty was meaningless.

Confederate authorities mainly focused on controlling the movements of soldiers, yet few civilians in the South escaped some measure of restriction over their spatial mobility. The main form of limitation was the passport system, which took root in Richmond but gradually encompassed the entire population of the Confederacy. The demand that all Southerners on the move carry passports had two main goals: the capture of deserters, stragglers, and draft dodgers and the apprehension of spies, who were assumed to be everywhere and were considered a grave danger to the Confederate cause.[123] While there was broad agreement that the government had to take strong measures to protect itself from its enemies, the requirement for travel documentation was both a considerable burden on the day-to-day life of civilians and a symbol of the white South's changing fortunes in times of war.

The passport system originated during the first months of the conflict, after the Confederate army encamped in Manassas. Civilians who lived in the capital and wanted to visit their relatives in uniform voluntarily applied to the War Department for some documentation they could present to pickets and guards they would meet on their way. Other Richmondites asked for passports when setting out on long trips to areas of the Confederacy where their status as strangers might expose them to suspicion or harassment. Due to the heavy demand, a passport office was established, and a special clerk was assigned to the task. No written orders were issued, but a mechanism for dispensing internal passports had effectively been formed.[124]

Following the declaration of martial law in Richmond, on March 1, 1862, carrying a passport ceased to be voluntary and became a prerequisite for anyone wishing to travel out of town. Until the end of the war the passport office issued a daily average of 1,350 passports to soldiers, civilians, and slaves. Passport clerks were stationed in the War Department as well as on each of the main roads leading out of the city. The offices were open day and night, sometimes until past one o'clock in the morning. Even so, in many cases the wait was so long that travelers missed their trains.[125] The clerks kept detailed logbooks of all passports they issued, including the name, origin, destination, and purpose of the trip a civilian sought to take.[126] When dealing with soldiers on furlough, the clerks went to greater lengths, verifying the signatures of the officers who signed the men's papers and sending them for further endorsement if doubt arose about the authenticity of the document at hand.[127] In addition railway companies were required to submit the names of people traveling into the city, and hotels were ordered to list the names and residences of their guests.[128] Guards were stationed in every railway depot and on railway cars, as well as on the ferries of the Rappahannock River, which had become popular gateways for men wishing to avoid conscription by escaping the city.[129] In the Confederate capital, authorities aimed at nothing less than monitoring the comings and goings of every single person moving through town.

Other cities followed Richmond's lead. In New Orleans a system of registry and passports was established in March 1862, following the declaration of martial law in preparation for a Federal invasion. After the Crescent City fell in April, the civil authorities in Charleston, South Carolina, declared martial law to prepare for a supposedly imminent Union attack. Colonel Johnson Hagood was appointed provost marshal and was told by his superior, General John C. Pemberton, that he was expected to set up "such a system of police that a *dog* could not enter the town without the knowledge of the provost marshal and his ability to lay hands upon said dog at any moment."[130] All over the Confederacy, provost guards were stationed on bridges, in entry points of cities, in railroad stations, and on railroad cars.[131] Arthur J. L. Fremantle, a British officer traveling through the South in 1863, described the procedures of boarding a train in Montgomery, Alabama: "A sentry stands at the door of each railway car, who examines the papers of every passenger with great strictness. Even after that inspection the same ceremony is performed by an officer of the provost-marshal's department, who accompanies every train." On his way out of Winchester he was denied passage because his passport was signed by the wrong official. The sentry who stopped him apologized but insisted, "If you were the Secretary of War, or Jeff Davis himself, you couldn't pass without a passport from the provost Marshall." Traveling across Mississippi, another British visitor was stopped by a Confederate officer "demanding some paper or other in succession from each passenger. Some were able to produce what he required; others were not. These last were at once ordered out of the car, and despatched, under guard, up the village."[132]

The passport system evolved into one of the defining features of wartime life, especially in urban centers and in locales close to military camps. The process of obtaining a passport often entailed questioning by a clerk or an officer, and applicants who feared they might not be approved arrived for the interview equipped with documentation to support their claims. Southerners presented to the passport office in Richmond a slew of different records, all of which were meant to establish their credibility in the eyes of the clerks vested with the power to authorize travel. Men visiting the capital regularly needed a local resident to vouch for their loyalty to the Confederacy, lest they be considered spies. Applications included statements such as "he is well known to me & is a true & loyal citizen of Montgomery County, Virginia" and "We have known Mr. W. T. Samuel for good many years, he is a resident of the county of King William and a good and loyal citizen of the Confederacy."[133] Even the sheriff of Richmond County in northern Virginia, who visited the capital in November 1864 on official business, needed a note from the government auditor's office in order to receive a passport on his way out.[134] Fathers wishing to visit their sons in the army needed a piece of paper verifying that they were above military age.[135] Youth too young to serve provided applications signed by parents or guardians.[136] Women also needed sponsorship from a local citizen of good standing, who provided them with notes consisting of statements such as "I certify that I have known Mrs. Margaret E. Cosgrove for several years past and that I regard her a person of excellent character. I therefore respectfully recommend that she be permitted to pass with her children to Stafford Co."[137] Men and women working in every industry in Richmond supplied documents in which their employers explained where they were going and why. Whether they labored for the Confederate cause in the Washington Woolen Mills, the Treasury Department, the Richmond Arsenal, or Tredegar Iron Works, white workers could no longer move without the recommendation of their superiors.[138]

The passport system in the Confederate capital was based on the premise that a white person seeking to travel needed approval from someone higher up in one of the social hierarchies that demarcated Southern society, whether that of gender, age, class, or an even more subtle hierarchy of reputation, which in this context was determined by a person's degree of attachment to a particular community. Thus men vouched for women, mothers for sons,

employers for employees, and locals for strangers. It was a system that acknowledged and relied on the mechanisms of social control to achieve its
goal of governing Southern space and keeping in check the menacing possibilities inherent in population movements.

Yet in the slave South the very notion of a passport system also invoked
the most conspicuous and intractable hierarchy of all. It was no secret that
the new configuration of movement both sprang from and resembled the
practices of human bondage. The documents required for white travel bore
an uncanny similarity to those carried by slaves. Some noted the height, hair
color, eye color, complexion, and scars of the traveler; others merely noted
the person's name, destination, and dates of permitted travel. Yet whatever
the exact configuration of the form a white person was required to carry, the
crux of the matter was that Confederates were now subjected to a practice
that had always been reserved solely for blacks. For some, this was a bitter pill
to swallow. On Christmas Eve 1861 Judith McGuire was traveling with her
family in a stagecoach between Winchester and Strasburg in the Shenandoah
Valley. When the passengers were stopped at a picket post and required to
present their passes, one woman responded with a rage born of a white person's sense of entitlement: "Passes! Passes for white folks! I have never heard
of such a thing. *I* ain't got no pass . . . we ain't no niggers to get passes."[139]
Confederate politicians, the consummate masters, also complained about
the humiliation of having to carry a pass like slaves and free blacks. Unhin-
dered travel was a basic right of a white man, and giving it up was an unmistakable sign of degradation.[140] Responding to their grumbling, the provost
marshal of Richmond freely admitted that the system infringed on the rights
of free men, but insisted that in the wartime South it was a burden everyone
must bear:

> That the system is obnoxious and trenches odiously upon personal lib-
> erty, there is no question, and that it should be abolished, unless sternly
> demanded by the exigencies of the War, and the safety of our cause,
> there is no doubt. Its operation includes, of course, the high and low,
> rich and poor, the loyal and the disloyal, and is attended frequently
> with vexatious delays, and sometimes with questioning and interviews,
> wounding to the self-respect of worthy and good citizens. It is just,
> however, to say, that much of the complaint it occasions arises, not so

much from any intentional disrespect on the part of officials, as from the offended pride and dignity of those inaccustomed to such restraints, and whose conscious integrity or high position, makes the interruption and questioning offensive. Nothing, however, can excuse or justify this interruption of personal liberty, but the sternest exigencies of the service.[141]

The situation was further complicated by the fact that the passport system for white people constantly overlapped and interlocked with the parallel system for blacks. This was evident first in the physical setting of the passport offices, which served the entire population of any given city, bringing together both slaves and masters in need of documentation for travel. Moreover the coexistence of the systems challenged the very concept of mastery. In wartime an owner's permission was no longer sufficient for a slave to travel. Enslaved Southerners were required to carry passes signed by a Confederate official and were thus incorporated into the same system that administered the movement of whites. This caused considerable confusion among slaveholders, who had always enjoyed an exclusive right to govern the movement of their property. The uncertainty about the boundaries of owners' authority was manifested in the applications they submitted to the provost marshal for their slaves. Some slaveholders filed requests for passes phrased in language such as "The bearer William has my leave to go to Richmond by the cars on central rail road . . . the provost marshal will please give him a permit to go" or "Please give to my servant woman Mary a passport to return to her home in Chesterfield."[142] By couching the documents they sent in the idiom of application, these owners were acknowledging the fact that a higher authority now had the power to control the movements of their slaves.

Other slaveholders, however, submitted to the passport office not applications but forceful decrees, in which they ordered the provost marshal to give their slaves passports. Under the title "notice" Robert Winter of King and Queen County, Virginia, announced to the provost marshal that his servant "has leave to pass and repass to Richmond . . . and not be disturbed on his way."[143] Owners routinely used directives such as "pass my boy" or "pass the bearer," expressing their assumption that they still had sole jurisdiction over the mobility of their slaves. Some owners treated the documents they penned as the actual passes their slaves were required to use, even if they then had to submit them to the clerks in the passport office for endorsement. "Let Isaac pass to Richmond and return. This pass to remain in force until 1st January," wrote Marion Stewart in a typical note.[144] Stewart and other owners had trouble adjusting to the fact that the travel documents they penned were now merely applications, that they had lost the absolute power they once had over the bodies of their chattel, and that they along with their slaves were subject to a state authority that determined who moved and how. The passport system introduced both slave and free to a new set of rules regarding freedom of movement, which simultaneously drew on and departed from its antebellum forerunner. While blacks traveled with passes as they did before, they were now required to obtain permission from a governmental authority rather than just from their owners; while slaveholders still retained considerable control over their own movements and over those of their property, they were forced to relinquish their unqualified powers and accept that the state had some say in their affairs. In the muddled reality of the Confederate South, slaveholders were both issuing passes for others and applying to receive passes for themselves. They continued to exercise their old mastery while facing the growing encroachment of wartime demands on what had always been their undisputable prerogatives as masters in a slaveholding world.

A far greater degree of coercion was applied against Southerners who lived under Confederate rule but were known to have Union sympathies. In areas of the South vulnerable to Northern invasion, the movements of Unionists were monitored and limited, both as a precautionary measure and as a means of punishment. In April 1862 Robert E. Lee ordered the officer commanding the town of Staunton to examine every person trying to cross Confederate lines and to read the letters they carried, after having learned that people were leaving the South "having in their possession a large number of letters directed to persons in various parts of the United States."[145] Lee never specified whether the captured letters actually contained any useful intelligence, but this measure made some sense since the Confederate army in the Shenandoah enjoyed a wealth of information regarding the whereabouts of the enemy, courtesy of pro-Southern civilians traveling up and down Valley roads.[146] Yet Unionists were also denied passports or harassed by pickets and guards even when they were moving within Confederate-controlled territory and were posing no threat to its security interests. In March 1862 Harriette Griffith, a young Quaker living in Winchester, recorded in her diary being stopped seven times while making her way to church with her father. Things got worse as the Confederate army prepared for Federal invasion; Unionists in the divided town were taken prisoner, either put in the local guardhouse or sent behind Confederate lines. Griffith's father narrowly avoided arrest; Julia Chase's father, Charles, was incarcerated in Harrisonburg with several other civilians hostile to the Confederate cause. He was eventually released and returned home, but in 1864 he left town altogether, looking for a place of safety out west. Two weeks later he was dead.[147]

In many ways these policies mirrored the Union army's treatment of Confederate civilians living under its rule. As is often the case in the workings of occupation regimes, the control of spatial mobility was a crucial means of subjugating the largely hostile civilian population the Northern army met when it entered the South. As soon as Federal soldiers overtook a Confederate community they introduced limitations on the freedom of civilians to come and go as they pleased. Strict curfews were enforced, and travel out of town required a pass from the Union provost marshal. "We can't go out at night any more we have to come in at eight o'clock, the Yankees have guards out every night," complained Margaret Miller, a teenager living under Union occupation in Winchester. After martial law was declared in the neighboring Front Royal, Lucy Buck's father attempted to get into town but was "halted by the sentinel and told that he would not be permitted to return home again if he should go within their lines—so he was forced to beat a retreat." A few months later Mary Lee attempted to step outside the city limits of Winchester to meet a relative who had arrived in town to check up on his family. The pickets would not let her pass, so she "determined to go out to the camp, & try to get a pass, though with very little hope of success": "When we got there, we found the Provost was in town & one of the Capts. went to head quarters, to make an appeal to the General, but in vain; after waiting a long time, he returned to say that the Genl. Would not allow any citizen of Winchester to leave town to-day, so there was nothing to do but return home."[148]

The restriction of movement served the Union army not only as a means of governing an unruly population, but also as a way to punish civilians who remained faithful to the rebellion. Passes were denied to men and women of known Confederate sympathies, and locales that proved resistant to Union rule suffered under more rigid controls. Southerners applying for passes tried to convince the local Union authorities that they had not assisted the enemy and therefore did not deserve the sanction of stasis. In February 1865 Susan Williams of Brookfield, Missouri, was left without any means of support as her husband was in the army and both of their fathers had died. Stranded in a guerrilla-stricken area with her four young children, she asked the provost marshal "to be permitted to go to my husband": "Not that I ever feed a bushwhacker or approve of their mode of warfare. If you will give me and my children permission to go to Miss. *Please* write me a permit with directions how to go and what I can take with me."[149] In the occupied South freedom of movement was often allotted according to a civilian's degree of ideological compliance and sectional loyalty.

In instances when Union officials were in fact willing to grant passes, they conditioned their approval on Confederate civilians taking the oath of allegiance. Provost marshal offices across the occupied South became the settings of lengthy and discordant negotiations between the Union army and the rebellious civilians living under its rule. In Winchester, recounted Mary Lee, "some citizens signed oaths of allegiance in return for receiving passes to leave town. There was a misunderstanding about the duration of the oath, which resulted in the passes being re-called." A few months later her sister-in-law Laura Lee reported that Union authorities had become "more strict . . . than ever before": "None is permitted to leave town in any direction without taking the oath, and no supplies are allowed to come except on the same conditions." On another occasion in western Virginia the local provost marshal attempted to compel a woman who used "notoriously disloyal" language to take the oath of allegiance in exchange for a pass. "She announced that she would do so," he testified, "[but] after a pause she asked me what kind of an oath it was she said she understood it was a honest oath that she had to take. I told her to come up to the office that I would read the oath to her she then said that if she did take the oath that she would always have the same opinion and stand out for the South as she had done, she said also that she would suffer death or any other torture rather than give up the south and her principles."[150]

The relationship between Confederate civilians and Union officers was further complicated by the fact that any man or woman allowed to travel outside of Federal lines and into Confederate territory was a potential security risk. Provost marshals assumed, with some justification, that civilians would willingly divulge information about the size, formation, and movements of the Union troops operating in occupied zones. A Confederate citizen in the embattled Kanawha Valley making an application on behalf of his sister-in-law openly addressed these suspicions: "No doubt but you have many such applications," he wrote the provost marshal, "but this is one that can do no one any harm, as she is a woman that has not been out of her own house for months & knows nothing of the situation of the Federal army or numbers, & is wiling to promise not to tell anything she might see or has seen."[151] The Union army's mistrust of civilians on the move stemmed in part from its own inclination to interrogate travelers arriving from the South, such as women who wanted to reunite with their husbands who had remained behind Union lines. Yet attempts to contain the flow of information seem to have had little effect; throughout the war Confederates found ways to smuggle out missives from occupied towns. Julia Chase, the Winchester Unionist, noted in frustration hearing every day "of persons going in and out of town with plenty of letters concealed about their persons."[152]

While obtaining permission to journey out of town was becoming an increasingly complicated ordeal, travel within city limits also offered civilians a fair amount of discontent. Too scared to leave her house after martial law was declared in Front Royal, Lucy Buck used her spyglass to watch "the citizens as they were every now and then arrested by the patrol and marched off to 'Headquarters'": "Could see the tents pitched in the Court House yard and all the bustle and confusion consequent upon the first forming of an encampment. Oh but 'tis galling to see them taking such cool possession of *our* town and our property." In Winchester it was not the commotion that startled civilians, but the eerie absence of their own people from the public domain. Wrote John Peyton Clark shortly after the first Union invasion of town, "The streets, however, are filled with Federal soldiers making it painful for any good citizen of the town to be on the street. In fact, few citizens, except in cases of necessity, are now seen on the street. They keep within doors and the town, except for the federal soldiers, seems deserted."[153]

On other occasions, however, downtown Winchester presented a sight considerably worse than emptiness. A major consequence of Union occupation was the overturning of the customary relations of power in public spaces, which had always been controlled solely by the master race. Now the community's freed slaves were everywhere to be seen. "Many in town have lost servants who walk the streets boldly, but are protected from seizure by threats of violence from the soldiers," wrote Robert Young Conrad. The white citizens of Winchester sat by their windows and watched in horror as the public arena was taken over by those who had always been forbidden to use it. "The streets are filled with runaways who have flocked to the town from all around the country and who lounge about in everybody's way. The Yankees walking and talking with them in the most familiar way," wrote Laura Lee in April 1862. The sudden emergence of black people on the streets of town was even more striking when compared to their masters' new suppression under the Union's movement regulations. "We are oppressed on every side, even the little school girls are dispersed if more than two stop to talk on the street on their way home," wrote Cornelia McDonald. "Negroes can assemble in any numbers, and if they choose can jostle and crowd ladies off the pavement into the gutter as may suit their convenience. They are the only people who have any rights or liberty, and of the latter they have an undue share." "The military regulations are far more rigidly enforced, & we are entirely cut off from the rest of the world," wrote Mary Lee. "These restrictions are more felt, each day, as our supplies become reduced; but that is a small matter, compared with the mental thralldom, & the annoyance of having the town filled with runaways; the wickedness that prevails is distressing to see & hear of—and there is no avoiding it unless one is blind and deaf." Such statements were most likely gross exaggerations of the actual situation on the ground. Even so, they reflect the fact that in occupied Southern towns a new configuration of race and space was coming into being. They also bespeak the extent to which white Southerners experienced Federal possession of their towns through the decline in their ability to move freely and the simultaneous rise in the possibilities of movement enjoyed by their former slaves.[154]

Unsurprisingly the new situation immediately conjured up the specter of human bondage. "We are certainly a free people now, cannot even go to Berryville," noted Matthella Page Harrison sarcastically on March 31, 1863. "I wonder if there was such a diabolical and absurd government concocted on earth before." Two months later she was attending a Sunday service in her church when a group of Northern soldiers surrounded the building and forbade the congregation to leave. "The horrors of our bondage seem to be thickening," she complained in her diary after being released. The relationship between life under enemy occupation and life under slavery was present in the minds of civilians no matter how old they were. Margaret Miller was thirteen in 1863, but not too young to understand the facts of life in the Civil War South. "I think it is so mean these yankees to not let anyone go out in the country unless they guard them," she wrote in her journal. "They say they came to free us but I rather think they are putting us in bondage."[155]

Yet on many opportunities Federal authorities took advantage of their ability to control civilian movement not in order to restrict Confederates who wanted to leave but to forcefully remove those who wanted to stay. Throughout the South's conquered cities, Union officers expelled citizens who refused to renounce their loyalty to the rebellion or to comply with Federal regulations. In Vicksburg, Mississippi, women who had violated military orders in May 1864 were released and given forty-eight hours to go beyond Union lines. If at the expiration of that time, warned the commanding general, they were found in town, they would be placed in close confinement.[156] The same fate awaited Mary Lee. Throughout the war Lee had experienced the loss of her mastery through spatial mobility. Her slaves had escaped and were using their freedom to occupy public places that used to be exclusively white; she could not leave town unless a Yankee officer assented; and in February 1865 she finally bore the full brunt of the Union's power to control her life through movement when General Phillip Sheridan ordered her to leave Winchester. Lee's open hostility toward Northern occupation had aggravated Federal commanders for years, but her collaboration with Confederate guerrillas operating outside of town was the last straw that brought her banishment. Lee, along with her sister-in-law Laura and the rest of their household, left Winchester on a cold and rainy day heading south, in the direction of Richmond. Traveling in a wagon with what she could take of her worldly goods, moving from one town to the next, Mary Lee had joined the ranks of the South's floating population. This was a remarkable change. Within three years she had been transformed from a confident mistress, a pillar of her thriving community, into a refugee whose circumstances might have seemed dangerously similar to those of her slaves who had preceded her in leaving town.[157]

The great majority of white Southerners did not share the fate of Mary Lee, yet daily life in the Civil War South was rife with struggles over the freedom to move and the right to enforce stillness. Undoubtedly neither the Union nor the Confederacy imposed on civilians in the South a burden impossible to bear. In the Confederacy the bulk of white civilians who wanted to travel were permitted to do so, and most Southerners adjusted to the new restrictions and accepted the passport system as another exigency of war. Even in Union-controlled territory, civilians were able to negotiate with the Federal army and extract concessions from officers and guards. Yet even if civilian movement was not altogether impeded, it was continuously monitored and curtailed. Whether they were standing in line for a passport or being escorted out of a train for the lack thereof, whether they were begging a Union official for a permit to leave town or trying to sneak through the woods without it, Confederates on the home front experienced another version of the contest over freedom of motion, a contest that both induced and reflected the social upheaval in the wartime South.

In May 1864 Emma Mordecai was traveling from suburban Richmond to the city center. On her way she observed what had become a common sight along the roads of the South's beleaguered sections, "several families moving with their servants, cattle, horses, sheep & c. to take refuge within the lines of fortification." When she returned later that evening, "some were preparing to camp out on a common, near the road. Ladies & children seated round a camp fire, while their carts, wagons, and a carriage were drawn up around them, with counterpanes arranged so as to make a sort of tent."[158] The campers on the road to Richmond numbered among the 250,000 white civilians who had become refugees in the course of the Civil War. Those who were not deported like Mary Lee had voluntarily fled the violence of battle and the prospect of enemy occupation. They formed another contingent of the South's wartime runaways, who moved about looking for safety in the midst of an ever-spreading conflagration.[159]

The first white refugees of the war left their homes in northern Virginia with the invasion of the Union army in the summer of 1861. As the war intensified and expanded, the small trickle of individuals on the run turned into a mass movement. In 1862 civilians left homes in the Shenandoah Valley, the Peninsula, Kentucky, Tennessee, and New Orleans; the capture of the Mississippi Valley in 1863 brought a second wave of refugees, and the third wave was propelled by Sherman's march through Georgia and the Carolinas.[160]

Everywhere in the Confederacy the driving force behind the decision of civilians to leave their homes was fear of enemy invasion. On the morning after the fall of Fort Donelson in February 1862, the Confederate population of Nashville was on the move, trying to beat the Union army's imminent arrival. "The streets were filled with carriages, horses, buggies, wagons, drags, carts, everything which could carry a human being from a doomed city," described Lizzie Hardin. "Men, women, and children, the rich, the poor, white and black, mingled in one struggling mass which gave way for nothing but the soldiers marching through the city." Among those leaving town in panic were Tennessee's governor and cabinet members, who packed up the state's archives and boarded a special train to Memphis. Members of the legislature were left to fend for themselves, making, according to one eyewitness, "rather a ludicrous appearance as they trudged off towards the depot of one or the other of the railroads, each one with this trunk on his back or carpet sack and bundle in hand."[161]

Thousands fled the northern Shenandoah Valley in March, when it became evident that Stonewall Jackson's small army could not defend them against an impending Union invasion. "Quite a number of our people are leaving town, frightened almost to death of the Yankees," wrote Julia Chase, the Winchester Unionist. "The Virginians have always said never surrender, that they never ran. Pretty good number are running now fast enough." Traveling on the turnpike, Jackson's topographer, Jedediah Hotchkiss, met "wagons of citizens loaded with furniture and carriages filled with families, many of them accompanied by servants moving up from the Lower Valley." Wives of high-ranking Confederate officers felt particularly threatened; Anzolette Pendleton, the wife of Brigadier General William Nelson Pendleton, spent many days in her Lexington home ready to leave at a moment's notice if she heard that Jackson had left the Valley or that the Yankees were on their way.[162]

In Staunton voluntary evacuation began on the night of April 19, when unsubstantiated rumors reached town that Jackson had ordered the removal of army stores as his forces were retreating to the Blue Ridge Mountains in the face of the enemy's advance. "Many persons, principally refugees from other places, had left in stages and all sorts of vehicles," noted Joseph Waddell, who also departed for Charlottesville in haste, fearing arrest. Even though the enemy had actually failed to arrive, the scene outside of town quickly turned chaotic. "Rain, rain all night and all Monday till evening. The road between C[harlotesville] and S[taunton] was full of wagons, Quartermasters &c, all anxiously seeking information, instructions where to go & what to do—Some teams abandoned on the road side. Everything and every body dripping wet, and the road almost impossible for loaded wagons."[163]

Spring brought mass flight also to central Virginia, where the Confederate army was evacuating its positions along the Rappahannock River and preparing to meet the enemy in Yorktown and Williamsburg. "Such an excitement!" recorded Fannie Braxton, who watched the exodus from her home in Orange Country. "A perfect caravan of 'refugees' passed up the road before dinner, carriages, wagons and horses." Her own family stayed put until August, at which time the war moved back to their neighborhood. "Soldiers everywhere—& Villagers all leaving," she noted in her diary on the day of her departure. In the autumn the town of Fredericksburg was abandoned by its inhabitants after it had become clear that the Federal army was on its way and that a large battle was about to take place. A soldier in Lee's army found the townspeople "all leaving and . . . carrying away everything they can possibly get of." He noted, "A large detail of wagons and ambulances is sent into town every day to help them to move." In the battle that ensued, Fredericksburg was burned and looted. Many of its residents remained refugees until the end of the war.[164]

In the lowlands of South Carolina the arrival of the Union army propelled some of the South's wealthiest families out of their homes. "We are now in a great state of excitement, all the low country getting into the upper country," reported Meta Grimball, the wife of a prominent planter. "Flying from our ruthless foes, we expect an attack and people are leaving their houses and families servants and furniture, crowding up to the railroad." Nearly three years later, as Sherman was approaching Columbia, Emma LeConte witnessed the same scenes: "The streets in town are lined with panic-stricken crowds, trying to escape. All is confusion and turmoil. . . . All day the trains have been running, whistles blowing and wagons rattling through the streets."[165]

All over the South civilians on the run intermingled with retreating soldiers in convoys of frantic escapees. "We were constantly in sight of, and often jostled by moving crowds of people and vehicles," wrote Cornelia McDonald of her flight from Winchester following the Southern defeat at Gettysburg. "Many wounded men were among them making their way to a place of safety, while fugitives of every grade and degree of misery were toiling on, on foot, or in any kind of broken-down vehicle."[166] On their way to a place of hiding, refugees leaving sheltered locales often received their first exposure to the horrors of war. "At the depot in Atlanta I caught the only glimpse of what actual war meant," remembered Katherine Polk Gale. "There we saw wounded, dead & dying soldiers, all lying side by side on the platform, waiting the attention of the hospital corps."[167]

Flight in the face of an advancing army was only the beginning of what in most cases was an agonizing journey, followed by a life of perpetual instability. Refugees mobilized whatever resources they had and could be seen traveling by train, wagon, by boat, or on foot. Southern roads had never been the region's strong suit, and years of intense military movement worsened their condition considerably. River travel was impeded by the presence of gunboats and by the scarcity of vessels. Trains were slow, crowded, and dangerous. Traveling in Mississippi in May 1863, Arthur Fremantle rode on what was considered "the very worst of all the bad railroads in the South": "It was completely worn out, and could not be repaired. Accidents are of almost daily occurrence, and a nasty one had happened the day before. After we had proceeded five miles, our engine ran off the track, which caused a stoppage of three hours. All male passengers had to get out to push along the cars." Refugees spent weeks on these trains and in wagons that broke down daily as they traveled hundreds of miles through swamps and woods and over run-down roads. They slept outdoors, in railroad cars, or in any kind of housing they could find.[168] In January 1863 a soldier serving in Fredericksburg reported that the refugees who had fled town the previous November were "still living in the country around, in the churches and outhouses, and not a few in tents, unwilling to trust themselves in the town as it is likely to be bombarded at any minute." A North Carolinian family who had fled from Wilmington to the countryside in the face of Sherman's march and contended with a series of raids by both Federal soldiers and Confederate deserters summed up their situation: "Our experience as refugees for the past month or more has been decidedly an unpleasant one, and has caused me to wish several times that we had remained in Wilmington, though what we could have done there to have warded off starvation, is more than I could foresee."[169]

Most refugees left their homes with a particular idea as to where they were going. Some escaped only for a short time to the surrounding countryside, like the neighbors of Ruth Hairston, who "left home & fled to the hills & hollows to hide themselves, until the Yankees should pass by."[170] The majority, however, searched for more permanent solutions. Wealthier planters rented property and attempted to resume production of crops with what remained of their enslaved workforce. Others moved in with relatives or friends. Tens of thousands flocked to Confederate cities, where they settled in cramped living quarters and coped with spiraling food and housing costs.[171] Yeomen and poor whites who were stripped of their livelihood and had no resources to fall back on roamed the country looking for housing and work. By 1865 as many as 80,000 had ended up in Union-occupied towns and cities, where they hoped to find employment and avoid the demands of the Confederate government. Some labored for the Union army; others received charity from Northern organizations.[172]

Refugees who stayed within the Confederacy were often uprooted multiple times, as the Union army extended its reach into Rebel territory. Earlier in the war Jorantha Semmes had fled Memphis for Canton, Mississippi, but by July 1863 the enemy had followed her there. "Each moment is so filled with fears of the advent of the enemy that we know no certainty from hour to hour," she wrote her husband. "For the past week we have lived in constant dread." In the last months of the war refugees who had flocked to central and southern Virginia to enjoy the protection of the large Confederate forces defending Richmond were uprooted again as Grant's Wilderness campaign ravaged the countryside. In March 1865 after hearing that the Union army was returning to Staunton, Joseph Waddell escaped farther south to Lynchburg. Yet shortly after his arrival "the local forces were called out to man the fortifications, and the Commandant of the Post notified officers having papers or public property to have them ready to move to a place of safety": "Where was there a safe place if Lynchburg should fall! For the first time my spirits gave way. I felt that our cause was hopeless." Things were even worse for the thousands who had fled to the interior of Georgia and the Carolinas and were now suddenly in the path of Sherman's wrathful march. "Where will it be safer than here?" asked Eliza Simkins in Anderson, South Carolina. "If any danger is apprehended, I am going to Florida, of course there is no safety there as it is at the mercy of the Yankees, to occupy it where they please, but I would rather meet them anywhere than in Columbia."[173]

While there was great diversity of circumstances among white refugees, the majority of those who left their homes belonged to the South's upper classes. Self-exile required substantial financial resources to pay for the trip, alternative housing, and living expenses.[174] As early as August 1862 Edmund Ruffin remarked that the only families remaining in his endangered section of Virginia were those "too poor to move." In May 1863 the itinerant Fremantle observed "signs of preparations for immediate skedaddling" on most plantations along the shores of the Mississippi River. When the moment to leave arrived, wrote the wife of one wealthy Louisiana planter, the Mississippi became "a seething mass of craft of all kinds and description that could be made into possible conveyances to carry away the terror-stricken people," who were "all making a mad rush for the mouth of the Red River."[175]

Large slaveholders were especially tempted to seek refuge in the face of an advancing Union army, as their human property was both increasingly vulnerable and highly movable. Those who were unable to take the majority of their slaves attempted to save other precious belongings from being destroyed. Writing from Louisiana on her way to Texas, Kate Stone observed refugee families who had "lost heavily, some with princely estates and hundreds of Negroes, escaping with ten or twenty of their hands and only the clothes they had on. Others brought out clothes and household effects but no Negroes, and still others sacrificed everything to run their Negroes to a place of safety."[176] Often the same wealthy families were also the most ardent Confederates, with sons and husbands in positions of military and political leadership. They feared both harsh vengeance for taking an active part in the rebellion and the humiliation of living as a defeated people.

Although this was a relatively small exodus in terms of the number of people involved, the hurried, frightened flight of the Southern elite in the face of its enemies was a critical episode in the history of the region. Even if just for a brief moment, an all-powerful ruling class was stripped of both material comforts and control of its own fate. Families that had dominated the region for generations were thrust from their mansions into the muddy roads of the Confederacy and would live as fugitives until the end of the war.[177] Years later a former slave perceptively recaptured the significance of that experience:

> Them whitefolks done had everything they had tore up, or had to run away from the places they lived, and they brung their Negroes out to Texas and then right away they lost them too. They always had them Negroes, and lots of them had mighty fine places back in the old states, and then they had to go out and live in sod houses and little old boxed shotguns and turn their Negroes loose. They didn't see no justice in it then, and most of them never did until they died. The folks that stayed at home and didn't straggle all over the country had their old places to live on and their old friends around them, but them Texans was different.[178]

Many a time the new itinerancy was even more shocking since it was forced on a subset of the white populace that was uniquely unprepared for the burdens of exile. The nearly total mobilization of military-age men in the Confederacy meant that an increasing number of planters-turned-refugees were female and that some had to undertake their journey without male escort. This was a radical departure from the traditional customs of Southern society. In the antebellum period elite women never traveled alone, and women of the yeomanry rarely traveled at all. Female movement was limited to particular destinations, such as church or the homes of relatives. Even a trip to the country store, which served as a regular outing, was a male chore. Long-distance travel was highly unusual and was normally reserved for the very wealthiest women of the planter class, who could afford to go on vacation or whose families owned multiple homes. The great majority of women lived their lives confined to narrow geographic spaces and did not have full control over their own movements. The culture of dependency that governed all aspects of gender relations in the South also prescribed that husbands and fathers supervise and restrict the physical mobility of women in their households.[179]

Yet in war this could no longer be the case. The advance of the Union army sent on the roads thousands of women whose male relatives were in the army and who were forced to join the world of Southern refugees without preparation and without the luxury of a chaperone. Some handled their new roles with poise and acumen; others were unabashedly helpless in the face of a new reality. For the latter, their suffering was very often exacerbated by the fact that men were either unreachable or equally powerless in confronting wartime conditions. "It will be impossible for me to give you any attention or help in your backwards march," wrote Colonel Edward Warren to his wife, Jennie, after she asked his permission to leave their farm in the beleaguered Shenandoah Valley. "You will have to make your own arrangements and be your own master in all things." Even when husbands provided advice, money, and logistical assistance from afar, women who abandoned their homes and got on the road were forced to deal with the hardships of displacement alone. They struggled with planning the trip, packing their belongings, and finding shelter for themselves and their children. They spent days and weeks on the roads of the Confederacy, coping with its dilapidated infrastructure and with the dangers of a trip through a war-ridden country.[180]

For most, this new experience was deeply upsetting. The records women left of their lives as refugees reveal a profound sense of helplessness and a great deal of bitterness. Jorantha Semmes, the wife of a Confederate commissary officer, sent her husband desperate letters asking to join him in camp, promising "to submit to many inconveniences to enjoy your society and protection." Emily Lovell, the wife of General Mansfield Lovell, moved to half a dozen locations in the lower South and hated every minute of it. In her long, sad, and often angry letters she complained about having been left alone and remarked that other generals sent aides to bring their wives closer to them. "If you can say that you are to remain two months longer where you are, or near where you are—I am going to ride heaven and earth to get to you," she wrote him from Marietta, Georgia. "Please try and get me some spot to stay in and if I cannot—this is enough—enough." When all else failed, she tried to get his attention by invoking the sickness of their daughter Caddie, who had been taken with "high fever and a dreadful cough night & day. . . . Today she is up—but looks miserably—your little thing—she says mother, tell dear father, I would be well if he would only come to see us."[181]

Like other couples separated by war, the Lovells and Semmeses may have suffered tensions in their marriage, but the novel experiences of wartime

movement did not weaken the commitment of the itinerant wives to patriarchy and did not translate into demands for greater freedom or for a recon-
sideration of traditional gender roles. Jorantha Semmes admitted to feeling
"rebellious" at her husband's insistence that she remain in Canton, but she
continued to follow his instructions and promised not to burden him. And
though she was clearly disappointed with the behavior of her spouse, Emily
Lovell expressed no hesitation about her ultimate desire. "Promise me that
at the end of this war," she wrote, "you will never ask me more to be separated,
I am determined to follow you where ever you see fit to go." White women
on the road did not embrace the opportunity for independence; they longed
for the return of the old order, with its promise of protection and stability.[182]

The exigencies of wartime did not instigate a revolution in gender relations
at large, but at the time they were not entirely without effect. The transformation of white men into soldiers and of white women into refugees radically reshaped customary relations of power in the realm of spatial mobility.
White men were now forced to ask for permission to move, as white women
were making their first independent decisions about travel. White men bore
a new burden of subordination to their officers, as white women coped with
the burdens of planning and executing prolonged stays away from home in
a time of danger and uncertainty. Neither men nor women welcomed this
upending of the social order. Men badgered their officers for furloughs and
escaped when those were denied; women protested their new role as masters
of households and begged for advice and protection as they departed from
their homes. Yet desirable or not, change was unavoidable. The combined
impact of mass mobilization and mass dislocation engendered a new reality
in which white men's freedom of motion was greatly curtailed whereas
white women were saddled with the responsibility of leading their families
on the road. Though both sides continued to uphold their commitment to
the traditional values of the antebellum South, the Civil War brought
about a new configuration of freedom and motion among families who
were caught up in the whirlwind of a long, bloody, and deeply disruptive
conflict.

As the war progressed, the arrival of the Union army also signaled the
possibility of an impending revolution in race relations. While some slaveholders remained confident of their slaves' devotion, others feared violent

retribution. In a remarkable reversal of the antebellum order, masters began to flee their slaves. "Everybody and everything trying to get on the
cars," reported Kate Stone from northeastern Louisiana. "All fleeing the
Yankees, or worse still, the Negroes." Her own family decided to abandon
its fine home and go to Texas after a neighboring plantation was ransacked
and its owners threatened with murder by their slaves and Union soldiers.
They left at night, in perfect silence, fearing that any noise "would bring the
Negroes down on us."[183]

Blacks who witnessed the flight of their masters fully appreciated its revolutionary meaning. A popular wartime song, "Kingdom Comin'," expressed
this sentiment better than most:

> Say, darkies, hab you see de massa
> Wid de muffstash on his face,
> Go along de road some time dis mornin'
> Like he gwine to leab de place?
> He seen a smoke way up de ribber
> Whar de Linkum gunboats lay.
> He took his hat, an' lef' berry sudden,
> An' I spec' he run away!
>
> CHORUS:
> De massa run! ha, ha!
> De darkey stay! ho, ho!
> It mus' be now de kingdom comin'
> An' de year ob Jubilo![184]

Yet if in some instances masters had become runaways while their slaves
stayed put, at other times black and white refugees were thrown together
on the road. The confluence of circumstances across racial lines was particularly visible among women, whose numbers among the ranks of Southern runaways rose steadily throughout the war and for whom wartime
mobility was a sharp departure from prewar norms. In the antebellum period mistresses and female slaves were both restricted in their movements,
compared to the men with whom they shared their lives. Although white

women were nominally free, their ability to move at will was severely limited by cultural mores that confined them to their homes. Within the
boundaries of slavery, females were substantially less mobile than their male
counterparts, and their geographic literacy was narrower. Black women did
not serve as drivers or teamsters and were less likely than men to be ordered
on tasks that required movement beyond the farm or plantation where they
were held in bondage. Men were also the ones who traveled to visit their
families when couples were living with different owners. Moreover before
the Civil War women were a minority among slave runaways, particularly
among those who attempted long-distance flight with the intention of never
coming back.[185]

Thus the revolution in the patterns of white women's mobility ran parallel
to the transformations that took place in the movements of bondswomen.
No doubt there were extraordinary disparities in their circumstances on the
road: the disruptions in white women's lives proved to be only temporary,
and the risks they took were much smaller; while many lost a great deal of
property, they still had some assets and connections to fall back on, whereas
black refugees were usually wholly destitute and could rely on nothing but
luck and their own resourcefulness. Nevertheless the war plunged both black
and white women into an entirely new experience of movement across space.
The escalation of the conflict gradually emptied black and white households
of men as the Confederate army stepped up its conscription efforts and as
the Union army actively sought the service of former slaves. Halfway through
the war black women escaping slavery and white women escaping invasion
found themselves alone on the road, seeking a place of refuge. Both relied on
networks of kin and friendship to support them through this ordeal, and
both sought the proximity of their husbands in the army. Fugitive slaves settled in the contraband camps around the bases where their spouses served
as workers or soldiers, and countless free women struggled to relocate as
close as possible to where their husbands were stationed. Black women
and white women clung to their earthly possessions with equal tenacity and
coped with disease, hunger, violence, and the difficulties of traversing the
treacherous Southern landscape.[186]

At different moments in the war the South was strewn with refugee convoys of both races, each composed of civilians who had gathered what
belongings they could and joined the mass departures from their neigh-

borhoods. Kate Stone described the planters of the Mississippi Valley attempting to escape, laden with their possessions: "Wagons, mules, horses, dogs, baggage, and furniture of every description, very little of it packed. It was just thrown in promiscuous heaps—pianos, tables, chairs, rosewood sofas, wardrobes, parlor sets, with pots, kettles, stoves, beds and beddings, bowls and pitchers, and everything of the kind just thrown pell-mell here and there." In Vicksburg, Isaac Shoemaker observed the arrival of a crowd of 5,000 former slaves into Union-held territory. "They came in all sorts of vehicles and all sorts of animals, remnants of massa's property," he wrote. "The vehicles were loaded with the odds + ends of their household duds, which were a motley mess, + on which were piled the little ones—all these duds were what could be put on the wagons in the hurry of departure." Both convoys were dominated by women and escorted by soldiers, white in Louisiana and black in Mississippi. Both were the sight of a social order crumbling down.[187]

But there was more than simple resemblance between the cavalcades; yet again the roads of the Confederacy provided the setting for an intersection between the rising tide of black freedom and the declining fortunes of the white South. While black women were practicing a new freedom of motion, white women were experiencing the hardships of involuntary relocation; while black women were abandoning places of bondage where they were degraded and dehumanized, white women were leaving cherished homes where they had usually enjoyed a measure of comfort and stability. For black women, movement away from the plantations signaled the beginning of a new life, while for whites it was the end of an era. The motion of refugees in the Confederate South was the essence of the simultaneous yet antithetical processes of change that the war had touched off. On the road black women and white women shared similar experiences of flight and displacement; at the same time the larger meaning of their movement was worlds apart.

James Southhall was one of the luckiest slaves in the antebellum South. Born in Tennessee during the 1850s, he belonged to a master who did not believe in owning human beings and decided to free his chattel before the Civil War. Decades later he told an interviewer what had transpired once the slaves

were set free: "He give 'em all freedom papers and told dem dat dey was as
free as he was and could go anywhere dey wanted. Dey didn't have no where
to go so we all stayed on wid him. It was nice though to know we could go
where we pleased even if we didn't take advantage of it."[188] Southall and his
fellow Tennesseans experienced freedom through a newly found right to
move at will. Whether or not they chose to exercise it was a different question; what mattered most was being in possession of their own bodies and
knowing that they could go where they chose. In a few years' time hundreds
of thousands of slaves would acquire freedom through movement, forever
changing the fate of their people and of their land.

Indeed African Americans' new freedom of motion remains the most
important and most durable legacy of the Civil War's universe of flight.
The departures of thousands of slaves ignited a revolution in race relations
that touched the life of every American and set the history of the United
States on a new course. Moreover, black Southerners who fled slavery displayed unparalleled courage, persistence, and moral conviction in their
quest for freedom. The dangers they overcame and the hardships they faced
exceeded anything that white Southerners ever experienced. And yet runaways from slavery were hardly alone on the roads of the Confederacy; nor
were they unique in their determination to move freely and seek a place
of refuge. The combined effects of mobilization, invasion, dislocation, and
emancipation sent entire populations on the run and made the movement
of the human body into the focal point of social conflict in the Confederate South. This by no means diminishes the significance of black self-
liberation during the Civil War or suggests that all forms of flight were the
same. In fact it is precisely the historical distinctiveness of black flight that
requires us to look at emancipation in conjunction with other forms of
dislocation and with other problems of social control in a theater of war.

For the duration of the Civil War, masses of men and women, enslaved
and free, civilians and soldiers, negotiated the limits of their right to move
and resisted the coercion of multiple authorities that worked to control them.
As blacks were fleeing their masters, soldiers were fleeing their officers; as
civilians living in occupied Union territory were refused a pass from a Northern officer, Confederate soldiers were refused a pass from their captains; as
planter women were seeking safety away from Union lines, enslaved women
risked all and fled to contraband camps that harbored the promise of free-

dom; and as provost marshals and conscription officers were hunting down white men in the woods, slave patrols were battling the growing numbers of fugitives from plantations.

This array of conflicts over freedom of motion amounted to nothing less than a general undermining of a social order that had grown and solidified over hundreds of years. While some areas of the South remained untouched and many Southerners remained in place, the pervasiveness of movement and the turmoil it brought on had a profound effect not only on the particular people who went on the road, but on Confederate society as a whole. The pathways of Dixie were the setting for parallel yet interlocking processes of change that profoundly challenged the balance of power between husbands and wives, masters and slaves, the rich and the poor. In the universe of flight that materialized across the Confederacy, slaves became free people and masters became fugitives; white men lost control over their own physical motion and white women gained it; the wealthiest families lost luxury and status on the run from the Union army, while their destitute slaves were on the path to deliverance as they ran toward the men wearing blue. In the Civil War South freedom and power were won and lost on the move.

Most of these changes would not last long. As the Civil War died down and Southerners began stitching their lives back together, race, class, and gender hierarchies were quickly and effectively restored. So were patterns of movement. Within weeks of the surrender at Appomattox, white Southerners enacted brutal vagrancy laws that restricted black people's freedom of movement and ensured that their former owners would retain a considerable measure of control over their spatial mobility. Soldiers returning home no longer had to submit to the limitations of military life and regained their right to move at will. Most white families quickly reverted to familiar gender roles that confined women to the household and restored the patriarchal hegemony of fathers and husbands. In the Reconstruction South the topsy-turvy world of runaways and their captors faded into distant memory as a new social order took hold.

Yet regardless of what happened next, the Civil War was a moment bursting with radical change. The very fabric of Southern life was torn asunder as multitudes ran, walked, and straggled along the roads of the Confederacy. Conflicts in the realm of mobility embodied the transformative impact of war on society at the same time that they generated even more chaos that pushed the system to the brink of collapse. For the first time since the seventeenth century, the notions of freedom and bondage were opened for redefinition and the entrenched hierarchies of the slave society had become obsolete. If only for a few brief years, the configuration of power in the South was fundamentally altered. On the roads and in the woods, it was a revolution in motion.

4

Dissolution in Motion

The End of the Confederacy

In February 1865 Samuel Moore of Staunton, Virginia, analyzed the state of affairs in the Southern Confederacy. The situation was undeniably bleak. A great Union army was amassed in front of Richmond, waiting for an opportunity to attack. Other enemy forces were advancing across the land, conquering cities, devastating farms, and crushing the feeble Rebel troops that tried to stop them. Bad news was arriving from all fronts, yet Moore was still hopeful. The Confederate nation could win the war if it would concentrate its forces and "whip them in a grand battle in which all the available men of both armies will meet for a settlement of the conflict." Like Moore, numerous Confederates expected that the outcome of the war would be determined in one final, colossal encounter, where one side would emerge as the indisputable winner and dictate the terms of peace to the other. In letters and diaries written during those last months of war, they spoke of the "culminating battle," "the next great battle," or the "great struggle," in which every soldier on both sides would fight to his last breath. This scenario gave the South a fighting chance against its powerful foe, as the Confederate army had repeatedly proven its ability to defeat a larger Union force on the battlefield. No less important, it was an appropriately epic ending to an epic struggle for national independence.[1]

The decisive battle never materialized. Instead the Southern experiment in nation building came to an end in a slow process of disintegration that took place in numerous settings, from the trenches in Virginia to far-flung plantations in the cotton states. Yet the looming defeat was most visible on the roads of the South. In the last months of the war, the armies, the government, and the labor system all collapsed in motion; soldiers, politicians, and freed slaves crowded the pathways of the war-torn region, their movements eroding the social and political order of the land. More than any official ceremony of surrender, human mobility announced that the Confederate States of America was gone.

The first clear indication of the imminent demise of the Southern army appeared in December 1864, following the defeat in the battle of Nashville. The Confederacy had enjoyed a string of military successes during the summer, but in September the tide had turned with the fall of Atlanta and a series of Union victories in the Shenandoah Valley. A few weeks later Southern hopes for an immediate end to the war were shattered when Northern voters reelected Abraham Lincoln to the presidency. Under these circumstances the new commander of the Army of Tennessee, John Bell Hood, embarked on an ambitious campaign to stop William Tecumseh Sherman's rapid and devastating advance across the Confederate interior. Hood moved north from Alabama on November 19 with 39,000 men. He hoped that Sherman would divert his march to follow him, but if that did not come to pass his alternative plan was to fight his way through Tennessee and Kentucky to the Ohio River and then march his men east and unite with Lee in Virginia. Sherman never arrived, but Hood still had to contend with George H. Thomas and his 60,000 troops in Tennessee. Within ten days the campaign turned into an unmitigated disaster for the Confederate army. On November 30 Hood ordered a frontal attack on a fortified Union force in the village of Franklin. The battle ended without a clear outcome, but Hood lost 6,300 men in casualties, three times the enemy's loss, including a dozen killed and wounded generals. Instead of retreating, he continued to Nashville and entrenched his weakened troops on the hills south of the city. Thomas attacked on December 1, overwhelming the Southern force and sending it on a panicked flight south. Union soldiers chased the survivors from the battle for two weeks, and stopped only on the banks of the Tennessee River. The fleeing Confederates did not halt until they reached Tupelo, Mississippi.[2]

This was not the first time Confederate soldiers had been defeated in battle, nor was it the first time they had fled the enemy in fear. Yet the retreat from Nashville was more than a mere rout. The Army of Tennessee fell apart in motion, as thousands of men scattered on the run. "Nearly every man in

Hood's Tennessee Campaign, December 1864

the entire army had thrown away his gun and accouterments," wrote Sam Watkins, a soldier in the 1st Tennessee Regiment. Thousands allowed themselves to be taken prisoner, while the rest kept going, "broken down from sheer exhaustion, with despair and pity written on their features. Wagon trains, cannon, artillery, cavalry, and infantry were all blended in inextricable confusion." The army, described another soldier, had become nothing more than a "demoralized wreck": "Nearly all without shoes & with worn out garments and added to this a ear of corn in each man's haversack to check the awful epidemic—hunger. . . . The retreat surpassed any thing I have ever experienced or ever read."[3] No further attempts at resistance were made. The only thing on the men's minds was getting away from the Union army and finding refuge behind Confederate lines. "The mob, for it was no longer an army, continued its rapid retreat day after day to the river, suffering as no soldier had done during this war from cold wet and hunger, and pressed for several days by the enemy," wrote Benedict Joseph Semmes, a commissary officer in the Army of Tennessee. Men told of comrades who left tracks of blood in the snow and of others who "sat on the road and wept from agony."[4]

Officers who did not join their men in flight failed miserably at stopping their units from dispersing and proceeded to fail at gathering the remaining troops into something resembling an army. Soldiers who arrived back in Confederate territory did not stop running and ended up leaving the service altogether. "One half at least of the Georgia, Mississippi, and Alabama troops have deserted and fill the whole country on their way home," wrote Semmes. In Richmond, John B. Jones was told by congressmen from Tennessee, "Hood's army is destroyed, . . . he will not get 1000 men out of the State, for the Tennesseans, Kentuckians, etc. refuse to retire farther south, but straggle and scatter to their homes, where they will remain." Fewer than half of the soldiers who started out on the campaign in November were present for duty in January. They would never again constitute an organized military force.[5]

Although the Army of Tennessee had ceased to exist, the Confederate government was determined to utilize its remnants to stop Sherman's advance. Soldiers who stayed in the service were sent east to the Carolinas, where they were expected to join the forces under Beauregard. Yet trying to move roughly 15,000 men across nearly eight hundred miles proved to be an impossible task. A combination of incompetent management and the dilapidated state of Confederate transportation infrastructure ensured that the army would continue to disintegrate on the move. The men traveled in trains that broke down incessantly and were stalled for days at a time in congested depots waiting for vehicles to arrive. Union raiders had destroyed the tracks along the route, and the travelers had to make up for gaps by marching. When they arrived in Augusta, Georgia, the soldiers got off the cars and started wandering around the country, as no one had a clear sense of where they were supposed to go or what they were supposed to do. The chaos on the road gave thousands more the opportunity to desert. Exhausted and demoralized after months of intense and unsuccessful campaigning, the soldiers who remained in the Army of Tennessee needed little incentive to leave. "The botched rail transfer rendered this mass exodus almost ludicrously easy," notes one historian. "It was frequently easier to get away from the army than to follow it on its journey." Merely 4,000 men from the Army of Tennessee eventually made it to North Carolina to face Sherman in the battle of Bentonville in March. The issue was no longer absenteeism or desertion; an entire army had dissipated in motion.[6]

In the last six months of the Confederacy's existence this phenomenon repeated itself all over the South. Rawleigh William Downman arrived in the Shenandoah Valley in October 1864 and soon discovered that "the infantry are all the time straggling over the country & don't seem to be under any command." By early January 1865 only one hundred men were left in his own regiment. Three weeks later Union officers in Louisiana reported seeing large Confederate forces going to Texas, accompanied by civilians searching for food. The New Year brought a continuous and uncontrollable wave of mass desertions even from the most disciplined units under the direct command of Robert E. Lee. Soldiers wrote to their families about "a great deal of desertion" and conveyed a sense of despair amid the dissolution of their commands. "I will go on but I think it of no use," wrote one North Carolinian to his brother. "I think we are a conquered people for the soldiers are coming home dayly."[7]

Though the Army of Northern Virginia had not been in motion for months, it was constantly bleeding men. In late March, Lee reported an average rate of at least one hundred desertions a night from his army and admitted that he did not know what could be done to stop it.[8] Neither his threats nor his

offers of amnesty had succeeded in deterring soldiers from departing. Entire units left together, either for enemy lines or in the direction of home, and
an increasing number of officers joined their men.[9] Traveling in southern
Virginia in late March, Joseph Waddell "repeatedly met soldiers, generally
three together," adding, "I inferred much that was bad from encountering so
many fugitives." The breakdown of the Confederacy's elite fighting force was
visible to everyone, from the commander in chief to civilians on the roads of
the Old Dominion.[10]

Even as desertion was becoming a crisis, as long as the soldiers were dug
in the trenches, the Army of Northern Virginia remained a functional military organization. This ended on Sunday, April 2. Active fighting on the
Petersburg-Richmond front had resumed the previous week, after a long
winter of stalemate. On March 25 Confederate soldiers attacked the Union
earthwork of Fort Steadman and were initially successful before being
repulsed by a heavy counterattack. Skirmishing continued during the next
few days, and on April 1 Union forces staged a flank attack on the Confederate right and defeated the Rebels in an open battle at the Five Forks crossroads. Half of the Confederate soldiers were killed, wounded, or captured;
the other half escaped in panic. This was the moment Grant had been waiting for. At dawn on the following day the Army of the Potomac opened an
assault along the entire Confederate line, forcing the Army of Northern Virginia to abandon the trenches and flee westward. The Confederates' first
stop was thirty-five miles away, at Amelia Court House, where a trainload of
rations was supposed to await them. No rations had arrived, and the army
was compelled to continue retreating west, in the direction of Lynchburg.
Lee's last hope was to unite in southern Virginia with Joseph E. Johnston's
army, which was in North Carolina trying to stop Sherman's march. According to this optimistic scenario, by joining forces the two decimated armies
might be able to face one Northern army at a time and defeat it in battle. But
it was already too late. Union soldiers pursued the retreating Confederate
army relentlessly, cutting its rail communications, burning its wagon trains,
and capturing entire units that had become isolated from the main body. On
April 8 the Army of Northern Virginia reached the village of Appomattox,
where Lee made one more attempt to break free of the vast force enveloping
his command. Realizing that he was completely encircled, he had no other
choice but to give up. On April 9 he raised the white flag.[11]

Appomattox Campaign

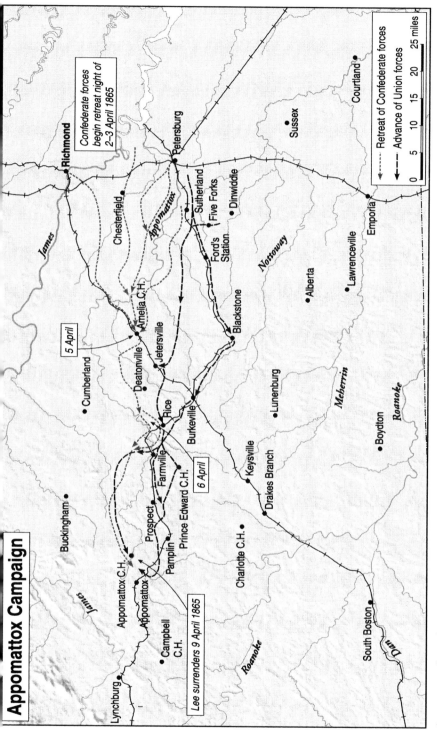

Confederate forces begin retreat night of 2–3 April 1865

Richmond

Petersburg

Chesterfield

Sutherland

Five Forks

Dinwiddie

Ford's Station

Appomattox

Blackstone

Nottoway

Amelia C.H.

5 April

Jetersville

Deatonville

Cumberland

Rice

Burkeville

Lunenburg

Alberta

Lawrenceville

Emporia

Sussex

Courtland

James

Buckingham

Farmville

6 April

Prince Edward C.H.

Keysville

Meherrin

Boydton

Roanoke

Prospect

Pamplin

Drakes Branch

Appomattox C.H.

James

Appomattox

Lee surrenders 9 April 1865

Campbell C.H.

Charlotte C.H.

Lynchburg

Roanoke

South Boston

Dan

	Retreat of Confederate forces
	Advance of Union forces

0 5 10 15 20 25 miles

Appomattox Campaign

By that point there was not much left to surrender. The Army of Northern Virginia had been destroyed by the week-long retreat. Approximately 58,000 soldiers had started out on April 2, but only about 10,000 were with Lee on the morning of April 9, according to his own estimate. During the next few days thousands who had left the march returned to receive their paroles, bringing the number up to 28,000, with an additional 4,000 men surrendering to Federal soldiers in Lynchburg and Farmville.[12] Even if precise figures for the entire army are impossible to ascertain, data collected in individual units also indicate a nearly general meltdown during the march. George Pickett had 9,500 men in his division on April 1, but only 500 on April 9. The eight Virginia brigades serving in the army numbered 12,865 men at the beginning of the campaign and 3,163 at Appomattox.[13]

While some soldiers who disappeared during the retreat were captured or killed by enemy fire, the majority of men who started from Petersburg but never made it to Appomattox simply dropped out of the column as it made its way west. By all accounts, the march was a hellish experience of starvation, exhaustion, and fear. Soldiers raced day and night without food or sleep, unable to escape the pursuit of the Union army. Many could simply not endure the physical exertion. "It is a fearful sight to see the state of our Army, hundreds upon hundreds lying in the road not able to move from hunger and fatigue," wrote one diarist.[14] A soldier who acted as rear guard remembered the stragglers lying asleep, "singly or in squads, in the woods and fields where they had dropped—dispirited and exhausted—and outnumbered us a hundred to one." Others were still standing but had been separated from their units in the confusion of flight and were roaming the countryside looking for food, friends, or a sense of where they should go.[15] Neither horses nor men had enough strength to carry the supplies of the army through quagmires of mud, and the roads were strewn with "broken down wagons, ambulances, caissons, cannon, baggage that had been thrown away. Papers, clothing, and utensils dropped by men who are breaking after four years of strain."[16] Another soldier remembered the roads and fields full of stragglers who "moved looking behind them, as if they expected to be attacked and harried by a pursuing foe. Demoralization, panic, abandonment of all hope, appeared on every hand. Wagons were rolling along without any order or system. Caissons and limber-chests, without commanding officers, seemed to be floating aimlessly upon a tide of disorganization." The Confederacy's toughest fighting force was turning into a chaotic mass of desperate men. "This retreat is doing terrible things to our mind," wrote one soldier on April 4.[17]

With every passing day regiments and brigades dissolved in motion, as some soldiers gave way, others got lost, and still more deserted. "I am staying with the wagon trains as I have no regiment," wrote George F. Clark on April 7. "Not more than a hundred men is left in the division except those that are connected with the wagon trains. Those that are left are going where ever they choose to go. The most of them have gone home." Indeed droves of men who had lost hope or refused to bear the humiliation of defeat took advantage of the complete breakdown in discipline and started on the long journey back to their families. It was painfully obvious that the army, and the nation it fought for, were in the process of final collapse. One officer wrote, "When I see the crowd of stragglers, & then look across at the Blue Ridge, & think that I must give up this beloved Virginia because of the faintheartedness and cowardice of these men, who have deserted their columns, my heart bursts with a sob."[18]

The Army of Northern Virginia had fought ferociously for four years to defend the South's northern border and its capital. Even in the last months of the war, when the Confederacy was running out of resources and a deep sense of despair prevailed across the land, these soldiers held their own in the face of the Union's much larger and better equipped Army of the Potomac. Despite the growing rates of desertion, Confederate divisions stayed in the trenches and did not give in. Yet once the army set out on the road, it came apart.[19] The most seasoned veterans could not withstand the power of retreat to break down an organized military body. The Army of Northern Virginia reached its end not in one great battle, but over a long and miserable week of flight. There were no heroic charges or brilliant maneuvers, just a host of worn-out men trying to escape their enemies in the dark. The road, as much as the battlefield, had become a locus of Confederate defeat.

Within hours of their departure, the men who had abandoned Lee's retreat were seen on the roads of central Virginia and in the farmhouses along the way. "The number of deserters crossing the river induced me to stop the ferry day before yesterday," wrote Christopher Tompkins, a mining engineer in the Dover coal pits on the James River. "Nevertheless they continue in crowds & are traveling the roads in all directions."[20] Days before they got word of the official surrender, civilians in the Old Dominion realized that the situation on the front lines was critical. "Stragglers and deserters have been passing in numbers giving most terrible accounts of the condition of Gen. Lee's army," wrote Mary Alice Downman to her husband. Years of experience with false rumors spread by stragglers had taught Virginians to be skeptical. Yet the sheer number of men on the road telling stories of suffering and hopelessness could not be ignored. "I know that such men are not to be relied on but hearing nothing else their tales should have *some* weight."[21]

Men on the road brought the news about the end of the war to civilians in many locales across the Confederacy. Mary Elizabeth Mitchell was in Tuscaloosa, Alabama, where definite news about the end of the war was slow to arrive. "It is certainly true that General Johnston has surrendered," she wrote in her diary on May 13. "His paroled soldiers have been passing through town on their way home." In South Carolina, Susan Jervey received confirmation of the rumors of surrender on April 23, when a "poor worn-out soldier from Lee's army begged for somewhere to rest, and something to eat." She wrote in her journal, "The news we heard has proved too true . . . Lee has surrendered!"[22]

Once Confederate soldiers had capitulated and received their paroles, they started en masse on their way home. Men from the Army of Northern Virginia embarked shortly after Lee's meeting with Grant on April 10. Three weeks later they were joined by Joseph Johnston's soldiers, who conceded to Sherman in North Carolina on April 26. In May Richard Taylor and Kirby Smith surrendered their men in the Deep South and Southwest. "For three weeks steady after the surrender people was passing from the War and for two years off and on somebody come along going home," recalled Irene Robertson, an ex-Louisiana slave.[23] Although many veterans entertained adventurous ideas of life after defeat, few ended up going to Mexico, South America, or Europe. Even if there was not much left of a farm or a plantation, soldiers who survived the war wanted to go home. "Soldiers began to scatter," recalled another former slave. "They was a sorry-lookin' bunch of lost sheep. They didn't know where to go, but most of 'em ended up pretty close to the towns they started from. They was like homing pigeons, with only the instinct to go home, and yet, most of them had no homes to go to."[24]

As there was no longer a Confederate government or a Confederate army to administer and pay for demobilization, the defeated soldiers were left to their own devices. Thousands went on the road with no food, no money, and no conveyances. Some were fortunate enough to be offered free transportation by federal officers or railway officials; others happened on civilians who still had the means and the inclination to feed soldiers on the move. Still others raided commissary stores or confiscated mules and horses from citizens along the way.[25] The rest scraped by. "Until last night I had not tasted bread for four days and drew but 1 lb of beef," reported a Georgian traveling home days after Appomattox. "We suffered much from hunger."[26]

Men living in Virginia or North Carolina reached their destination within a week or two of hard marching; soldiers from the trans-Mississippi west could travel for two months before getting to their final destination. Many had not recovered from the experience of the last retreat before they had to move again. Kena King Chapman started for Richmond on April 14 with men who were "suffering greatly from fatigue and the want of suitable food," while others were "footsore and almost broken down." Henry Bahnson had lost thirty-eight pounds since he left Petersburg, and by the time he got home three weeks later he was so emaciated and filthy his own father did not recognize him.[27]

The thousands of men trudging wearily along the roads of Dixie created a powerful spectacle of defeat. In 1861 soldiers marching to Virginia embodied the new Southern nation and its fight for independence; returning in 1865 they were the living proof of the Confederacy's demise. The contrast between what they once were and what they had turned into was blindingly obvious to some. Isaac Coles of the 6th Virginia Cavalry remembered nostalgically that bright day in the beginning of the war when "a blithe company of Pittsylvania County's young blood-thirsting" men left for war, "well-mounted and looking upon the venture as more of a lark or picnic. . . . Naturally and fortunately they could little foresee the return of that depleted company, four years later, seeking home again—a company in remnants and shreds, broken down in ranks and in fortune." Southern men, like the land they had fought for, were a pale shadow of their old selves. "Each day . . . they came," wrote Emma Holmes in South Carolina, "homeless, penniless, clotheless, with the past an awful quivering wreck, the future a blank whose gloom was only made deeper by memory of former happiness

& peace." A Northern reporter described them as "homesick boys and exhausted men wandering about in threadbare uniforms, with scanty outfit of slender haversack and blanket roll hung over their shoulders, seeking the nearest route home; they have a care-worn and anxious look, a played out manner."[28] The image of Southern men at the end of the war was even more striking when compared to that of the victorious Northern army marching through the conquered land. "We alas saw *miles* of his four horse wagons pass before this gate," wrote a woman in North Carolina of Sherman's army. "Day after day battalion after battalion marched by, all well clad, fully armed and looking like men well fed & ready to *commence* the war—these were only 12 hours behind our ragged war-worn gallant men." Standing by the roadside and watching the armies passing by, Confederates encountered the downfall of the South and the triumph of the North.[29]

The scenes of Confederate soldiers traveling home evoked not only the defeat of a nation, but also the decline of a ruling class. War transformed white Southern men from a caste of proud masters into a crowd of broken-down losers. This was visible to everyone, most of all to their slaves. Well into the twentieth century African Americans remembered in detail the sight of their owners coming back from war. "I can still see dem soldiers of ours coming across Broad River, all dirty, filthy, and lousy," said one former South Carolina slave. "Dey was most starved, and so poor and lanky. And deir hosses was in de same fix." Most Confederate veterans did not even own an animal to ride. "The Yankees was in front—they was the horsebackers," remembered Bernice Bowden. "Then come the wagons and then the Southern soldiers comin' along in droves." George Simmens saw throngs of men "walkin' on the road, sometime dey had ol' wagons, but mos' times dey walk."[30] In the antebellum South, riding was a defining feature of white mastery and an essential instrument of domination over the enslaved. Now white men were no longer on horseback, no longer riding patrol or escorting a coffle of human chattel going south. At the end of the Civil War they were the ones trudging along on foot.

No less shocking was the state of the bodies making the journey home. "Young master bin in de big battle in Virginia, and he git hit, and de git sick, and when he come home he jest lak a old man he was so feeble," remembered a former slave from Texas. Alice Cole's master returned to his plantation after having been wounded twice: "Maser he was poor, his face was pale and looked like death." The difference between the soldiers' jubilant departure and their despairing homecoming struck a powerful note with those who had suffered most from their authoritarian rule. "I seen our 'Federates go off laughin' an' gay; full of life an' health," remembered a man who was enslaved in Alabama. "Dey was big an' strong, a singin' Dixie an' dey jus knowed dey was agoin' to win. An' boss, I seen 'em come back skin an' bone, dere eyes all sad an' hollow, an' dere clothes all ragged. Boss, dey was all lookin' sick. De sperrit dey lef' wid jus' been done whupped outten dem." Tom McAlpin, whose father was sent to war with his master, remembered both returning as different people: "De massa an' pap what had gone off mad an' healthy an' ridin' fine beastes comes back walkin' an' dey looked sick. Massa am white as cotton an' so help me, iffen my pap, who wus black as sin, ain't pale too."[31]

Slaves were particularly attuned to the changes in the physical appearance of their masters since their lives in the antebellum period were in many ways governed by the white man's absolute control over black bodies. The frail, gaunt veterans who returned from war were the same men who used to beat, whip, and chain people and nail them to trees; the same men who had an unconditional right to abuse their female slaves; the same men who had the power to sell the bodies of husbands, wives, and children on the auction block. The conspicuous breakdown of their own physiques was a revelation. It was also an unmistakable sign that the previous relationship between blacks and whites could be no more.

While several hundreds of thousands of slaves were able to attain freedom during the war, the great majority of black Southerners were still enslaved when the Confederate army surrendered. Millions of bondspeople learned of emancipation in the plantations and farms where they were held, either from their masters or from Union soldiers. In numerous cases their initial reaction to the news was to pack some belongings and get on the road. Slavery in the United States came to its end with a mass exodus, which was seen and felt all over the South. "When the War over," recalled one ex-slave, "you'd see men, women and chillun walk out of their cabins with a bundle under their arms. All going by in droves, just going nowhere in particular." "After freedom, folks scattered out just like sheep," remembered Lidia Jones, who was enslaved in Arkansas. "A heap left, dey jes' broke ranks and left," recalled another ex-slave.[32] Harriett Robinson's master convened his freed slaves and promised each ten dollars if they would continue to work until harvest time. "Don't you know before he got half way thoo' over helf them niggers was gone."[33] Many slaves who had not been informed of the change in their status remained in their master's home for weeks and months after the war ended, working under the same regime of bondage. They too often chose to leave as soon as word came that they were free. Dora Franks was in Choctaw County, Mississippi: "When de war was over my brother Frank slipped in de house where I was still a-stayin'. He tol' me us was free an' for me to come out wid de res'. 'Fore sundown dere warnt one Nigger lef' on de place." Slaves had spent a lifetime fantasizing about freedom. When the day finally came, they wasted no time in realizing their dream.[34]

In the Civil War South motion of the human body was deeply intertwined with the concept of freedom. Yet at no other time were the two as closely related as they were in the immediate aftermath of the surrender. By getting on the road, freed people assumed control of their bodies. It was the first and most crucial step toward realizing their new status in the world.[35] Men and women who had been enslaved all their lives were allowed for the first time to use their own limbs as they saw fit and to explore their surroundings. There was no need to flee, or move through the woods, or ask for a pass, or hide from a patrol. It was an enormous, breathtaking change. "Desertion is the order of the day," wrote Christopher Tompkins at the Dover coal pits in Virginia. "All the negroes are going or have gone, quick for Richmond. Never was change accomplished so silently & so completely."[36] Emma Mordecai recorded in her diary, "The negro movement is still a most vexatious and mischievous one and its effects are painfully felt in every Southern household."[37] Most Southern households, of course, never included any slaves to begin with, but wherever slaves had lived and worked, the roads were thronged with freed people on the move. The slow and uneven disintegration of the system during the war was turning into a rapid and permanent collapse. Any hopes of preserving the old order under a new name were shattered in the face of black people's determined use of their freedom to move.

Freed people's movement in the immediate aftermath of the Civil War remains clouded by the lack of reliable statistics and by the deep prejudice evident in the accounts written by white Southerners who witnessed it unfold.[38] It is virtually impossible to estimate how many actually left the plantations as soon as the war ended, nor is it easy to assess their motivations, destinations, and intents. Their former owners described their departures as senseless and impulsive, the result of a wholly irrational urge. "Poor wretches, they seem possessed with mania," wrote Joseph Waddell. A woman in North Carolina claimed "the creatures were intoxicated at what they heard . . . they abandoned their former homes & flocked to town." Yet white Southerners were grossly mistaken. Postemancipation black mobility was a complex and varied phenomenon, encompassing an untold number of individuals who used mobility in the service of many different priorities and goals. Their decision to set out constituted a calculated attempt to address a unique set of desires and anxieties prevalent among a people whose world had been radically, and often suddenly, transformed. Yet what was clear back then and remains clear now is that whenever they left and however far they traveled, the very act of leaving their place of bondage was the consummate realization of emancipation. It is precisely why their former owners were so enraged.

For most Southerners, black and white, the need to put bread on the table was the most pressing concern in the first few months after the war. Yet some freed people decided that their longing to experiment with spatial mobility and to put some physical distance between themselves and their former masters outweighed material considerations. "When the war ended mother went to old master and told him she was goin' to leave," recalled one former slave. "He told her she could not feed all her children, pay house rent, and buy wood, to stay on with him. Master told father and mother they could have the house free and wood free, an' he would help them feed the children, but ma said, 'No, I am goin' to leave. I have never been free and I am goin' to try it.'"[39] Similar conversations took place in innumerable households across the South. "The negroes in this part seem to have a general desire to leave their old homes and hunt new ones," testified a Texas judge as the year drew to a close. "It is also appearend that the negroes will rather work for low wages among the German population, then to take high prices from their former owners where they don't feel 'free.'"[40]

Many former slaves were driven to leave by the yearning to locate family members from whom they had been separated during slavery. Against all odds, they embarked on journeys to look for wives, husbands, or children, some of whom had vanished from their lives decades earlier. A Northern reporter met one man "who had walked from Georgia in the hope of finding in Salisbury a wife from whom he had been separated years before by sale. In Louisiana, I met men and women who since the war had made long journeys in order to see their parents or their children."[41] Nettie Henry's father had been forced to leave his family in Meridian, Mississippi, when his master tried to get away from the Union army. "After de War he come back to us, walked mos' all de way frum Texas," she recounted. Former slaves never forgot these reunions, which were often the sweetest reward of their liberation from bondage. William Curtis remained with his master in Georgia after he was freed: "After a while my pappy come home to us. Dat was de best thing about de war setting us free, he could come back to us."[42] In the antebellum era the forced mobility of the slave trade had broken their families and their hearts. Their new freedom of movement gave them the hope that they could reverse the process, undo the damage.

Another very popular motive for leaving a farm or plantation was the attraction of city life. This tendency would remain strong for years to come, but it was evident from the earliest days of freedom. As soon as word of Lee's surrender reached the slaves working in the Dover coal pits, "the fever was so high that every soul who had legs to walk was running to Richmond, even old Eliza with her 4 little children was anxious to go, but . . . she was ready to leave her children behind sooner than fail to go." "All the negroes in the country were making for Richmond, with their 'things,'" remembered a Confederate veteran of his journey home in May 1865. "They did not feel free until they had left the plantations."[43] Postbellum cities offered blacks schools, churches, and fraternal societies, as well as a chance to work as wage laborers. Urban centers also harbored the promise of greater protection from the violence and abuse of rural folk. The presence of Union soldiers and Freedmen's Bureau agents often assured blacks a safer existence than the one they could expect at the mercy of their masters-turned-employers. The black population of the ten largest Southern cities doubled between 1865 and 1870, while the white population rose by only 10 percent. In smaller towns the rate of increase in the size of black communities was even greater.

The quest for safety in the volatile postwar South led some former slaves away from areas where they were a minority and into black belt counties, where their large numbers could potentially serve as a shield against white aggression. Also on the move were former slaves who had been relocated by their masters during the war but were determined to return to their old homes as soon as the war ended. A Northern journalist in South Carolina met "parties of hungry, ill-clad Negroes moving towards the coast country. . . . They wanted to get back to the region with which they were familiar, or they thought to find employment in labor which they understood better than that which they were leaving."[44] Going in the other direction were men and women who were lured by the promise of abundant land and high wages in the Southwest, and were willing to take a long journey to an unknown land for better economic prospects.[45]

Yet the majority of freed people who moved in the aftermath of the war did not seek to travel long distances or to restart their lives in entirely new surroundings. They chose instead to move to an adjacent county or to a different plantation within the same area. Only rarely did they migrate to another state or to the North; often they ended up only a few miles from where they started.[46] Although the land they had lived on belonged to the people who kept them in bondage, freed men and women nevertheless had a profound sense of belonging to a particular place. They were attached to their home, the natural environment, and the local slave community. Moving some distance from their master and exploring the world that had previously lain beyond their reach were one thing; leaving everything behind was another. "The people would be glad to stay here on the soil of K[entuck]y if they could stay and not have the life tormented out of them," noted a superintendent of a refugee home in Camp Nelson, Kentucky.[47]

Freed people who set out in the wake of emancipation belonged to every subgroup within the black community. There were men and women, young and old, married and single. Those who had been obedient slaves left with those who were the most rebellious; those who labored under cruel masters were joined by those who lived with the most humane slaveholders in the South. Yet more often than not, the freed men and women who led the migration were the able-bodied house servants and artisans and those who had acquired special skills as slaves. "A portion of Miss Archers' numerous negroes went off lately," wrote Edmund Ruffin in his diary on April 28, "of course, of the more able & profitable class." Frequently these were also the family's favorites, and their manifest desire to depart as quickly as possible shocked their owners. "I did not believe Dave would leave," wrote John Kimberly in North Carolina, after a trusted slave departed with some of his money. "Rosina is really and greatly distressed at parting with the foolish creatures," noted Emma Mordecai in Richmond, as the household's workforce was discovered to be preparing to go away. Joseph Waddell woke up in Staunton one morning in early May to find out that the Yankee army was leaving town, accompanied by a "negro exodus." Among the departing were "negroes of all ages, and some who," he thought, "had too much family pride or attachment to go off with the Yankees." Waddell was especially offended by seeing that "A. A. H. Stuart's Peyton was among them, who was identified with the family, and was really as free as his master, and who leaves a comfortable home and the kindest treatment for the uncertainties of freedom among Northern *friends*—freedom to starve and die, but hardly freedom to labor."[48] After a lifetime of self-delusion, slaveholders finally faced the truth about the men and women whom they had kept in bondage. They were not content, they were not grateful, and most of all, many of them wanted to get away from their masters as soon as possible. The mass movement of newly freed slaves was an unequivocal manifestation of their true feelings toward their former owners and toward the institution itself. For many white people, this amounted to nothing less than a betrayal. Their basic convictions about the life they had lived were falling to pieces with every departure of a privileged slave.

In numerous cases the disappointment and disillusionment quickly turned into violence and rage. Owners who refused to come to terms with their property's new ability to move at will used the most brutal means available to keep the freed people in their place. Planters chased their former slaves, unleashed their wrath on those who were caught, and forced them back into the fields and cabins they had sought to escape. In Mississippi a chaplain of a black regiment heard of former slaves who had run away but were overtaken by their owners, "arrested & brot back, & flogged—They ran away again, & were again caught & flogged more severely—They were the third time punished by having an ear cut off." In Georgia the freedwoman Betsey Lexley attempted to smuggle her three children from the plantation where they were still kept as slaves in June 1865, but their owner outstripped them on the road, "beat them severely, knocked her son Edward, on the head with a gun, and carried the party back with him."[49] Yet even slaves who did not attempt to leave their masters but merely moved around their neighborhood often reaped a violent reward. Lydia Turner, a freed slave in

Greene County, Virginia, defied her employer one Saturday when she chose to go to Stanardville to "be present at a 'Tournament'" against his wishes. When she returned, he punished her by "shaking her severely" and "admonished her if she left again without leave she might be subjected to more severe punishment."[50]

Southern whites intent on stopping black movement did not only act as individuals, but were also quick to organize civic groups for the same purpose. Neither the shock of defeat nor the trauma of Union occupation deterred former slaveholders from reviving the old techniques of movement control, including the violence, humiliation, and intimidation that had served them so well in the past.[51] In Opelousas, Louisiana, a local police force outlawed the presence of black people in town unless they had written permission from their employers. Blacks were also banned on the streets after 10 PM on weekdays and past 3 PM on Sundays, and the only African Americans allowed to reside within city limits were those employed by white persons. In eastern Texas local white residents formed committees charged with preventing freed people from going back to their homes in other states, as well as whipping those who attempted to relocate in order to live with their families.[52]

Yet even as former slaveholders were desperate to keep some freed people from leaving, they did not hesitate to utilize the opening created by black mobility to get rid of other slaves who were no longer deemed sufficiently profitable. Planters routinely expelled from their property the old, the young, and the infirm, either because they did not want to spend money on their subsistence or as punishment for the departure of stronger workers. In late May William H. Sims reported to his aunt that he had "driven off" some of the men on his plantation "as they were worthless." A few days later Joseph Waddell declared, "It is preposterous to imagine that the master, in a majority of cases, can maintain the aged and young slaves, when deserted by all the able-bodied." A Northern reporter on his way to Richmond in the summer of 1865 met an old black man going to the city after his former master threw him out of his plantation: "He said he'd no use fo' old wore-out niggers. I knowed I was old and wore-out, but I growed so in his service. I served him and his father befo'e nigh on to sixty year; and he never give me a dollar. He's had my life, and now I'm old and wore-out I must leave."[53]

At the same time that the scenes on Southern roads created an impression that every former bondsperson was on the move, in reality numerous freed people chose at first to stay where they were. "After de surrender us colored people didn' have no whar to go but out on de road," recalled Arthur Greene, a former Virginia slave. "Folk jes' stayed on wid dair masters an' mistresses." "Mr. Spence told me I was free," recalled a former Missouri bondswoman. "I didn't leave. I didn't have sense to know where to go. I didn't know what freedom was." Agricultural workers, especially those who had lived on large plantations, were particularly prone to remaining behind even as members of their community left. Realizing the tremendous difficulties that awaited them on the road, they opted for the security and familiarity of their former masters. "Us didn't want no more freedom than us was gittin' on our plantation already," remembered Ezra Adams, who was enslaved in South Carolina. "Us knowed too well dat us was well took care of, wid a plenty of vittles to eat and tight log and board houses to live in."[54] Yet choosing to stay on a farm or plantation did not denote rejection of freedom. Nor did it mean that freed people who stayed behind failed to take advantage of their right to move at will. Alice Cole remembered in vivid detail how she had come to experience emancipation through motion, in the very same household where she was once enslaved:

> I'se never tasted freedom until Maser told us we was just as free as he was and then we asked him if we could go and come without asking him and he said that was exactly what he meant, that he in no way had any string on us now. We could hardly go anywhere for a long time after freedom without first asking our Maser. If we did go without asking him we was scared all the time or would be looking for the patter roller to come and get us cause you'se knows we did not have any pass. Of course, son, we finally got use to coming and going without asking Maser or him giving us a pass so'es the patter rollers would not get the poor old negro.[55]

Freed slaves who chose to stay with their former masters and await further developments often made a wise decision. Four years of war had left large parts of the former Confederacy impoverished, if not devastated. Agriculture, industry, and transportation were at a standstill; there was little currency in circulation and few opportunities for employment besides field labor. Freed people who chose to make their way through this desolated landscape suffered greatly from hunger, disease, and the absence of shelter. With few possessions and no money, they tried to make a life in urban shanty-towns and improvised camps along the road. H. R. Brinkerhoff, a Northern officer commanding a detachment of black soldiers stationed by a railroad near Clinton, Mississippi, witnessed throngs of freed slaves passing by, "hungry, naked, foot sore, and heartless, aliens in their native land, home-less and friendless. They are wandering up and down the country, rapidly becoming vagabonds, and thieves from both necessity and inclination."[56] Their deserted owners openly gloated at their misfortunes. "They sat in squads about the streets, then crowded into empty houses, lived upon ra-tions scantily given out by the Yankee army," wrote a white woman in the summer of 1865. "The air has become gradually impure sickness is the re-sult and yellow jaundice an epidemic now prevailing." Another former slaveholder in North Carolina described the freedmen as "destitute, dirty, ragged": "[They] had not slept in a house since leaving Chapel Hill, and were receiving from the commissary each three crackers a day. Moreover, the negroes are dying here in droves from a malignant fever."[57] In Richmond, Susan Hoge declared the "poor creatures" doomed, as "in a few generations there will none be left—they are dying from neglect by hundreds all over the country."

Freed men and women were not expiring at the rate some white South-erners might have hoped for, but the hardships on the road forced many to return to their old habitats. "They soon found out dat freedom ain't nothin', 'less you is got somethin' to live on and a place to call home. Dis livin' on liberty is lak young folks livin on love after they gits married. It just don't work." The sight of those coming back deterred others who had hesitated to leave. "Freedom meant we could leave whar we'd been bawn en bred, but hit also meant, we had to scratch for ourselves," said a former Mississippi slave. "Dem what left de ole plantation seemed all so fired glad to git back dat I made up my mind to stay put."[58] A Freedmen's Bureau officer in Beaufort, South Carolina, observed in late July that former slaves who realized they could not procure work in town "soon return to their old homes, make con-tracts with the planters and again work better than ever before. In fact this is most universally the case."[59]

Freed people on the move faced not only the economic realities of a war-torn land and the violence of their former masters, but also fierce opposition from those who were supposed to protect their new liberties. Freedmen's Bureau agents and Union officers frequently attempted to stem the tide of mobility that swept through the South and force black people to remain in their place. In various cities across the former Confederacy Federal officers issued strict orders preventing freed people from entering their domain and actively tried to banish those who had already arrived. The superintendent of the Freedmen's Bureau in Memphis issued an order in mid-July directing all freed people who had left their employers and reached the city to "return and resume their labor at once." Moreover he threatened, "All freed people coming to this city under such circumstances, or who come here and make complaints, which upon careful examination shall prove false or malicious, will be arrested as vagrants and compelled to return to their employers or be otherwise dealt with as justice require." In Petersburg, Virginia, the local military commander informed the freedmen that it was "much better" for them to remain in the countryside than "to come to the already over stocked city, and that they will not be permitted to come here for work or subsistence, unless they cannot obtain it where they are."[60]

In their effort to hold back the surge of black movement, Union authorities felt no compunction about reinstating the pass system for African Americans, a distinctive feature of the same slave system that had supposedly just been abolished. A circular issued in west Tennessee warned, "Negroes from the country will not be permitted to visit military posts without a pass from their employer," while the local commander in northern Louisiana prohibited "all transports and private steamboats running on Red River" from carrying freed slaves "except upon a military pass, which will be given only in exceptional cases."[61] While this particular officer was referring to former plantation hands, in reality the vicious struggle over black people's freedom of movement permeated every echelon in the black community, consuming even those who had been free before the war and who had always enjoyed the right to move at will. "In the city of Richmond, the military and police authorities will not allow us to walk the streets by day or night, in the regular pursuit of our business or on our way to church, without a *pass*," wrote a group of black denizens to President Andrew Johnson in June. "And passes do not in all cases protect us from arrest, insult, abuse, violence, and imprisonment." In Memphis one resident testified, "Collored people that have lived in this city all there life more or less cannot walk the streets without being halted by the guards and asked for the pass. . . . The oldest citizens of collor in this city are hunted down like brutes—and taken to a corall like beasts to be hired or sold to the highest bidder."[62]

Free or freed, black people in Memphis were hounded as if slavery had never ceased to exist. Captain Edward C. Lovell, inspector general of the bureau in western Tennessee, confirmed black residents' complaints, using even stronger language to describe the state of affairs in town: "[Colored persons] are daily arrested by armed patrols, wearing the uniform of the U.S. corralled together until a sufficiently large number is obtained and then sent to the country for employment, generally to work for their former masters whether willing or no." And lest soldiers lose their motivation for the task of man hunting, they received five dollars for every laborer they brought in. The severity of the situation in Memphis caused a Northern clergyman living in the city to wonder whether the Freedmen's Bureau was "established for the purpose of thus acting the blood-hound & press-gang over again—on behalf of those who have wrought the damning crime of treason & rebellion in order to keep these poor people in perpetual bondage."[63]

In the countryside Freedmen's Bureau agents and army officers often assisted planters in forcing former slaves into signing exploitive labor contracts and encouraged them to stay where they were regardless of how they were treated. In Camden, Arkansas, the bureau announced, "The season is now so far advanced that freed-people are advised to remain where they now are, for the remainder of this year. They will not be allowed to congregate in towns, and about military camps, to spend their times in idleness and vagrancy." In Shreveport, Louisiana, the same officer who proscribed black travel on the Red River also enjoined freed people to "remain for the present with their former masters, and by their labor secure the crops of the present season. The only place where they can obtain a living for themselves and their families is in the feild, where they have been accustomed to work."[64] The occupation forces were concerned with stabilizing life in a tension-ridden society that had just gone through a revolution. They were also interested in resuming crop production and preventing widespread starvation. Yet the same practical considerations, combined with a healthy measure of virulent racism, led them in many cases to cooperate with planters in limiting African Americans from using the most basic right emancipation had granted them: the right to come and go as they pleased.

Some Northern officials expressed their sympathy toward Southern planters by espousing the notion that black movement equaled indolence, laziness,
and refusal to work. Instead of treating the right to move at will as the most
basic prerogative of freedom, they shared the planters' anger and contempt
toward those who dared to leave and reinforced the image of blacks on the
move as criminals and tramps. "A large portion of the able bodied are already vagrants, and more daily becoming so," wrote a Union officer in Mississippi, in a particularly hostile report. "The slightest friction of the home
harness is enough to drive them into vagabondism." In Helena, Arkansas,
the bureau superintendent claimed, "One sixth of the crops stand a fair
chance of being lost and most of it is occassioned by the hands coming to
town in droves for amusement or on the most trivial excuses and wasting
whole days."[65] Not all officers and agents shared this view, and some repeatedly pointed out that movement was the essence of freedom and that confin-
ing former slaves to plantations was unjust and unlawful. Yet in the postemancipation South there were more than a few Northerners who were eagerly
involved in delegitimizing black mobility and accepting the white Southern
vision of what the freed people's geographical future should be.[66]

But no matter how hard they tried, neither planters nor bureau agents were
able to prevent former slaves from exercising their right to move at will. In
many ways the mass movement of freed people in the spring of 1865 was
what turned emancipation in the American South from an idea into a reality with which every person, white or black, had to contend. It would take
decades before free labor in the region would actually be free. But the ability
of black people to move at will and the parallel inability of white people to
control their movements were palpable and meaningful from the very first
day. Freedom of motion transformed the former slaves into their own masters. That is why so many were willing to face the hunger, exposure, and violence on the road; that is also why former slaveholders were so infuriated by
the sight of their former chattel setting out. Freed slaves did not have to abandon their owners to trigger a violent attack. Even a one-day excursion into
town or an unauthorized visit to a farm nearby was enough to demonstrate
that black people were no longer captives in the hands of white folks. Often
the distance traveled or purpose of the trip made no difference at all. Any
form of black mobility served as a stark reminder of the new reality taking
hold over the slaveholders' former domain.

The movement of freed slaves out of the plantations also coincided with the return of their masters from the war. For a few weeks in the spring and summer of 1865 the roads of the South were simultaneously inundated with the defeated and the triumphant, with those who were leaving home and those who were going back. A former Virginia slave remembered "long lines of tired men straggling back to their homes" followed by "great droves of negroes" passing by the plantation "singing as they went." On April 22 Lizzie Hardin recorded in her diary the passage of "crowds of soldiers and refugees who had escaped. . . . Droves of Negroes, horses, mules, cattle, and hogs were pouring through town to seek refuge at some point on the Madison road." At the end of the Civil War blacks and whites once again formed one wave of motion. "The country is full of poor deluded negroes crazed by the idea of freedom and deserters," wrote a diarist in Virginia. At a time when saving what remained of one's private property often mattered more than anything else, both groups were suspected of posing the same threat. "The country is filled with stragglers and negroes who have left their owners," wrote John Kimberly. "They must subsist, and will do it by pillage and robbery. Misery and suffering await us, unless the federal government will soon furnish us with supplies." In South Carolina one white resident looking for some missing horses told the Union provost marshal he believed that his property "had been stolen by rebel scouts, robbers, or negroes." In the minds of war-weary Southerners, liberated blacks and subjugated whites often fell into the same category of mobile people who existed by preying on others for money, transportation, or food.[67]

While the motion of former slaves and former soldiers embodied the downfall of the Old South, in the twilight of the Confederacy's existence human mobility also harbored a promise of salvation. For four years white Southerners had kept their nation alive by shifting their armies, their slaves, and their supplies from one place to another. When defeat finally became an inescapable reality in the spring of 1865, Confederates resorted to motion as the last available means to turn the tide and win the war. Watching their strategic assets disappearing one by one, Confederate patriots clung to space and movement as other nations have clung to imaginary secret weapons. As long as Southerners could move around their land, there was still hope.

The idea that mobility could save the Confederacy had been in the air
for a long while. In August 1863 Benedict Semmes predicted that the enemy would eventually overrun "every important portion of the Confederacy" but that this "would not be subjugation by any means": "To over run a
country and hold it are very different things. Our army would still keep in
the field—move from one strong portion of the land to another, give them
battle or retreat from time to time as Washington did." The war of movement would go on until the enemy would become "worn out by empty successes. Always catching the eel and the eel always skipping away when
caught." When Semmes was writing, the South still had a fighting chance at
victory, but he was correct in realizing that the advance of the Union army
across the land could not be stopped. The only way he saw to resist it was
to keep the armies in motion and constantly move the war between theaters until the invaders gave up. The geography of the South would win
the war.[68]

As the Confederacy's prospects darkened over the next twenty months,
this notion crystallized into a plan to relocate the theater of operations from
the eastern Confederacy to the west. By the beginning of 1865 many Confederates could no longer ignore the true nature of the military situation in
Virginia and the Carolinas. With Sherman's army advancing north from
Georgia and Grant's massive forces concentrating in front of Richmond, it
was becoming alarmingly clear that drastic measures would have to be taken
to prevent a complete capitulation of the army and the nation. After the fall
of Columbia in February, John B. Jones reported from the War Office, "Letters are beginning to come in from the South, advocating the abandonment
of Richmond, and the march of Lee's army into East Tennessee and Northern Georgia, and so on down to Montgomery, Ala."[69]

Roughly at the same time, General John Bell Hood submitted to Jefferson Davis a document outlining a strategy for the upcoming spring offensive. Hood had good reason to show some creative thinking, as not much
else had remained of his reputation in the wake of the embarrassing failure
of the Tennessee campaign he had led a few weeks earlier. After the battle of
Nashville his army fell apart, and Hood himself resigned his command on
January 23. Yet even if the blundering general had ulterior motives for coming up with bold ideas, his plan for saving the Confederacy from surrendering to its powerful foe reflects the kind of possibilities white Southerners

imagined as they watched their country cave under the weight of Union invasion.

Hood began with the prediction that by the middle of April the shortage of food and the force of the enemy would compel the Army of Northern Virginia to abandon Richmond. "The question," he said, "is not what should be done when that pressure comes, for it will then be too late, but what would be done now with time just sufficient to arrange relief." The answer lay in what Hood saw as a hitherto unprecedented opportunity for the Confederacy to concentrate its armies and move. "Kentucky and Tennessee are denuded of hostile forces. Alabama, Mississippi, and Georgia, are freed from the presence of a Federal Army except along the exterior water lines. The Confederate forces are in three bodies under Taylor, Johnston, and Lee. There is no enemy between them." The point of concentration for the three armies would be central Tennessee. Marching in that direction, he argued, would relieve the Confederacy from its most pressing difficulties. "Each day's march would increase the distance from the enemy. Rations could be easily supplied and distributed. Supplies on hand in Richmond can be placed at convenient intervals for the troops to receive as they march on to Lynchburg." With a working railway connection and abundant provisions available in eastern Tennessee, the march of Lee's army from Richmond "can be safely and surely made." Hood professed unlimited confidence in the promise of the West: "Each army will move with no enemy in front or on flank, each on a line of rail-road as a conduit of supplies, and they will continue with improving roads, propitious weather, and abundant hope, to converge until the smoky mountains only separate them." The Federal army would then have no choice but to hasten after the Confederates, thus freeing large parts of the South from its presence. In the battles that would follow, the Confederacy would obtain the great victories it so desperately needed.[70]

With its mixture of sound military thinking and sheer fantasy, Hood's plan for the spring campaign was a professional articulation of a popular idea. Not only could armies be shifted around; the war itself was moveable. Stretching across one million square miles, the South was a vast land. There was no obligation to win its independence in Virginia or North Carolina. The struggle could be taken elsewhere and be conducted with the same men and the same spirit and for the same cause. If beating the Yankees in the Old Dominion proved to be impossible, it might still be done in Tennessee, Kentucky, the trans-Mississippi West, or in a generic "farther South." By the end of the Civil War, space had become more meaningful than place.[71]

The readiness to sacrifice particular locales for the sake of national existence originated in the sense that life under Yankee occupation would be insufferable and that anything was preferable to defeat. But the idea that place was immaterial and that the war could be fought anywhere emerged from a broader experience with the contraction and expansion of Southern spaces.[72] From the outset of the war, Confederate territory was in constant flux. Union armies came and went, occupying ground and then retreating from it in haste. Some portions of the South existed as no man's land, and others changed hands frequently. Some occupied cities remained staunchly Confederate even under prolonged Union rule, while others gradually drifted away from the Confederacy as a comfortable coexistence with the conquerors developed into de facto Unionism.[73] By 1865 the South had become a highly fragmented space. The penetration of Federal forces deep into the Confederate interior and the rapid deterioration of the communication infrastructure left states and counties disconnected from one another and out of the national administration's reach. The telegraph network had become virtually nonfunctional as wires were cut by Union armies and new ones could not be put up. Regular mail service gradually fizzled out, leaving only the express service of wagons traveling between cities as a reliable means of transmitting information. The transportation network was in similar shape, as rail lines had been destroyed, wagons confiscated, and horses killed. As the war approached its finale, the territorial cohesion of the South was a thing of the past. "I can tell you nothing of our friends and relations," wrote Eldred Simkins to his fiancée from South Carolina in March. "Each portion of the country is now effectually isolated from the other—and every body is in the dark."[74] Confederates who had watched parts of the South invaded and occupied at every stage of the war had become accustomed to the idea that cities and states were dispensable. While the country had been torn to pieces, there was always another point to fight for. As long as there were armies that could move in the field, the Confederacy was still alive.

Yet even if the supremacy of space over place was an established principle in the Confederate South, abandoning Richmond and moving the war west was a different matter. From the very beginning of the conflict, the capital had been the focal point of the contest between North and South. The rallying cry for the Army of the Potomac, the Union's largest fighting force, was "On to Richmond." The Confederacy allocated a great proportion of its limited means to defend the capital, often at the expense of other significant theaters. For white Southerners, Richmond had acquired unmatched practical and symbolic importance. Aside from serving as the administrative center of the nation, it was also a hub of transportation, communications, manufacturing, and medical care, as well as a haven for thousands of refugees who had fled from other places. But even more significant, in its four short years as a capital it had become the foremost symbol of Southern pride and independence. The process that started in 1861 with the mobilization of the Southern army had come to a head. By war's end, Richmond was firmly established as the nucleus of the Confederacy, the sine qua non of national survival.

This sentiment was equally common both inside and outside the capital. As Federal armies swept across the land and conquered the Confederacy's other strongholds, Richmond remained the sole bastion of massive resistance. "It is now . . . a common sentiment with intelligent and firm-minded men," wrote a Virginian to his wife from the city in January 1865, "that the fate of the Confederacy depends upon the fate of Richmond." Travelers from the cotton states who arrived in the capital reported, "The feeling in Georgia is not despondency—it is absolute *despair*—and . . . in Mississippi it is worse. All admit that there is no 'back bone' out of Virginia." Even in the war's last and worst days the city's white population did not succumb to hopelessness. Whether they were natives or newcomers, the men and women who tied their fate to the capital were avid rebels who were willing to endure great hardship for victory. They seemed to think, wrote Anne Hobson, "that Richmond meant the South." Indeed many Confederates viewed the evacuation of Richmond as a synonym for defeat. "If we have to give up Richmond, the war, in my humble opinion, is at an end," wrote a soldier from the trenches of Petersburg in March.[75]

The significance of Richmond to the Southern struggle for independence makes it all the more remarkable that the surrender of the city did not automatically signify an end to the war. Realizing that he could no longer hold the Petersburg-Richmond line of defense, on April 1 Robert E. Lee embarked on a march west in an attempt to unite with Joseph E. Johnston's army. Such a move had been on Lee's mind for a while. He had hoped to accomplish this feat without relinquishing the capital altogether, by drawing

Grant after him and forcing a confrontation in southern Virginia. Yet Lee pursued the same course even after Richmond had fallen. The surrender of the capital did not entail the capitulation of his army. With his back against the wall, Lee essentially tried to do what Hood had advised him a few months earlier: go west, join forces with Johnston, and continue the war elsewhere. The week-long retreat proved that the Army of Northern Virginia was incapable of either marching or fighting, yet the notion that Richmond was expendable and that the war could be prolonged by using space was powerful enough to fuel an attempt to continue the struggle after the loss of the city.

Joining the movement west was the Confederate government. Lee sent an order to evacuate the capital shortly before starting on the march, leaving politicians and clerks little time to digest the news and prepare for departure. Jefferson Davis received Lee's dispatch while attending Sunday services in St. Paul's Episcopal Church. Within hours he and his cabinet were in the Danville depot, the only functional railway terminal in the besieged city. They were among hundreds of men, women, and children who were desperately trying to get on board the last trains going south. "Both trains were packed," remembered a Confederate officer, "not only inside, but on top, on the platforms, on the engine—*everywhere*, in fact, where standing room could be found. . . . I placed sentinels at the doors of the depots finally, and would not let another soul enter." The government's cars were stacked with papers and the remnants of the Confederate treasury, roughly half a million dollars in gold and foreign currency. "This poor train is so over loaded it can hardly move, but moving we are," wrote Charles Chewning, a commissary officer.[76]

The train's destination was Danville, a tobacco town on the Virginia–North Carolina border, 140 miles southwest of the capital. It took the rickety, overburdened train sixteen hours to make the trip. A soldier observing the journey from the roadside saw "a government on wheels. It was the marvelous and incongruous debris of the wreck of the Confederate capital." Upon arrival, the government was greeted by cheering citizens and local dignitaries, but even an enthusiastic welcome could hardly make up for the dire circumstances. "We have arrived in this miserable little town to find there is no fuel or food," wrote Chewning. "Our fate awaits us here whatever it will be. There is much talk of making a stand then firing the train when it is hopeless. I await my time in quiet desperation."[77]

Retreat of the Confederate Government

OHIO

Ashland

KENTUCKY

WEST VIRGINIA

Charleston

Staunton

Lynchburg

Christiansburg

Roanoke

Clinch

Bristol
Kingsport

Fancy Gap

TENNESSEE

Winston-Salem
High Point

Statesville

Asheville

Spartanburg
Greenville

Cross Keys

Martin's Depot

Cokesbury

Abbeville

Athens

Washington

Powelton

GEORGIA

Macon

Columbus

Hawkinsville

Abbeville

Albany

Irwinville

Sandersville

Dublin

Vidalia

Rome

Atlanta

Sanders
Yorkville

Fort Mill

Unionville

Columbia

Augusta

SOUTH CAROLINA

Charleston

Beaufort

Savannah

Darien
Brunswick

Jacksonville

FLORIDA

St. Augustine

Gulf of
Mexico

Harpers Ferry

Winchester

Baltimore

Annapolis

Washington

Dover

MARYLAND

Fredericksburg

Charlottesville

VIRGINIA

James

Richmond

Appomattox

Petersburg

Norfolk

Danville

Greensboro

Durham

Lexington

Raleigh

Salisbury

Concord

Charlotte

NORTH CAROLINA

Goldsboro

Fayetteville

Wilmington

Florence

Georgetown

Atlantic

Ocean

Roanoke

Pee Dee

Broad

Savannah

Ocmulgee

Oconee

Altamaha

Chattahoochee

Tennessee

Ohio

Potomac

Rappahannock

Dan

0   50   100   150 miles

treat of the Confederate Government

The commissary officer was wrong. The purpose of the departure from Richmond to Danville was not to surrender, but to continue the fight. However improbable Danville might have seemed as a capital city, Davis, his cabinet, and numbers of ordinary civilians were willing to give it a chance. It was an eleventh-hour attempt to rescue the government from submission. At the same time, going to Danville revealed the prevalent notion that the capital, and the nation itself, were moveable entities. Inspired by similar successes of Americans during the War for Independence and by their own recent experience with the power of motion to shape events during wartime, these unyielding Rebels placed the last vestiges of hope in moving their country's focal point to a new location. The Confederacy might have lost almost everything, but it still had land.

This spirit was evident in the April 4 proclamation that Jefferson Davis issued to the citizens of the Confederacy from Danville. Acknowledging the "great moral as well as material injury to our cause that must result from the occupation of Richmond by the enemy" and the importance of preserving a capital "which is usually regarded as the evidence to mankind of separate national existence," he pointed out, "The loss which we have suffered is not without compensation." Richmond was in fact a burden: "For many months the largest and finest army of the Confederacy ... has been greatly trammeled by the necessity of keeping constant watch over the approaches to the capital, and has thus been forced to forego more than one opportunity for promising enterprise." That had finally ended. "We have now entered upon a new phase of a struggle," he claimed.

> Relieved from the necessity of guarding cities and particular points, important but not vital to our defense, with an army free to move from point to point and strike in detail the detachments and garrisons of the enemy, operating on the interior of our own country, where supplies are more accessible, and where the foe will be far removed from his own base and cut off from all succor in case of reverse, nothing is now needed to render our triumph certain but the exhibition of our own unquenchable resolve.

Davis suggested that additional retreats were unavoidable, but even the abandonment of the Old Dominion did not signify defeat. "If by stress of numbers we should ever be compelled to a temporary withdrawal" from Virginia, "again and again will we return, until the baffled and exhausted enemy shall abandon in despair his endless and impossible task of making slaves of a people resolved to be free."[78]

Regardless of Davis's other intentions when publishing his proclamations, his plea for continued resistance is a powerful expression of the notion that space could give the Confederacy a new lease on life. With the fall of the capital, the army would be free to take advantage of the Southern land, without the limitation of being anchored to a particular place. Cities and states would be meaningless; the war could be fought and won by movement. Writing from a remote town on the Virginia border, Davis was trying to convince himself and his subjects that space was more important than place. For Davis, the war had indeed entered a new phase, one in which the president had been driven out of his capital and sent out on the road, but his country still existed and his army was still in the field. Undoubtedly his April 4 proclamation contained a fair measure of both political propaganda and self-delusion, but it also conveyed the potency of his faith in the possibilities that Southern expanses opened for him and his country.[79]

Few Southerners actually heard about the proclamation at the time, as all forms of communication in the Confederacy were in shambles by April 1865. Yet even if word had gotten out of Danville loud and clear, it is unlikely that great numbers would have responded with enthusiasm. After four years of hard war the white South had reached the point of exhaustion. Death and destruction had worn out both soldiers and civilians, and it was becoming increasingly evident that even the greatest sacrifices had failed to bring victory. Nevertheless coming to terms with defeat was a complicated process. Fervent Rebels were easily tempted by the illusion that the war might be won elsewhere if Virginia proved to be indefensible and that the North would never be able to triumph over the enormity of Southern spaces. In the beginning of April, after Union possession of the Old Dominion had become a fact, some Confederates shifted their hopes from western Virginia and eastern Tennessee to the great land lying beyond the Mississippi River. "The way things look now the trans Mississippi seems our ultimate destination," wrote Varina Davis, wife of the Confederate president, on April 7. The idea that within a week the Confederate army "would stack arms at Appomattox, surrender, and then be disbanded did not enter into my mind even then," wrote an officer in hindsight about the first week of April. "I still thought that it would retreat, and abandoning Richmond, fall back to some new position, where it would fight many other battles before the issue was decided."[80] The same spirit persisted in the capital even after Grant and Lee had met at Appomattox. "No intelligent person supposes, after Lee's surrender, that there will be found an army anywhere this side of the Mississippi of sufficient numbers to make a stand," wrote John B. Jones in Richmond on April 13. "No doubt, however, many of the dispersed Confederates will join the trans-Mississippi army under Gen. E. Kirby Smith, if indeed, he too does not yield to the prevalent surrendering epidemic." Francis Lubbock, an aide to Davis, remembered that by late April he was still certain that the government would end up going west "to join, if possible, Generals Taylor and Forrest in Alabama, and with those commanders, and such troops as they might be able to hold together, retreat across the Mississippi into Texas, and there marshal another army and continue the war."[81]

In fact on April 9, when Lee's decision to lay down his arms became known to his soldiers, hundreds left the army and started west, hoping to reach the trans-Mississippi army, which was thought to consist of 60,000 men, though in reality its numbers were roughly half that. "I shall start on my journey very soon to the other side of that river, and try to join the Confederate Army there, still in arms and try and strike a last blow for honor and liberty," recorded one soldier in his journal. "I would not surrender with Lee and I will not with Johnston." Thomas Rowland told his mother he expected "to remain in Virginia for a month longer at least. I may then go South, perhaps as far as Texas. I will follow the fortunes of the Confederacy as long as there is any hope of retrieving our fallen fortunes. Wait patiently—hope & pray."[82]

The West remained a promised land of Confederate independence even when defeat had become an indisputable fact. "We still have an army in the West, and as dark as everything is, we *must* hope," wrote Emma LeConte in South Carolina on April 23. "I can't give up yet!" exclaimed Lizzie Hardin in her diary on April 25. "I think the Trans-Mississipi will save us." On May 6 Jefferson Davis's niece acknowledged in her diary the surrender of Southern armies, but said, "I feel sure this is not the end of the war. Uncle Jeff, I know, will not submit so tamely, and if he can succeed in crossing the Mississippi River he will, I hope, take command of the army on the other side and yet achieve our independence." Weeks after Appomattox, refugee planters in

Texas were still hoping that Davis was on his way to save them and that his arrival would breathe new life into the cause. Southerners who refused to accept defeat constructed their fantasies of national rejuvenation around territory and the ability of men to move across it. One soldier on his way to the trans-Mississippi in early May wrote, "Who knows but what from the ashes of the Confederacy, a new phoenix may arise, clothed with brighter hues than its parent." Like so many other Americans in the nineteenth century, white Southerners in the final weeks of the Civil War held on to the notion that the West was a space of unlimited opportunity and bright hopes. In their imagination the army and the government might be beaten, but the land and its magnitude could not be.[83]

In Danville the Confederate government waited impatiently for news from Lee. Couriers came and went, but no definite word on the state of the army arrived until the morning of Monday, April 10, when paroled soldiers on their way home began to appear. Later that afternoon a messenger from Lee finally reached the president with an official dispatch announcing the surrender of the Army of Northern Virginia. Stunned and alarmed, Davis and his cabinet took to the road again, hoping against hope to reach a place of safety and regroup. At eleven o'clock that evening they joined other refugees on a ramshackle train heading south, barely escaping Union raiding parties who were burning the bridges behind them. Their next destination was the town of Greensboro, some fifty miles away in the North Carolina piedmont. Greensboro had been a center of anti-Confederate sentiment throughout the war, and its residents had little interest in serving as a provisional capital or even in hosting a group of men who no longer ruled the country and were likely to face charges of treason. No welcoming crowds appeared at the train station, and the only member of the government who was offered housing was Secretary of the Treasury Trenholm, who was very ill but was also assumed to be carrying some of the Confederate gold. Davis was able to procure a room through his nephew, while the rest of the cabinet was forced to take up residence in a leaky train car and subsist on what remained in the commissary stores. A runaway government in a land of runaways, they experienced a small portion of the harsh realities of refugee life that countless Southerners had faced during the previous four years of war.

After a few days in Greensboro it was obvious that the government had to keep moving. A meeting with Generals Johnston and Beauregard revealed that the officers had lost all hope and were determined to surrender their men, leaving Davis and his cabinet no army to protect them or to keep fighting.[84] Sherman was fifty miles away, and the railroad tracks leading out of town had been destroyed by Federal cavalry. Davis was still hoping to reach the trans-Mississippi and continue the struggle, while the rest of the government was merely hoping to escape capture and avoid standing trial. With railway travel no longer available, the Confederate government left Greensboro on April 15 in wagons and on horseback. Dragging their vehicles and animals along muddy roads, they slowly made their way to Charlotte, eighty miles to the southwest. There, on April 26, they received the news that Johnston had surrendered his army to Sherman. From that moment on, Davis and his cabinet shed the last vestiges of governmental authority. All that was left to do was run. Now even the wagons and ambulances disappeared, as each member of the cabinet rode his own horse and carried his own baggage. Secretary of War John C. Breckinridge organized a force of 3,000 cavalry that was supposed to see Davis and him safely out of Union-controlled territory. After leaving Charlotte, the government and its retinue began to dissolve, as politicians, soldiers, and clerks chose not to join the fleeing president and started for their homes or for the coast. "Disintegration has set in rapidly, everything falling to pieces," wrote John Taylor Wood, an aide of Davis from Charlotte. "Officers of all ranks & from every quarter are going home." The Confederate government, like the army and the labor force, fell apart in motion.[85]

Much like Confederate soldiers, whose pitiful journeys home were the geographical and visual inverse of their joyful, confident deployment at the beginning of the war, the movement of the Confederate government south was a mirror image of its triumphant journey in May 1861. Back then the leaders of secession who traveled from the South's first capital in Montgomery, Alabama, to its permanent seat in Richmond, enjoyed a hero's welcome in every train station along the way. "No matter where the cars stopped," described the *Richmond Enquirer* at the time, "even though it was only for wood or for water, throngs of men, women and children would gather around the cars, asking in loud shouts, '*Where is President Davis?*' '*Jeff Davis!*' '*the old hero!*' and he was forced to his appearance and frequently to address them. Then we could see handkerchiefs waving, and gay flags and bouquets."[86] Four years later, things could not have looked more different. The Confederate executive, wrote the head of the Bureau of War, was reduced to "a fugitive government which gave no orders, getting constantly farther from home, without means of any sort and many without transportation."[87] The government that had traveled to Richmond in fanfare was fleeing back south in fear. The pride and exaltation of the movement to Virginia were succeeded by the shame and desperation of seeking shelter in the Southern heartland, after having suffered a terrible defeat. For those who hoped to continue the war out west, these sights of dissolution were a slap in the face. "This day I will remember as the one on which our Gov't. went to pieces," wrote a soldier who witnessed its final dispersal. "The President went one way some of his cabinet remained in town, others with Gen. Bragg went home, the troops disbanded at least most of them, and the whole concern ended in a disgraceful panic and break up. From the sights I saw that day I gave up all hope of our Gov't or people doing anything."[88]

On May 2 Davis and the remnants of his government reached the town of Abbeville in western South Carolina, where the fleeing president held his last council of war. For the first time he heard from his men the unequivocal and unanimous opinion that the military struggle between North and South was over and that he had to find a way to leave the country. The next day he started toward Washington, Georgia, where his family was supposedly waiting for him. By that time Breckinridge could no longer control the cavalry guards, most of whom demanded to be paid in specie and allowed to go home. On May 4 Davis finally succumbed to reality and officially dissolved the nonexistent Confederate government. An officer who followed him to Washington recorded in his diary that day a distressing silence, interrupted only by the "impatient pawing and neigh" of his horse. "[A] death pall, a plague seems to rest on the town. All have gone that were attached to the Government and the straggling soldiers have followed their example."[89]

Jefferson Davis was now nothing more than a fugitive, seeking the same things that Southern fugitives, both black and white, had sought throughout the war: safety from their pursuers and the proximity of their families. On May 6 he finally caught up with his wife, Varina, and together they continued on to Florida. The small party now traveled swiftly on back roads and avoided contact with civilians along the way. In the wake of Lincoln's assassination, Andrew Johnson had placed a reward of $100,000 on Davis's head and Federal units in the area were in hot pursuit. On May 10, while camping outdoors in the piney woods near Irwinville, Georgia, Davis and his party were captured. Two Union cavalry regiments, searching for the presidential party, raided their camp at daybreak with no specific knowledge of who was staying there. In the confusion of the raid, Davis tried to escape from his tent and into the woods, but a Federal officer noticed him attempting to get away and called him to stop. With a carbine gun pointed at him, Davis had no choice but to surrender. Much has been made of the fabricated story that he was dressed as a woman when caught. Yet the true significance of the circumstances of his capture lies in the fact that he was apprehended not only in flight, but in the woods. Davis was forced to follow the ways of his former slaves and take refuge within the alternative geography they had used for generations to hide from the bloodhounds and armed patrollers who chased them without mercy. The Civil War did not end with Robert E. Lee's dignified surrender at Appomattox. It ended with Jefferson Davis, in the forest, staring in fear at a group of white men who were coming to get him. The war had reduced even the most elevated of masters, the Confederate president, to a desperate runaway.[90]

The Confederate States of America disintegrated in motion. From the fall of 1864 onward, the armies of the South dissipated on the move, as one body of men after another succumbed to exhaustion, hunger, and a feeling of impending doom. Confederate armies never made it to the pivotal battlefield where the war was supposed to culminate and end. They fell apart on the way, rendering Southern roads the quintessential site of Confederate defeat and turning flight into the most popular way for Confederate soldiers to lay down their arms. While men in uniform were straggling away from the army and toward their homes, the government that had led them was also on the run. Jefferson Davis and his cabinet never surrendered in an official ceremony but fled the capital as Union forces approached. Much like the Confederate army, the nation's political leadership dissolved on the move, with members of the government and their armed escort gradually dropping out of the column, until any pretense of national existence had become impossible to maintain.

While white men were fleeing before the Federal army or trying to get home, a second wave of human beings on the move began to emerge on the South's beaten paths. Black men and women got on the road as soon as news of freedom reached the farms and plantations where they were kept as slaves. Theirs was an immensely diverse and complicated movement. Some freed slaves traveled hundreds of miles in an attempt to return to the homes from which they had been forcibly removed or to locate family members from whom they had been brutally separated. Others moved to the nearest town in search of a new way of life, and many left their place of bondage but remained in the same county or rented a patch of land only a few miles from where they had previously lived. Still more stayed with their former masters but experimented with their new freedom by going on short excursions beyond the boundaries of the farm or plantation and familiarizing themselves with the geography that had formerly lain outside their reach. Regardless of the form it took, the physical act of movement was a realization of freedom. Both simple and tangible, it allowed black men and women to experience the freeing of their bodies from captivity and put into practice their new ability to link their volition to their limbs. This was hardly lost on white Southerners and their Northern allies, who responded immediately by launching a ruthless operation to stop freed people from exercising their liberty to move at will. The struggle over black movement, waged between former slaves and former masters, between army officers and bureau agents, between supporters of freedom and champions of a new slavery, would remain a feature of Southern life for decades to come. Yet its roots lay in the first months after the Confederacy's defeat, when each black person setting out was partaking in the demolition of racial slavery and the creation of a postemancipation world.

Hence even as fervent Rebels were hoping that space and the ability to move across it would save their country from Union conquest, at the end of the Civil War human mobility was instrumental in both precipitating and embodying the Confederacy's collapse. The motion of soldiers leaving the army, of slaves abandoning the fields, and of a government escaping the capital formed the physical dimension of the process of disintegration that engulfed the Southern nation in 1865. At the same time these movements created a series of striking images that represented the total destruction of the Confederate project and of the social order it strove to protect. Once again the two dimensions of human mobility fused to create a potent effect. Motion, as act and as symbol, lay at the heart of the Old South's remarkable death.

Epilogue
Memory and Movement

Nine years after the collapse of the Confederacy, Napier Bartlett, a Confederate veteran from New Orleans, published a memoir of his exploits during the Civil War. Putting his thoughts down on paper had taken him a while. In the immediate postwar period, he was eager to forget and start anew. But Bartlett, like numerous other men and women who lived through the sectional conflict, could not let go. The sights he had seen and the sounds he had heard remained etched in his memory as a permanent, living record of the horrors of war. Equally durable, however, was his recollection of the conflict as a series of movements:

> Whether we will or not, in our dreams or daily ideas we are constantly hearing the command to "March"; to pack up our slender baggage and go vagabondizing from one miserable town to another searching for food, shelter and rest for your tender ones if you are a woman; or, if a man, to take your place in line of battle, and receive the bullet that has already been moulded for your breast. The old ideas cannot be rubbed out—will come back; some unseen influence will march you over the well-tramped, fenceless, grassless and herbless fields—through the forests whose trees have been cut down or completely killed by the volleys of musketry.[1]

Bartlett's reminiscing reflects what has often been left hidden both in public memory and in the historical literature. Movement, in all its shapes and forms, was a fundamental dimension of the human condition in the Confederate South. It is hardly surprising that in 1874 this old soldier was still hearing voices telling him to march.

Spatial mobility was very much on the mind of another Southern writer contending with the drama of the Civil War. In 1938 William Faulkner published *The Unvanquished,* a novel set during the war period in northern Mississippi. *The Unvanquished* is considered one of Faulkner's minor works and has attracted only limited attention from literary critics.[2] Yet because it is his only novel dealing with the war itself rather than with its long-lasting impact, it is of significant interest for historians. Faulkner was no Civil War scholar, but growing up in Mississippi during the early twentieth century he had imbibed a great deal of Civil War history from local folks who told their stories both in person and in writing.[3] The imagery he uses and his sense of how war appeared, felt, sounded, and smelled carry their own meaning and merit a closer look. What this look reveals is a world teeming with motion.

The Unvanquished consists of seven episodes taking place during the Civil War and Reconstruction. The novel opens in 1862, introducing the twelve-year-old Bayard Sartoris; his slave and companion, Ringo; his father, John; his grandmother, Rosa; and various other family members and slaves who make up the Sartoris household. The story moves from comedy to tragedy, from the hopeful days of Confederate victories to the desolation and decline of the postwar era, from the confines of the plantation to the war-ravaged countryside surrounding it. Throughout the novel's twists and turns, the protagonists encounter the incessant mobility that shaped the Civil War South. Faulkner's fictional representation of these movements is as powerful as was their reality.

Embarking on a journey to Alabama, where they hope to recover some property that had been confiscated by the Union army, Bayard, Ringo, and Rosa enter a land overrun by armies on the march and slaves on the run. Riding through a devastated landscape of burned houses and empty fields, they come face to face with the flight of enslaved men and women and with their unflinching determination to reach the promised land of freedom. "They were coming up the road. It sounded like about fifty of them; we could hear the feet hurrying, and a kind of panting murmur. It was not singing exactly; it was not that loud. It was just a sound, a breathing, a kind of gasping, murmuring chant and the feet whispering fast in the deep dust. I could hear women, too, and then all of a sudden I began to smell them."[4] In hindsight an older Bayard fully understands the momentous nature of the black exodus and its significance to Ringo, his trusted slave:

The motion, the impulse to move which had already seethed to a head among his people, darker than themselves, reasonless, following and seeking a delusion, a dream, a bright shape which they could not know since there was nothing in their heritage, nothing in the memory even of the old men to tell the others, "This is what we will find"; he nor they could not have known what it was yet it was there—one of those impulses inexplicable yet invincible which appear among races of people at intervals and drive them to pick up and leave all security and familiarity of earth and home and start out, they don't know where, empty-handed, blind to everything but a hope and a doom.[5]

Further along, the travelers stop at the Hawkhurst plantation, where the family's cousins reside. Hawkhurst rests near a now torn-up railroad that had recently been the scene of a heroic locomotive chase. Cousin Drusilla tells the story of how Confederates stole a train engine from Atlanta and rode it to Chattanooga, Tennessee, pursued all the way by a Yankee locomotive. Bayard and Ringo are transfixed by Drusilla's tale, by the images of iron, velocity, and smoke, by the shrieking sounds of engines, by the "flash and glare of indomitable spirit starved by three years of the impeding flesh."[6]

Because this was it: an interval, a space, in which the toad-squatting guns, the panting men and the trembling horses paused, amphitheatric about the embattled land, beneath the fading fury of the smoke and the puny yelling, and permitted the sorry business which had dragged on for three years now to be congealed into an irrevocable instant and put to an irrevocable gambit, not by two regiments or two batteries or even two generals, but by two locomotives.[7]

This is the kind of war story Bayard had long been yearning for, a feat of audacity that conformed to his romantic ideas of war, a venture of sufficient élan to demonstrate that there was more to war than the depressing realities of the home front.

So we knew a war existed; we had to believe that, just as we had to believe that the name for the sort of life we had led for the last three years was hardship and suffering. Yet we had no proof of it. In fact, we had even less than no proof; we had had thrust into our faces the very shabby and unavoidable obverse of proof, who had seen Father (and the other men too) return home, afoot like tramps or on crow-bait horses, in faded and patched (and at times obviously stolen) clothing, preceded by no flags nor drums and followed not even by two men to keep step with one another . . . sneaking home to spend two or three or seven days.[8]

Bayard's conflicting visions of war are articulated through the visual language of motion. The modernity, dynamism, and speed of the locomotive chase stand in sharp contrast to the slow, haphazard, painfully unglamorous movement of the men creeping home to work on their crumbling farms and save their families from hunger. The fictional Bayard conceives of wartime motion in ways similar to those we have seen among real-life Southerners during the Civil War. He notices the state of men's bodies, uniforms, and animals. He closely follows the pace and formation of the movement, and he does not fail to note the fact that these once proud men had been reduced to a life of straggling and skulking. Bayard reads into the details of movement, and he understands what they mean.

Back home on the plantation, the Sartoris family cannot escape the new forms of wartime motion that evolve as the conflict wears on. Bands of roving deserters appear, wreaking havoc on the countryside and its people:

They called themselves Grumby's independents—about fifty or sixty of them that wore no uniform and came from nobody knew where as soon as the last Yankee regiment was out of the country, raiding smokehouses and stables, and houses where they were sure there were no men, tearing up beds and floors and walls, frightening white women and torturing Negroes to find where money or silver were hidden . . . and now women who had lived alone for three years surrounded by invading armies were afraid to stay in the houses at night, and the Negroes who had lost their white people lived hidden in caves back in the hills like animals.[9]

It is doubtful that many African Americans bereft of their owners were as helpless as Faulkner describes them, and it is impossible to know how many were actually hiding not from Grumby's men but from their own brutal masters. Yet Faulkner's depiction of a social order in a state of disintegration places the appropriate emphasis on flight from the plantations, desertion from the army, and the growing chaos originating from both.

Finally, Bayard Sartoris also has something to say about the return of Confederate veterans. Recounting his last meeting with a Union officer, taking place shortly before the invading army departs the area, he remarks, "This was to be the last time we would see any uniforms at all except as the walking symbols of defeated men's pride and indomitable unregret."[10] In both the fictive and the factual South, soldiers coming home in 1865 were the living embodiment of the Confederacy's downfall. The memory of their pitiful appearance during their journey back would persist in the minds of both black and white Southerners for years to come. And so the older Bayard, who narrates the story, remembers too.

What is remarkable about Faulkner's engagement with the world of wartime motion is the fact that the Sartoris family does not live in the midst of a battle zone, nor are the heroes of the novel deserters, runaways, refugees, or soldiers serving in a particularly peripatetic unit. None of the novel's events takes place in the heartland of Confederate movement, which was the focus of this book. Yet throughout the narrative men and women, young and old, enslaved and free, experience the conflict through the tides of motion swirling around them: the movement of whole armies, the arrivals and departures of raiding parties, the homecomings of Confederate men, the flight of bondspeople from the plantations, and the wanderings of deserters, skulkers, and stragglers. Multiple times over the course of the novel the lives of Bayard, Ringo, Rosa, and others are transformed by motion. In Faulkner's northern Mississippi the boundaries between stasis and movement are as difficult to demarcate as they were in central Virginia. His imagined Civil War is a venture of itinerancy, a period defined by departures and arrivals, advances and retreats, galloping horses and rumbling trains, the scurrying of women and the roving of men.

And so it was. As this book has attempted to show, marching, straggling, fleeing, and traversing formed the heart of the lived experience in the Confederate South. Movement was not merely an interlude between battles or a prelude to social and political change, but rather an essential component in each of the different realities that combined to form the matrix of the Civil War.

In the spring and summer of 1861 movement was pivotal to the formation of the Confederacy as an independent country. The volunteers who traveled from the far-flung corners of the South to the front lines in Virginia served as a powerful symbol of the South's transformation from a section into a nation and mobilized the citizenry for the struggle ahead. The journeys of thousands along roads and railways provided the settings for civic rituals in which both civilians and soldiers played out their new roles as members of the Confederate polity and as enemies of the United States. The balls, barbeques, and receptions Southerners staged for the wayfaring men stoked a nascent national sentiment and promoted devotion to a revolutionary and controversial cause. Simultaneously the movement north reversed the decades-long shifts in the demographic and political makeup of the region. Since the beginning of the century Southerners had gazed westward, to the new lands where cotton was king and where unlimited opportunity seemed to beckon. Going to the front lines the volunteers refocused the emotions and energies of the entire section on its historic birthplace. Their journeys spurred the political reconfiguration of Southern space and its concentration around the city of Richmond.

As the military conflict intensified in 1862, movement emerged as a formative power in the lives of men in the army and civilians on the home front. Fast, efficient mobility lay at the heart of the Confederate army's strategy against a larger, better-armed foe. As they struggled to thwart the Union's multiple invasions, generals marched their men back and forth across Virginia's terrain, using their bodies as living barriers to the Union's advance and as vehicles for moving the war northward. The constant, peripatetic motion of the armies turned Virginia into a theater of war and transformed its towns and villages into battlefields, hospitals, transportation hubs, and supply depots. Whether willingly or not, civilians living along the routes of war were swallowed up by armies on the move and their incessant demands for food, shelter, transport, and medical care. At the same time the effect of military movement extended from the material dimension of wartime life and percolated into the realm of the cultural and symbolic. Civilians rarely had a chance to witness combat, but they regularly got to observe military movement in all its shapes and forms. Standing by the roadsides, watching the soldiers filing by, they read every detail of their motion and analyzed its hidden meanings. Advances and retreats, marching and straggling, running and hobbling, all served as the living embodiments of victory and defeat, honor and shame, strength and weakness. Military movement evolved from the physical act of shifting men between battlefields into a visual language that represented abstractions and generated emotions. For bodies and minds in the eastern theater, movement was the heart of the wartime world.

While armies were marching back and forth across the land, other powerful currents of human mobility were gaining a momentum of their own. The arrival of the Union army below the Mason-Dixon Line instigated a massive wave of flight among enslaved Southerners, who took advantage of the sudden proximity of sympathetic whites to the farms and plantations where they were held. At the same time white flight from the Confederate army was also evolving into a mass phenomenon, as an increasing number of soldiers tired of the service or were called by their families to come back home. Also on the roads were white civilians fleeing the enemy's advance and seeking a place of safety behind Confederate lines. The result was the transformation of the South into a world of runaways, a space in which multitudes of men and women, black and white, rich and poor, were on the move. Their desires and motivations differed widely; the risks they took and prospects they faced were hardly the same. Yet all staged their different struggles for freedom and power in the realm of mobility, by using their bodies to escape oppression, real or imagined, by asserting their right to move at will, and by resisting the authorities that tried to restrict them. The new configuration of movement in the Confederate South formed a physical expression of the parallel yet inverted processes instigated by war: the inception of black freedom on the one hand and the constriction of white freedom on the other. These complex and variegated metamorphoses took shape in thousands upon thousands of conflicts over movement, staged between slaves and masters, soldiers and officers, deserters and provost marshals, civilians and passport clerks. They turned the freedom to come and go into the most widely contested issue among Southerners of all circumstances and hues.

Movement remained an equally powerful force in the processes that formed the essence of the Confederacy's collapse. The flight of the government from

Richmond and its dissolution on the roads of the South formed one stage in a process that began months before, with the dissipation of armies on retreat, and would continue for years, with the movement of African Americans from the farms and plantations where they were held as slaves to the new homes they would build as free people. With soldiers leaving the army, slaves escaping the fields, and the government abandoning the capital, there was nothing to keep the ancien régime from dying a slow but inevitable death. Even as fervent Confederates continued to cling to space and movement in a last-ditch effort to thwart a calamitous defeat, the very structures that held the Confederacy together fell apart on the road.

While the roles and meanings of wartime mobility were in constant flux, its most salient features were present and important from the very beginning of the conflict to its very end. During four years of ups and downs, the army's motion had a potent effect on the citizenry's mind-set and perceptions of the war. In 1861 the movement of volunteers to the front lines galvanized the population and turned the Confederacy from a mere idea into a living reality. As the war escalated and armies began to move across the land, the images of soldiers marching, retreating, and straggling created a visual language that civilians employed to make sense of the conflict upending their world. And when the war finally wound down and the veterans made their way home, their emaciated, broken-down frames incarnated the white South's humiliating downfall. Whenever soldiers went on the road, the citizenry was there to watch, learn, and draw its own far-reaching conclusions. In the Confederate South bodies in motion served as flesh-and-blood icons, epitomizing the best hopes and worst fears in a time of uncertainty and change.

Simultaneously, movement figured prominently in an entirely different arena of wartime upheaval: the destabilization of the Southern social structure. The right to govern one's own physical movement had always been a marker of freedom in the slave South. Denied to African Americans and white women, it was generously awarded to white men, who were entitled to control both their own bodies and those of their dependents and slaves. Yet the onset of war shook this order to its core. Armed service diminished white men's previously unassailable claims to self-ownership while granting women and the enslaved new agency, possibilities, and roles. This overturning of social convention produced wide-ranging and conflicting results. On the one hand, it encountered massive resistance. The stragglers who dropped out of the columns during the Maryland campaign and the deserters who left the service altogether toward the end of the war were reluctant to accept the idea that someone was authorized to prevent them from moving as they saw fit. On the other end of the social spectrum, runaway slaves used movement to break away from their brutal captivity, attaining with their own bodies the freedom they had never been allowed to enjoy. Once officially liberated from bondage, movement remained the former slaves' most immediate and palpable means to effectuate their new status as freed people. Multitudes went on the road, some only for short excursions, others for long and difficult journeys in search of new lives. Only four short years had elapsed since the first runaway slaves reached Fortress Monroe in May 1861. Yet during that time movement had emerged as a realization of freedom, the physical manifestation of innumerable desires, motivations, and rationales that pushed both black and white Southerners on the roads of a war-torn land.

Over the course of the war, movement of the human body figured both as cause and as symbol, and herein lies its greatest complexity and its most profound meaning as a historical force. Volunteers traveling to Virginia formed the army that would stave off Union invasion, but their appearance on the roads of the South also served as a powerful metaphor for a nation on the rise; the movement of soldiers on their way to battle was meaningful because it determined to a large extent the outcome of the contest but also because the sight of men on the march created in the minds of citizens different ideas about the army and the nation; slaves who left the plantations in April 1865 participated in the creation of a new system of labor, but their movement also signified their freedom to white people who were observing them in dismay. In these instances, as in many others, the material and symbolic dimensions of movement were indissolubly intertwined. Southerners on the move simultaneously functioned as vehicles for some of the conflict's most significant dynamics as well as a living embodiment of the strange new world created by war.

Finally, while the contours of space shaped the movement taking place within its boundaries, in the Civil War South movement had an equally powerful effect on the transformation of space. One dimension of this phenomenon was the creation of theaters of war, which occurred with the armies' advances and retreats. Whereas battles took place in confined locations and impacted limited stretches of land, the movement of armies reached far and wide, into lives and landscapes extending across a great expanse. The moving columns of men in uniform carried the sectional conflict with them wherever they went, delineating with their bodies the borders of combat zones, determining which granary would be emptied, which farm would be devastated, which railroads torn apart. Equally important, the movements of soldiers were instrumental in the making and unmaking of political space. The journeys of volunteers in 1861 to Virginia fashioned the slave states into a coherent entity and created a focal point for the new nation in the capital city of Richmond. Yet soon thereafter the process of territorial and political consolidation began to unravel as Federal armies moved into Southern territory, carving out enclaves of freedom within a slave country and converting Confederate locales into Union-occupied terrain. The fracturing of Southern space, which eventually culminated in Confederate defeat, occurred in motion, through numerous incursions that chipped away at the new nation until it finally foundered and ceased to exist.

As act or as symbol, as a means of liberation or as a vehicle of subjugation, en masse or on one's own, movement was omnipresent in the lived experience of individuals, communities, and the Confederate nation itself. And so it has continued to our own day. The Civil War is long over, but other vicious conflicts have taken its place. As bloodshed keeps ravaging lands and peoples around the world, the dreary motion of wartime presses forward, carrying tumult and misery along newer, faster routes of war.

NOTES

ACKNOWLEDGMENTS

INDEX

Notes

Abbreviations

BR	Robert Alonzo Brock Collection, Huntington Library, San Marino, California
BRB	Beinecke Rare Book and Manuscript Library, Yale University
CRC	Confederate Research Center, Hill College, Hillsboro, Texas
DL	Rare Books, Manuscripts, and Special Collection Library, Duke University, Durham, North Carolina
DOCS	Documenting the American South, University Library, University of North Carolina, Chapel Hill
GLC	Gilder Lehrman Collection, New York City
HL	Henry E. Huntington Library, San Marino, California
JWE	James William Eldridge Collection, Huntington Library, San Marino, California
LC	Library of Congress, Manuscript Division, Washington, D.C.
LVA	Library of Virginia, Richmond
MAYU	Manuscripts and Archives, Yale University Library
MOC	Eleanor S. Brockenbrough Library, Museum of the Confederacy, Richmond, Virginia
NA	National Archives and Records Administration, Washington, D.C.
NYHS	New-York Historical Society, New York City
OR	U.S. War Department, *The War of the Rebellion: A Compilation of the Official Records of the Union and Confederate Armies*, 128 vols.
PL	Manuscripts Division, Department of Rare Books and Special Collections, Firestone Library, Princeton University
RG	Record Group, National Archives and Records Administration, Washington, D.C.
SBJ	Stuart Bell Junior Archives, Handley Regional Library, Winchester, Virginia
SHC	Southern Historical Collection, Wilson Library, University of North Carolina, Chapel Hill

UPMF Union Provost Marshal Files, National Archives, Washington, D.C.
UVA   Special Collections, University of Virginia, Charlottesville
VHS   Virginia Historical Society, Richmond
VOTS   *Valley of the Shadow: Two Communities in the American Civil War,*
         Virginia Center for Digital History, University of Virginia

Prologue

1. Leo Tolstoy, *War and Peace*, trans. Anthony Briggs (New York: Penguin, 2006), 1263.

2. On mobilization in the summer of 1914, see Jeffrey Verhey, *The Spirit of 1914: Militarism, Myth and Mobilization in Germany* (Cambridge, U.K.: Cambridge University Press, 2000), 102–103; Adrian Gregory, "Railway Stations: Gateway and Termini," in *Capital Cities at War: Paris, London, Berlin 1914–1919*, ed. Jay Winter and Jean-Louis Robert (Cambridge, U.K.: Cambridge University Press, 2007), 2:28.

3. Mark Mazower, *Dark Continent: Europe's Twentieth Century* (New York: Vintage, 1998), 214; Michael Robert Marrus, *The Unwanted: European Refugees in the Twentieth Century* (New York: Oxford University Press, 1985), 209–239, quote on 299–300. See also Eugene Michel Kulischer, *Europe on the Move: War and Population Changes, 1917–47* (New York: Columbia University Press, 1948), ch. 9.

4. Jonathan E. Gumz, *The Resurrection and Collapse of Empire in Habsburg Serbia, 1914–1918* (Cambridge, U.K.: Cambridge University Press, 2009), 4–5; Hanna Diamond, *Fleeing Hitler: France 1940* (Oxford: Oxford University Press, 2007), 1–111.

5. For an example of how mobility can be studied as a central feature of the human experience, see the highly influential Michel de Certeau, *The Practice of Everyday Life* (Berkeley: University of California Press, 1984), 91–130.

6. Historians have dedicated a great deal of time and effort to surveying, analyzing, and explaining the different aspects of wartime violence, producing some exceptionally rich and stimulating studies of war and culture. Among notable works in this field, see Paul Fussell, *The Great War and Modern Memory* (New York: Oxford University Press, 1975); John Keegan, *The Face of Battle* (New York: Viking, 1976); John A. Lynn, *Battle: A History of Combat and Culture* (Boulder, Colo.: Westview Press, 2003); Stéphane Audoin-Rouzeau and Annette Becker, *14–18: Understanding the Great War* (New York: Hill and Wang, 2002); Isabel V. Hull, *Absolute Destruction: Military Culture and the Practices of War in Imperial Germany* (Ithaca, N.Y.: Cornell University Press, 2005); Modris Eksteins, *Rites of Spring: The Great War and the Birth of the Modern Age* (Boston: Houghton Mifflin, 1989); Joanna Bourke, *An Intimate History of Killing: Face-to-Face Killing in Twentieth-Century Warfare* (New York: Basic Books, 1999); J. M. Winter, *Sites of Memory, Sites of Mourning: The Great War in European Cultural History* (Cam-

bridge, U.K.: Cambridge University Press, 1995); David W. Blight, *Race and Reunion: The Civil War in American Memory* (Cambridge, Mass.: Belknap Press of Harvard University Press, 2001).

7. A notable exception can be found in the recent scholarship on Eastern Europe in the era of the First World War. Historians in this field are producing a growing body of work on the region as a land of movement and are urging others to focus on persons on the move and their impact on the major historical developments of the period. See Nick Baron and Peter Gatrell, "Population Displacement, State-Building, and Social Identity in the Lands of the Former Russian Empire, 1917–1923," *Kritika: Explorations in Russian and Euroasian History* 4, no. 1 (2003): 51–100; Peter Gatrell, *A Whole Empire Walking: Refugees in Russia during World War I* (Bloomington: Indiana University Press, 1999); Vejas G. Liulevicius, *War Land on the Eastern Front: Culture, National Identity and German Occupation in World War I* (Cambridge, U.K.: Cambridge University Press, 2000); Eric Lohr, *Nationalizing the Russian Empire: The Campaign against Enemy Aliens during World War I* (Cambridge, Mass.: Harvard University Press, 2003), ch. 6; Joshua A. Sanborn, "Unsettling the Empire: Violent Migrations and Social Disaster in Russia during World War I," *Journal of Modern History* 77, no. 2 (2005): 290–324.

8. Ira Berlin, *The Making of African America: The Four Great Migrations* (New York: Viking, 2010), 45.

9. Joshua Sanborn, who has studied the migratory experiences of soldiers, notes, "Military sociologists, who might have been expected to remind their colleagues both in sociology and in history of the importance of mobility for soldiers and their worldviews, have focused their attention elsewhere. Amid the thousands of articles written in the field of military sociology in recent years on the mechanisms of combat cohesion, the professional attitudes of officers, and the impact of military training on modern political and industrial habits, the number that have explored migration can be counted on one's fingers" ("Unsettling the Empire," 297).

10. The topic of death in the American Civil War has recently received meticulous examination in Drew Gilpin Faust, *This Republic of Suffering: Death and the American Civil War* (New York: Knopf, 2008) and Mark S. Schantz, *Awaiting the Heavenly Country: The Civil War and America's Culture of Death* (Ithaca, N.Y.: Cornell University Press, 2008). Faust argues that "for those Americans who lived in and through the Civil War, the texture of the experience, its warp and woof, was the presence of death" (xiii). For a new estimate of the number of men who died in the Civil War, see J. David Hacker, "A Census-Based Count of the Civil War Dead," *Civil War History* 57, no. 4 (2011): 306–347.

11. An exact assessment of the number of people who traveled on the roads of the South during the war is impossible, but rough estimates are available. The Confederate army mobilized approximately 850,000 men; about 200,000 took

part in the demobilization of the Southern army in 1865. Historians have calculated that about 500,000 enslaved men and women reached the Union army
during the conflict, though this estimate remains highly debatable and open to
reinterpretation. David Blight, for one, has recently suggested that the number of
slaves who reached Union lines by early 1865 was 600,000 to 700,000. Regardless,
it is difficult to quantify how many of them fled and how many came under Union
rule when the Federal army occupied their places of residence. It is equally difficult to estimate how many slaves left their homes in the immediate aftermath of
the Confederacy's surrender. For the lack of a better option, we must rely on an
accumulation of evidence suggesting that in areas of relatively dense settlement,
large numbers of freed people took advantage of slavery's collapse to explore a
geography they had previously been banned from accessing. The numbers of deserters and stragglers from the Confederate armies are as hard to calculate. The
official figure for desertion is 103,400, though all evidence suggests that the actual
number of men who left the army without permission at different times and different circumstances was several times higher. On the number of soldiers in the
Confederate army, see James M. McPherson, *Ordeal by Fire: The Civil War and
Reconstruction* (Boston: McGraw-Hill, 2001), 202; on slaves, see Joel Williamson,
After Slavery: The Negro in South Carolina during Reconstruction, 1861–1877
(Chapel Hill: University of North Carolina Press, 1965), 3; Eugene D. Genovese,
Roll, Jordan, Roll: The World the Slaves Made (New York: Pantheon Books, 1974),
90; W. E. B. Du Bois, *Black Reconstruction: An Essay toward a History of the Part
Which Black Folk Played in the Attempt to Reconstruct Democracy in America,
1860–1880* (New York: Russell & Russell, 1935), 66; David W. Blight, *A Slave No
More: Two Men Who Escaped to Freedom: Including Their Own Narratives of
Emancipation* (Orlando, Fla.: Harcourt, 2007), 160. On official estimates of desertion, see Mark A. Weitz, *More Damning than Slaughter: Desertion in the Confederate Army* (Lincoln: University of Nebraska Press, 2005), ix. The figure for refugees
is from George C. Rable, *Civil Wars: Women and the Crisis of Southern Nationalism* (Urbana: University of Illinois Press, 1989), 183.

12. Space is an extensively researched and theorized concept. One particularly
useful formulation is from the geographer Yi-Fu Tuan: "In experience, the meaning of space often merges with that of place. 'Space' is more abstract than 'place.'
What begins as undifferentiated space becomes place as we get to know it better
and endow it with value. Architects talk about the spatial qualities of place; they
can equally well speak of the locational (place) qualities of space. The ideas 'space'
and 'place' require each other for the definition. From the security and stability of
place we are aware of the openness, freedom, and threat of space, and vice versa.
Furthermore, if we think of space as that which allows movement, then place is
pause; each pause in movement makes it possible for location to be transformed
into place." Yi-Fu Tuan, *Space and Place: The Perspective of Experience* (Minneapolis: University of Minnesota Press, 1977), 6. Other important works include Da-

vid Harvey, "Between Time and Space: Reflections on the Geographical Imagination," *Annals of the Association of American Geographers* 80 (September 1990): 418–434; David Harvey, *Justice, Nature, and the Geography of Difference* (Cambridge, Mass.: Blackwell Press, 1996); Doreen Massey, *Space, Place, and Gender* (Minneapolis: University of Minnesota Press, 1994). Two influential historical works on changing perceptions of space are Wolfgang Schivelbusch, *The Railway Journey: The Industrialization of Time and Space in the 19th Century* (Berkeley: University of California Press, 1986); Stephen Kern, *The Culture of Time and Space* (Cambridge, Mass.: Harvard University Press, 1983).

1. Nation Building on the Road

1. Cornelia Peake McDonald, *A Woman's Civil War: A Diary with Reminiscences of the War from March 1862*, ed. Minrose Gwin (Madison: University of Wisconsin Press, 1992), 253–254.

2. Several terms are used interchangeably to refer to the South during the Civil War: nation, section, region, and country. They all describe the aggregation of slave states that seceded from the Union and formed the Confederacy: Virginia, North Carolina, South Carolina, Georgia, Alabama, Mississippi, Louisiana, Florida, Texas, Arkansas, and Tennessee.

3. Emory M. Thomas, *The Confederate Nation, 1861–1865* (New York: Harper & Row, 1979), 56. Nation building in the South was a haphazard process that ended in defeat and disaster, prompting generations of historians to ask whether white Southerners had sufficient faith in their cause to see the process through. This study does not attempt to take a stand on whether white Southerners developed a strong enough sense of Confederate nationalism or what role the lack thereof played in their eventual defeat. My focus here is on the process of constructing a new nation and the role of mobilization in this process. Major studies of Confederate nationalism that have informed this discussion are David M. Potter and Don E. Fehrenbacher, *The Impending Crisis, 1848–1861* (New York: Harper & Row, 1976), 17–18; Thomas, *Confederate Nation*, 20–60; Avery Craven, *The Growth of Southern Nationalism, 1848–1861* (Baton Rouge: Louisiana State University Press, 1953); John McCardell, *The Idea of a Southern Nation: Southern Nationalists and Southern Nationalism, 1830–1860* (New York: Norton, 1979); Richard E. Beringer, *Why the South Lost the Civil War* (Athens: University of Georgia Press, 1986), ch. 4; Drew Gilpin Faust, *The Creation of Confederate Nationalism: Ideology and Identity in the Civil War South* (Baton Rouge: Louisiana State University Press, 1988); Paul D. Escott, *After Secession: Jefferson Davis and the Failure of Confederate Nationalism* (Baton Rouge: Louisiana State University Press, 1978); Gary W. Gallagher, *The Confederate War* (Cambridge, Mass.: Harvard University Press, 1997), 3–111; William W. Freehling, *The Road to Disunion*, 2 vols. (New York: Oxford University Press, 1990); Manisha Sinha, *The Counterrevolution of*

Slavery: Politics and Ideology in Antebellum South Carolina (Chapel Hill: University of North Carolina Press, 2000), ch. 3; Anne S. Rubin, *A Shattered Nation: The Rise and Fall of the Confederacy, 1861–1868* (Chapel Hill: University of North Carolina Press, 2005), 1–42; Robert E. Bonner, *Southern Slaveholders and the Crisis of American Nationhood* (New York: Cambridge University Press, 2009); Stephanie McCurry, *Confederate Reckoning: Power and Politics in the Civil War South* (Cambridge, Mass.: Harvard University Press, 2010), ch. 2; Carl N. Degler, "Thesis, Antithesis, Synthesis: The South, the North, and the Nation," *Journal of Southern History* 53 (1987): 3–18; James M. McPherson, "Antebellum Southern Exceptionalism: A New Look at an Old Question," *Civil War History* 29 (1983): 220–244; Edward L. Ayers, "What Do We Talk about When We Talk about the South?" in *All Over the Map: Rethinking American Regions,* ed. Edward L. Ayers et al. (Baltimore: Johns Hopkins University Press, 1996), 62–82. Two classic formulations of the idea that nation building is a process are Clifford Geertz, "After the Revolution: The Fate of Nationalism in the New States," in *Interpretation of Cultures: Selected Essays* (New York: Basic Books, 1973) and Benedict R. O'G. Anderson, *Imagined Communities: Reflections on the Origin and Spread of Nationalism* (London: Verso, 1983).

4. Thomas, *Confederate Nation,* 73–74; James M. McPherson, *Battle Cry of Freedom: The Civil War Era* (Oxford: Oxford University Press, 1988), 317–318.

5. Joseph Waddell Diary, August 2, 1861, VOTS, http://valley.lib.virginia.edu/papers/AD1500; Thomas C. DeLeon, *Four Years in Rebel Capitals: An Inside View of Life in the Southern Confederacy, from Birth to Death* (Mobile, Ala.: Gossip Print Co., 1890), 77; Nicholas A. Davis, *Chaplain Davis and Hood's Texas Brigade: Being an Expanded Edition of the Reverend Nicholas A. Davis's The Campaign from Texas to Maryland, with The Battle of Fredericksburg (Richmond, 1863),* ed. Donald E. Everett (Baton Rouge: Louisiana State University Press, 1999), 42; William Clegg Diary, GLC; Davis, *Chaplain Davis and Hood's Texas Brigade,* 42.

6. George P. Rawick, *The American Slave: A Composite Autobiography,* 19 vols. (Westport, Conn.: Greenwood Press, 1972), suppl. ser. 2, vol. 9, pt. 8, Texas narr., 3570.

7. John W. Stevens, *Reminiscences of the Civil War* (Hillsboro, Tex.: Hillsboro Mirage Print, 1902), 12; Napier Bartlett, *A Soldier's Story of the War; Including the Marches and Battles of the Washington Artillery, and of Other Louisiana Troops* (New Orleans: Clark & Hofeline, 1874), 16–17; Amanda Virginia Edmonds, *Journals of Amanda Virginia Edmonds: Lass of the Mosby Confederacy, 1859–1867,* ed. Nancy Chappelear Baird (Delaplane, Va.: N. C. Baird, 1984), 48; Rufus J. Woolwine, "The Civil War Diary of Rufus J. Woolwine," ed. Louis A. Manarin, *Virginia Magazine of History and Biography* 71 (1963): 418.

8. W. D. Pritchard, "War Remembrances," 3, W. D. Pritchard Papers, CRC; Joseph B. Polley Diary, June 29, 1861, Joseph B. Polley Papers, CRC. On flag presen-

tation ceremonies as community events that were meant to foster support for the Confederacy, see Wayne K. Durrill, "Ritual, Community and War: Local Flag Presentation Ceremonies and Disunity in the Early Confederacy," *Journal of Social History* 39, no. 4 (2006): 1105–1122.

9. Joseph B. Polley Diary, June 29, 1861; "Our Holy Springs Correspondent," *Charleston (South Carolina) Mercury,* June 15, 1861.

10. On women's participation in antebellum public festivities, see Mary P. Ryan, *Women in Public: Between Banners and Ballots, 1825–1880* (Baltimore: Johns Hopkins University Press, 1990). On white Southern women's involvement in the politics of secession, see Drew Gilpin Faust, *Mothers of Invention: Women of the Slaveholding South in the American Civil War* (Chapel Hill: University of North Carolina Press, 1996), 10–17; Victoria E. Ott, *Confederate Daughters: Coming of Age during the Civil War* (Carbondale: Southern Illinois University Press, 2008), ch. 2; McCurry, *Confederate Reckoning,* 89–93.

11. John L. Wilson to Mr. Cross, May 17, 1861, Thomas Cross Papers, DL.

12. Samuel Rush Watkins, *"Co. Aytch"* (Chattanooga, Tenn.: Times Printing Company, 1900), 15; Thomas Gorree to Mother, June 23, 1861, Thomas Jewett Gorree Papers, CRC.

13. J. Roderick Heller, Carolynn Ayres Heller, and Milton Barrett, *The Confederacy Is on Her Way Up the Spout: Letters to South Carolina, 1861–1864* (Athens: University of Georgia Press, 1992), 25; Augustus D. Dickert, *History of Kershaw's Brigade, with Complete Roll of Companies, Biographical Sketches, Incidents, Anecdotes, etc.* (Newberry, S.C.: E. H. Aull Co., 1899), 41–42.

14. Mary Chesnut, *Mary Chesnut's Civil War,* ed. C. Vann Woodward (New Haven: Yale University Press, 1981), 79; Thomas W. Cutrer and T. Michael Parrish eds., *Brothers in Gray: The Civil War Letters of the Pierson Family* (Baton Rouge: Louisiana State University Press, 1997), 17.

15. Lafayette McLaws, *A Soldier's General: The Civil War Letters of Major General Lafayette McLaws,* ed. John C. Oeffinger (Chapel Hill: University of North Carolina Press, 2002), 86–87; Cutrer and Parrish, *Brothers in Gray,* 17.

16. Chesnut, *Mary Chesnut's Civil War,* 79; Myra Inman, *Myra Inman: A Diary of the Civil War in East Tennessee,* ed. William R. Snell (Macon, Ga.: Mercer University Press, 2000), 101, 107–108; Elizabeth Pendleton Hardin, *The Private War of Lizzie Hardin: A Kentucky Confederate Girl's Diary of the Civil War in Kentucky, Virginia, Tennessee, Alabama, and Georgia,* ed. G. Glenn Clift (Frankfort: Kentucky Historical Society, 1963), 18–19.

17. Dickert, *History of Kershaw's Brigade,* 42; Bartlett, *A Soldier's Story of the War,* 25; Watson D. Williams to Unknown, September 13, 1861, Watson Dugat Williams Papers, CRC.

18. George L. Mosse, *The Nationalization of the Masses: Political Symbolism and Mass Movements from the Napoleonic Wars to the Third Reich* (New York: H. Fertig, 1975), chs. 4–5; Mona Ozouf, *Festivals and the French Revolution,* trans.

Alan Sheridan (Cambridge, Mass.: Harvard University Press, 1988); Sean Wilentz and Shelby Cullom Davis Center for Historical Studies, *Rites of Power: Symbolism, Ritual, and Politics since the Middle Ages* (Philadelphia: University of Pennsylvania Press, 1985).

19. OR, ser. 1, vol. 51, pt. 2, 168. On the reception of Confederate soldiers in east Tennessee, see Thomas Gorree to Mother, June 23, 1861, Thomas Jewett Gorree Papers; William Cowan McClellan, *Welcome the Hour of Conflict: William Cowan McClellan and the 9th Alabama*, ed. John C. Carter (Tuscaloosa: University of Alabama Press, 2007), 22; G. Ward Hubbs, *Voices from Company D: Diaries by the Greensboro Guards, Fifth Alabama Infantry Regiment, Army of Northern Virginia* (Athens: University of Georgia Press, 2003), 6.

20. Pritchard, "War Remembrances," 2; Hubbs, *Voices from Company D*, 4; W. A. Nabours, "Active Service of a Texas Command," *Confederate Veteran* 24 (1916): 69.

21. Malachia Reeves, "Reminiscences," Malachia Reeves Papers, CRC.

22. Rawick, *American Slave*, suppl. ser 2, vol. 9, pt. 8, Texas narr., 3610–3611.

23. Samuel K. Carrigan to Brother William, April 31, 1861, folder 1860–1866, Carrigan Family Papers, DL.

24. OR, ser. 1, vol. 2, 857.

25. John B. Floyd, untitled order, August 13, 1861, box 1, Entry 119, RG 109, NA.

26. Heller et al., *The Confederacy Is on Her Way Up the Spout*, 18.

27. Joseph B. Polley Diary, date missing; Oscar J. Downs Diary, August 9, 1861, Oscar J. Downs Papers, CRC; William Henry King et al., *No Pardons to Ask, Nor Apologies to Make: The Journal of William Henry King, Gray's 28th Louisiana Infantry Regiment* (Knoxville: University of Tennessee Press, 2006), 5; Rawick, *American Slave*, suppl. ser. 2, vol. 9, pt. 8, Texas narratives, 3611; DeLeon, *Four Years in Rebel Capitals*, 79.

28. Hubbs, *Voices from Company D*, 5.

29. DeLeon, *Four Years in Rebel Capitals*, 72–73. For a modern account of this journey, see Terry L. Jones, *Lee's Tigers: The Louisiana Troops in the Army of Northern Virginia* (Baton Rouge: Louisiana State University Press, 1987), 14–17.

30. Louis-Hippolyte Gache, *A Frenchman, a Chaplain, a Rebel: The War Letters of Pere Louis-Hippolyte Gache, S.J.*, ed. Cornelius M. Buckley (Chicago: Loyola University Press, 1981), 43.

31. Stevens, *Reminiscences of the Civil War*, 14; J. T. Hunter, "When Texas Seceded," *Confederate Veteran* 24 (1917): 363.

32. William Watson, *Life in the Confederate Army, Being the Observations and Experiences of an Alien in the South during the American Civil War* (New York: Scribner & Welford, 1888), 126; "Departure of the Marshall Guards," *Texas Republican*, June 8, 1861; Hardin, *The Private War of Lizzie Hardin*, 17.

33. Faust, *Creation of Confederate Nationalism*, 1–22, quote on 14. See also Rubin, *Shattered Nation*, 3.

34. Patricia Kelly Hall and Steven Ruggles, "Restless in the Midst of Their Prosperity: New Evidence on the Internal Migration of Americans, 1850–2000," *Journal of American History* 91 (2004): 844.

35. Peter McClelland and Richard J. Zeckhauser, *Demographic Dimensions of the New Republic: American Interregional Migration, Vital Statistics and Manumissions 1800–1860* (Cambridge, U.K.: Cambridge University Press, 2004), 51; David Hackett Fischer and James C. Kelly, *Bound Away: Virginia and the Westward Movement* (Charlottesville: University of Virginia Press, 2000), 137; James David Miller, *South by Southwest: Planter Emigration and Identity in the Slave South* (Charlottesville: University of Virginia Press, 2002), 19. Studies of smaller sample groups give further evidence of this trend. Fifty-four percent of the residents of Albemarle County, Virginia, left during the 1830s. John D. Majewski, *A House Dividing: Economic Development in Pennsylvania and Virginia before the Civil War* (Cambridge, U.K.: Cambridge University Press, 2000), 20.

36. D. W. Meinig, *The Shaping of America: A Geographical Perspective on 500 Years of History* (New Haven: Yale University Press, 1986), 2:232–236. In 1860 the superintendent of the U.S. Census Bureau commented, "The almost universal law of internal migration is, that it moves west on the same parallel latitude. . . . Men seldom change their climate, because to do so they must change their habits." Quoted in Frank Lawrence Owsley, *Plain Folk of the Old South* (Baton Rouge: Louisiana State University Press, 1982), 55. Donald Schaefer complicates the picture by proving that migrants who went to Arkansas and Texas deviated considerably from the east-west axis. Those who chose to diverge were usually better educated and wealthier and could afford taking a greater risk. Donald F. Schaefer, "A Statistical Profile of Frontier and New Migration: 1850–1860," *Agricultural History* 59 (1985): 563–578.

37. Adam Rothman, *Slave Country: American Expansion and the Origins of the Deep South* (Cambridge, Mass.: Harvard University Press, 2005), 46.

38. Ira Berlin, *Generations of Captivity: A History of African American Slaves* (Cambridge, Mass.: Belknap Press, 2003), 130.

39. Rothman, *Slave Country*, 220–221; Randolph B. Campbell, *An Empire for Slavery: The Peculiar Institution in Texas, 1821–1865* (Baton Rouge: Louisiana State University Press, 1989), 191. Although cotton became the predominant crop across the Deep South, in some areas planters stuck to other traditionally profitable crops. In Louisiana sugar remained central despite the popularity of cotton. Louisiana's sugar producers increased their output tenfold between the 1820s and 1850s. Simultaneously, planters on the South Carolina coast continued to profitably grow rice, as they had done for generations.

40. Schaefer, "A Statistical Profile," 567; Charles C. Bolton, *Poor Whites of the Antebellum South: Tenants and Laborers in Central North Carolina and Northeast Mississippi* (Durham, N.C.: Duke University Press, 1994), 70 ; Bruce Collins, *White Society in the Antebellum South* (London: Longman, 1985), 86–88.

41. James Oakes, *The Ruling Race: A History of American Slaveholders* (New York: Knopf, 1982), 69–95. See also Miller, *South by Southwest*, ch. 1; Roger G. Kennedy, *Mr. Jefferson's Lost Cause: Land, Farmers, Slavery, and the Louisiana Purchase* (New York: Oxford University Press, 2003), 11–16, 21–23; Fischer and Kelly, *Bound Away*, 221–222; Catherine Clinton, *The Plantation Mistress: Woman's World in the Old South* (New York: Pantheon, 1982), 167; Rothman, *Slave Country*, 184–186. On the configuration of age, gender, and matrimony in planters' decision to migrate, see Jane Turner Censer, "Southwestern Migration among North Carolina Planter Families: The Disposition to Emigrate," *Journal of Southern History* 57 (1991): 407–426; Joan E. Cashin, *A Family Venture: Men and Women on the Southern Frontier* (New York: Oxford University Press, 1991), 32–34; Miller, *South by Southwest*, 68.

42. Daniel Walker Howe, *What Hath God Wrought: The Transformation of America, 1815–1848* (Oxford: Oxford University Press, 2007), 414–423.

43. Cashin, *Family Venture*, 32–51.

44. The institution of slavery facilitated western migration in other ways as well. Since slaveholders' property was mostly tied up in slaves, they could more easily relocate than nonslaveholding farmers whose fortunes were invested in land. Slaves were easily movable, giving their masters the flexibility to migrate without having to give up their most significant possession. Historians have also argued that since slaveholders' primary attachment was to their human property they had a weaker emotional connection to their land and could easily trade one tract for another. See James Oakes, *Slavery and Freedom: An Interpretation of the Old South* (New York: Knopf, 1990), 99–100; Miller, *South by Southwest*, 140. For a stimulating analysis of slaveholders' lack of attachment to a particular place, see James H. Justus, "The Lower South: Space and Place in Antebellum Writing," in *Southern Landscapes*, ed. Anthony J. Badger et al. (Tübingen, Germany: Stauffenburg, 1996). In his recent study of the Southern economic imagination, John Majewski discredits these explanations, arguing that land abandonment in the South was a rational response to specific environmental factors such as the soil's high level of acidity and erosion. John D. Majewski, *Modernizing a Slave Economy: The Economic Vision of the Confederate Nation* (Chapel Hill: University of North Carolina Press, 2009), 22–39.

45. Berlin, *Generations of Captivity*, ch. 5. Scholars of the slave South are putting increasing emphasis on the centrality of mobility to the lives of the enslaved, particularly from the perspective of the internal slave trade. Through the work of these historians, we have come to see the black experience in the South as taking place not merely on the farm and the plantation, but also on the road. See Walter Johnson, *Soul by Soul: Life inside the Antebellum Slave Market* (Cambridge, Mass.: Harvard University Press, 1999); Steven Deyle, *Carry Me Back: The Domestic Slave Trade in American Life* (Oxford: Oxford University Press, 2005); Edward E. Baptist, *Creating an Old South: Middle Florida's Plantation Frontier before the*

Civil War (Chapel Hill: University of North Carolina Press, 2002), ch. 3; Robert H. Gudmestad, *A Troublesome Commerce: The Transformation of the Interstate Slave Trade* (Baton Rouge: Louisiana University Press, 2003). Lacy K. Ford has suggested that the scholarship on the slave trade and its impact constitutes the most serious challenge to Eugene Genovese's theory of slaveholders' paternalism. Lacy K. Ford, "Reconsidering the Internal Slave Trade: Paternalism, Markets, and the Character of the Old South," in *The Chattel Principle: Internal Slave Trades in the Americas,* ed. Walter Johnson (New Haven: Yale University Press, 2004). For a comprehensive summary of the recent scholarship on slavery and its emphasis on the mobile nature of the institution in the nineteenth century, see Anthony E. Kaye, "The Second Slavery: Modernity in the Nineteenth-Century South and the Atlantic World," *Journal of Southern History* 75 (2009): 627–650. For Ira Berlin's most recent definition of African American history as a series of movements, see *The Making of African America: The Four Great Migrations* (New York: Viking, 2010).

46. Michael Tadman, *Speculators and Slaves: Masters, Traders, and Slaves in the Old South* (Madison: University of Wisconsin Press, 1989), 41–42.

47. Scholars have offered radically different estimates of the ratio between slaves sold to the Lower South and slaves who migrated there with their masters. In *Time on the Cross: The Economics of American Negro Slavery* (Boston: Little, Brown, 1974), 1:47, the economic historians Robert Fogel and Stanley Engerman argue that only 16 percent of the slaves who moved west were sold there. Most historians have come up with much higher figures. In *Slave Trading in the Old South* (Baltimore, Md.: J. H. Furst Company, 1931), 397–398, Frederic Bancroft calculated that fully 70 percent of the slaves who relocated were sold in the interregional slave trade. Tadman, in *Speculators and Slaves,* 31, similarly estimated that 60–70 percent of the slaves who moved to the Lower South got there through the trade. The economist Jonathan B. Pritchett set the number at 50 percent in "Quantitative Estimates of the United States Interregional Slave Trade, 1820–1860," *Journal of Economic History* 61 (2001): 467–475. The most recent and complete analysis of the controversy over the magnitude of the internal slave trade can be found in Deyle, *Carry Me Back,* 283–289. Deyle adopts the numbers suggested by Tadman and notes, as did Tadman, that had subregional sales also been accounted for, the percentage of slaves sold would have been even higher.

48. Charles L. Perdue et al., *Weevils in the Wheat: Interviews with Virginia Ex-Slaves* (Bloomington: Indiana University Press, 1980), 153, 323.

49. Deyle, *Carry Me Back,* 42–43. See also Berlin, *Generations of Captivity,* 213.

50. William Blair, *Virginia's Private War: Feeding Body and Soul in the Confederacy, 1861–1865* (New York: Oxford University Press, 1998), ch. 1. Blair disputes the claim that Virginia was gradually distancing itself from slavery, despite the drop in the slave population. While slaves were being sold south for record prices, the economic recovery of the 1850s fostered small farmers'

aspirations to become slave owners. In the western part of the state, the newly arrived railways brought prosperity and a 10 percent rise in slave ownership. See also Majewski, *Modernizing a Slave Economy*, ch. 1; William A. Link, *Roots of Secession: Slavery and Politics in Antebellum Virginia* (Chapel Hill: University of North Carolina Press, 2003), 29–39; Scott Nesbit, "Scales Intimate and Sprawling: Slavery, Emancipation, and the Changing Nature of Slavery in Virginia," *Southern Spaces*, July 19, 2011, http://southernspaces.org/2011/scales-intimate-and-sprawling-slavery-emancipation-and-geography-marriage-virginia. On the changing character of slavery on the Atlantic Seaboard, see Berlin, *Generations of Captivity*, 219–225.

51. McPherson, *Battle Cry of Freedom*, 138. Four slave states located in the Upper South (Maryland, Delaware, Kentucky, and Missouri) ended up staying in the Union.

52. In fact some of the radical secessionists who orchestrated the founding of the Confederacy supported leaving the Upper South states out of the new nation altogether to serve as a buffer zone between the Deep South and the Union. See Thomas, *Confederate Nation*, 43–44. On the secession process in Virginia, see Link, *Roots of Secession*, ch. 7.

53. Davis, *Chaplain Davis and Hood's Texas Brigade*, 37; Hardin, *The Private War of Lizzie Hardin*, 21; William Gilmore to Henry W. Whitcomb, November 13, 1861, folder 32, box 200, BR.

54. Mark Smither to mother, September 12, 1861, Mark Smither Papers, CRC; Nicholas Pomeroy, "Reminiscences," 4, Nicholas Pomeroy Papers, CRC.

55. Pomeroy, "Reminiscences." The political and cultural distance between Texas and the Upper South was evident to soldiers from Texas, who enjoyed their status as representatives of the South's roughest frontier. In the fall of 1861, when a Marylander was appointed colonel of one of the Texas regiments, Dugat Williams, an officer, wrote home, "All say he is not the man to lead them into a battle, that he is from a state too far North and too near Yankeedom for Texans to trust as their Commanding Officer . . . the men all know that Texans are claimed as the best Soldiers in the Army and they think the position of Colonel is too high for a Marylander to hold over Texas." Dugat Williams to Laura, October 7, 1861, Watson Dugat Williams Papers, CRC.

56. "By the Governor of Virginia," *Richmond Enquirer*, April 27, 1861.

57. Samuel A. Burney, *A Southern Soldier's Letters Home: The Civil War Letters of Samuel A. Burney, Cobb's Georgia Legion, Army of Northern Virginia* ed. Nat S. Turner (Macon, Ga.: Mercer University Press, 2002), 11; McClellan, *Welcome the Hour of Conflict*, 22–23; DeLeon, *Four Years in Rebel Capitals*, 38; Thomas Gorree to Mother, June 23, 1861, Thomas Gorree Papers; David W. Blight, *A Slave No More: Two Men Who Escaped to Freedom: Including Their Own Narratives of Emancipation* (Orlando, Fla.: Harcourt, 2007), 186.

58. DeLeon, *Four Years in Rebel Capitals*, 96.

59. Watson D. Williams to Laura, September 22, 1861, Watson Dugat Williams Papers; Cornelia McGimsey, *My Dearest Friend: The Civil War Correspondence of Cornelia McGimsey and Lewis Warlick*, ed. Mike and Carolyn Lawing (Durham, N.C.: Carolina Academic Press, 2000), 11; Edwin Anderson Penick to Mary, March 11, 1862, Edwin Anderson Penick Letters, VHS.

60. "Regular and Volunteers Appointments," *Richmond Enquirer,* June 11, 1861; "Crops in the South—Troops on Their Way to Virginia," *Richmond Enquirer,* June 16, 1861; "The Journey of President Davis to Richmond," *Richmond Enquirer,* May 31, 1861.

61. Cyrus F. Jenkins Civil War Diary, 12, Georgia Digital Library, http://dlg .galileo.usg.edu/jenkins/; "Troops," *Richmond Enquirer,* June 7, 1861; "City and State News," *Richmond Enquirer,* July 11, 1861.

62. Berry Benson, *Berry Benson's Civil War Book: Memoirs of a Confederate Scout and Sharpshooter*, ed. Susan Williams Benson (Athens: University of Georgia Press, 1962), 4; "Encampments," *Richmond Enquirer,* July 13, 1861; "City and State News," *Richmond Enquirer,* July 11, 1861.

63. DeLeon, *Four Years in Rebel Capitals,* 86. The extensive correspondence between the Confederate War Department and officials across the South in regard to the mobilization of the army is in OR, ser. 1, vol. 51, pt. 2, 16–220; OR, ser. 4, vol. 1, 140–240.

64. McDonald, *A Woman's Civil War,* 26; Fannie A. Beers, *Memories: A Record of Personal Experience and Adventure During Four Years of War* (Philadelphia: Lippincott, 1888), 26.

2. Armies on the March and the Languages of Motion

1. Fanny Braxton Diary, March 22, 1862, April 3, 1862, VHS.

2. The literature on military campaigns in Virginia is vast in scope and detail. Major works include James M. McPherson, *Battle Cry of Freedom: The Civil War Era* (New York: Oxford University Press, 1988); Herman Hattaway and Archer Jones, *How the North Won: A Military History of the Civil War* (Urbana: University of Illinois Press, 1983); Russell Frank Weigley, *A Great Civil War: A Military and Political History, 1861–1865* (Bloomington: Indiana University Press, 2000); B. Franklin Cooling, *Counter-Thrust: From the Peninsula to the Antietam* (Lincoln: University of Nebraska Press, 2007); Joseph T. Glatthaar, *General Lee's Army: From Victory to Collapse* (New York: Free Press, 2008); James I. Robertson, *Civil War Virginia: Battleground for a Nation* (Charlottesville: University of Virginia Press, 1991); James I. Robertson, *Stonewall Jackson: The Man, the Soldier, the Legend* (New York: Macmillan Library Reference USA, 1997); Robert G. Tanner, *Stonewall in the Valley: Thomas J. "Stonewall" Jackson's Shenandoah Valley Campaign, Spring 1862* (Garden City, N.Y.: Doubleday, 1976); Peter Cozzens, *Shenandoah 1862: Stonewall Jackson's Valley Campaign* (Chapel Hill: University of North

Carolina Press, 2008); James M. McPherson, *Crossroads of Freedom: Antietam* (Oxford: Oxford University Press, 2002); Stephen W. Sears, *To the Gates of Richmond: The Peninsula Campaign* (New York: Ticknor and Fields, 1992); Brian K. Burton, *Extraordinary Circumstances: The Seven Days Battles* (Bloomington: Indiana University Press, 2001); *The Richmond Campaign of 1862: The Peninsula and the Seven Days,* ed. Gary W. Gallagher (Chapel Hill: University of North Carolina Press, 2000).

3. OR, ser. 1, vol. 11, pt. 3, 397.

4. Ibid., 412.

5. Ibid., 506, 557.

6. Ibid., 634.

7. Ibid., 673–674.

8. OR, ser. 1, vol. 12, pt. 3, 913.

9. OR, ser. 1, vol. 11, pt. 3, 676.

10. OR, ser. 1, vol. 19, pt. 2, 711.

11. OR, ser. 1, vol. 12, pt. 3, 905–906. Lee is referring to Brigadier-General James Shields, who commanded one of the Union forces operating in the Shenandoah Valley.

12. OR, ser. 1, vol. 19, pt. 2, 622.

13. Ibid., 619.

14. Ibid., 614, 633, 718, 721.

15. Ibid., 709.

16. J. William Thomas Diary, May 22, 1861–July 10, 1862, SBJ; Randolph Fairfax to Jenny, June 7, 1862, Fairfax Family Papers, LVA; H. Watters Berryman to Ma, February 25, 1863, H. Watters Berryman Papers, CRC; Thomas Petty Diary, April 8, 1862, MOC. For additional examples of soldiers' diaries that contain daily enumeration of distance, see John P. Hite Diary, Charles J. Lillis Collection, SBJ; Gilmer W. Crutchfield Diary, UVA; John Simmons Shipp Diary, VHS; M. Shuler Diary, LC.

17. James Langhorne to Mother, January 12, 1862, section 1, Langhorne Family Papers, VHS; Randolph Fairfax to Mamma, January 9, 1862, Fairfax Family Papers; James Langhorne to Pa, January 16, 1862, section 1, Langhorne Family Papers; George K. Harlow to Family, February 8, 1862, George K. Harlow to Family, January 9, 1862, section 2, Harlow Family Papers, VHS.

18. Henry Kyd Douglas, *I Rode with Stonewall, Being Chiefly the War Experiences of the Youngest Member of Jackson's Staff from the John Brown Raid to the Hanging of Mrs. Surratt* (Chapel Hill: University of North Carolina Press, 1940), 56; Robert T. Barton, "Sketch of a Battle at Winchester," 7, VHS.

19. Benjamin Farinholt Diary, August 23, 1862, VHS.

20. William Ross Stilwell and Mollie Stilwell, *The Stilwell Letters: A Georgian in Longstreet's Corps, Army of Northern Virginia,* ed. Ronald H. Moseley (Macon, Ga.: Mercer University Press, 2002), 37.

21. John F. Sale to sister Jenny, note at the end of a letter by John H. Sale to Jenny, October 17, 1862, John F. Sale Papers, LVA.

22. Richard Ewell to Lizzie Ewell, May 13, 1862, Richard Stoddert Ewell papers, 1838–1896, LC. The enthusiastic fanatic he is referring to is General Jackson.

23. Jedediah Hotchkiss to Dear Brother, December 4, 1862, Jedediah Hotchkiss Papers, 1835–1908, LC.

24. Douglas, *I Rode with Stonewall*, 70; G. Ward Hubbs, *Voices from Company D: Diaries by the Greensboro Guards, Fifth Alabama Infantry Regiment, Army of Northern Virginia* (Athens: University of Georgia Press, 2003), 85; Samuel H. Walkup Diary, September 19, 1862, DL.

25. Randolph Fairfax to Sister Jenny, June 7, 1862, Fairfax Family Papers; James Dinwiddie to wife, June 29, 1862, James Dinwiddie Letters 1862, LVA.

26. Kenneth Radley, *Rebel Watchdog: The Confederate States Army Provost Guard* (Baton Rouge: Louisiana State University Press, 1989), 102.

27. William Blair, *Virginia's Private War: Feeding Body and Soul in the Confederacy, 1861–1865* (New York: Oxford University Press, 1998), 64–66; Mark A. Weitz, *More Damning than Slaughter: Desertion in the Confederate Army* (Lincoln: University of Nebraska Press, 2005), 96. The topic of white men's freedom of movement within the army is treated in detail in Chapter 3.

28. OR, ser. 1, vol. 19, pt. 2, 601.

29. Tanner, *Stonewall in the Valley*, 50.

30. OR, ser. 1, vol. 11, pt. 3, 503; Watkins Kearns Diary, vol. 2, June 1, 1862, VHS; Jedediah Hotchkiss, *Make Me a Map of the Valley: The Civil War Journal of Stonewall Jackson's Topographer*, ed. Archie P. McDonald (Dallas: Southern Methodist University Press, 1973), 78; Samuel H. Walkup Diary, November 21, 1862.

31. Albert B. Ross Diary February 1862–September 1862, March 9, 1862, NYHS; William Randolph Smith Diary, April 10, 1862, SBJ; Rufus Felder to Sister, July 14, 1862, Rufus Felder Letters, CRC.

32. Lucius C. Haney to Dear Friend, June 22, 1862, Jacob B. Click Papers, DL.

33. OR, ser. 1, vol. 12, 895, 891, 903.

34. John Sale to Uncle, November 30, 1862, John F. Sale Papers.

35. Benjamin Farinholt Diary, August 23, 1862; Henry M. Talley to Mother, May 11, 1862, Henry M. Talley Papers, VHS; William Randolph Smith Diary, May 5, 1862, SBJ.

36. Glatthaar, *General Lee's Army*, 167, 209–210, 211. On the purchase of shoes during the Maryland campaign, see OR, ser. 1, vol. 19, pt. 2, 605–614.

37. Henry M. Talley to Mother, November 30, 1862, Henry M. Talley Papers; William Cowan McClellan, *Welcome the Hour of Conflict: William Cowan McClellan and the 9th Alabama*, ed. John C. Carter (Tuscaloosa: University of Alabama Press, 2007), 198. See also William Randolph Smith Diary, May 15, 1862; Nicholas Pomeroy, "Reminiscences," 32, Nicholas Pomeroy Papers, CRC; Ujanirtus Allen, *Campaigning with "Old Stonewall": Confederate Captain Ujanirtus*

Allen's Letters to His Wife, ed. Randall Allen and Keith S. Bohannon (Baton Rouge: Louisiana State University Press, 1998), 207.

38. For some examples of straggling practices, see Watkin Kearns Diary, March 25, June 18, 1862, VHS; James Bradfield Diary, typescript, July 10, 1862, SBJ; Charles William McVicar Diaries, December 1862–May 1865, June 23, June 29, June 30, 1863, LVA; J. William Thomas Diary, April 19, April 20, April 21, 1862; Watson D. Williams to Laura, February 27, 1863, Watson Dugat Williams Papers, CRC; Thomas J. Selman Diary, March 19, 1862, September 22, 1862, Thomas J. Selman Papers, CRC.

39. Thomas J. Selman Diary, March 8, 1862, Thomas J. Selman Papers; McClellan, *Welcome the Hour of Conflict*, 156. Other soldiers casually reported in their diaries about their activities as stragglers, with short entries describing the people who gave them food or places where they had obtained food. See, for example, Watkins Kearns Diary, vol. 2, June 1, 2, 5, 6, 1862; William Randolph Smith Diary, April 10, 11, 1862; J. William Thomas Diary, April 20, 21, 22, 1862.

40. Radley, *Rebel Watchdog*, 103, 121–122; Tanner, *Stonewall in the Valley*, 50.

41. OR, ser 1, vol. 19, 143.

42. Randolph Fairfax to Mamma, October 3, 1862, Fairfax Family Papers; Francis Key Shaaff to mother, September 25, 1862, Letters from Captain F. K. Shaaff CSA to His Mother, PL; Allen, *Campaigning with "Old Stonewall,"* 167. See also William Ransom Johnson Pegram to Jennie, October 1862, section 1, Pegram-Johnson-McIntosh Family papers 1825–1941, VHS; Edwin Anderson Penick to dear family, September 29, 1862, Edwin Anderson Penick Letters, VHS; Richard Woolfolk Waldrop to father, September 22, 1862, folder 1, Richard Woolfolk Waldrop Papers, SHC.

43. Stonewall Jackson Letter Book, 1862, May 13, 1862, quoted in Tanner, *Stonewall in the Valley*, 179; Thomas Jonathan Jackson, Charge and specifications preferred by Maj. General T. J. Jackson against Maj. Gen. A. P. Hill, September 1862, Henry Brainerd McClellan Papers, VHS.

44. General Orders by Robert E. Lee, September 4, 1862, item 78, box 2, J. E. B. Stuart Papers, HL; OR, ser. 1, vol. 19, pt. 2, 592, 597.

45. OR, ser. 1, vol. 19, pt. 2, 1143.

46. "Augusta County: Burr to Macon (Georgia) Daily Telegraph," October 25, 1862, VOTS, http://valley.lib.virginia.edu/papers/A1101; Francis Key Shaaff to Mother, September 25, 1862, Letters from Captain F. K. Shaaff CSA to his mother; Edgeworth Bird and Sallie Bird, *The Granite Farm Letters: The Civil War Correspondence of Edgeworth and Sallie Bird*, ed. John Rozier (Athens: University of Georgia Press, 1988), 71; Sara Agnes Rice Pryor, *Reminiscences of Peace and War* (New York: Macmillan, 1905), 161; W. C. Corsan, *Two Months in the Confederate States: An Englishman's Travels through the South*, ed. Benjamin H. Trask (Baton Rouge: Louisiana State University Press, 1996), 44.

47. On Richmond as the Confederate capital, see Emory M. Thomas, *The Confederate State of Richmond: A Biography of the Capital* (Austin: University of Texas Press, 1971); Ernest B. Furgurson, *Ashes of Glory: Richmond at War* (New York: Knopf, 1996); Mike Wright, *City under Siege: Richmond in the Civil War* (Lanham, Md.: Madison Books, 1995); Nelson D. Lankford, *Richmond Burning: The Last Days of the Confederate Capital* (New York: Viking, 2002).

48. Thomas C. DeLeon, *Four Years in Rebel Capitals: An Inside View of Life in the Southern Confederacy, from Birth to Death* (Mobile, Ala.: Gossip Print Co., 1890), 147; Corsan, *Two Months in the Confederate States*, 78.

49. James Dinwiddie to Bettie, April 14, 1862, James Dinwiddie Letters 1862; Judith White Brockenbrough McGuire, *Diary of a Southern Refugee, During the War* (Richmond: J. W. Randolph & English, 1889), 282.

50. J. B. Jones, *A Rebel War Clerk's Diary at the Confederate States Capital* (Philadelphia: Lippincott, 1866), 1:132; DeLeon, *Four Years in Rebel Capitals*, 193; Joseph Waddell Diary, August 13, 1862; Julia Chase and Laura Lee, *Winchester Divided: The Civil War Diaries of Julia Chase and Laura Lee*, ed. Michael G. Mahon (Mechanicsburg, Pa.: Stackpole Books, 2002), 60; Joseph Waddell Diary, September 23, 1862.

51. John H. Sale to Jenny, October 17, 1862, John F. Sale Papers; Jones, *Rebel War Clerk's Diary* 1: 141. See also Joseph Waddell Diary, August 13, 1862; "Augusta County: Burr to Macon (Georgia) Daily Telegraph," October 25, 1862; Sally Lyons Taliaferro Diary 1859–1864, December 2–3, 1862, LVA.

52. Richard S. Ewell to Dear Lizzie, July 20, 1862, Richard Stoddert Ewell papers, 1838–1896, LC.

53. Sigismunda Stribling Kimball Diary, March 12, 19, 20, 21, 23, April 15, 16, June 18, 27, July 6, September 7, 23, 28, October 1, 2, 4, 9, 12, 14, 17, 30, 31, 1862, LVA; Fannie Braxton Diary, April 3, 8, July 18.

54. Fannie Braxton Diary, April 12, August 24, 1862; Hugh Terrance to sister, February 16, 1863, folder 1863–1864, box 2, Davidson Family Papers, DL.

55. Thomas J. Selman Diary, September 20, 1862; OR, ser. 1, vol. 25, pt. 2, 632; Harold B. Simpson, *Gaines' Mill to Appomattox: Waco and McLennan County in Hood's Texas Brigade* (Waco, Tex.: Texian Press, 1988), 118; H. Carrington Watkins to William Henry Lyons, March 2, 1863, folder 3, box 36, BR. Even soldiers were often shocked by the Texans' brazenness. A South Carolinian who served in Hood's Texas Brigade described them: "The Texas regiments is the most diapated foot soldiers in servis and it takes the tites dissipland to keep them rite and we are in a Texans brigade and when we are in rome we have to do like rome . . . tha are like a spriet horse. tha are hard to madge." J. Roderick Heller, Carolynn Ayres Heller, and Milton Barrett, *The Confederacy Is on Her Way Up the Spout: Letters to South Carolina, 1861–1864* (Athens: University of Georgia Press, 1992), 55.

56. Robert Young Conrad to T. J. Jackson, September 15, 1862, section 16, Holmes Conrad Papers, VHS; Joseph Waddell Diary, September 24, 1862.

57. Fanny Braxton Diary, August 29, 1862; Benjamin Farinholt Diary, September 3, 1862.

58. OR, ser. 1, vol. 19, pt. 2, 617–618.

59. Ibid., 624.

60. John Daniel Imboden to Robert Y. Conrad, November 20, 1863, section 16, Holmes Conrad Papers.

61. John Peyton Clark Diary, June 2, 1862, Louisa Crawford Collection, SBJ; Mrs. Hugh Lee Diary 1862–1865, March 11, 1862, p. 1, SBJ, hereafter cited as Mary Lee Diary; Joseph Waddell Diary, May 7, June 18, 1862. The Shenandoah Valley loses altitude from south to north, and its rivers flow north to the Potomac. Therefore the Valley's residents have long used a peculiar terminology to describe the region: "down the Valley" means going north, while "up the Valley" means heading south.

62. Lucy Rebecca Buck, *Shadows on My Heart: The Civil War Diary of Lucy Rebecca Buck of Virginia*, ed. Elizabeth Roberts Baer (Athens: University of Georgia Press, 1997), 158; Cornelia Peake McDonald, *A Woman's Civil War: A Diary with Reminiscences of the War from March 1862*, ed. Minrose Gwin (Madison: University of Wisconsin Press, 1992), 95.

63. Alexander S. Pendleton to Father, March 6, 1862, folder 21, box 2, William Nelson Pendleton Papers, SHC; OR, ser. 1, vol. 12, pt. 3, 847.

64. On Union occupation in the Valley, see Jonathan M. Berkey, "In the Very Midst of the War Track: The Valley's Civilians and the Shenandoah Campaign," in *The Shenandoah Valley Campaign of 1862*, ed. Gary W. Gallagher (Chapel Hill: University of North Carolina Press, 2003). The 1864 Shenandoah campaign brought a range of harsher policies and greater violence to the Valley, as the Union army struck at the Confederate infrastructure rather than merely at the army. See William G. Thomas, "Nothing Ought to Astonish Us: Confederate Civilians in the 1864 Shenandoah Valley Campaign," in *The Shenandoah Valley Campaign of 1864*, ed. Gary W. Gallagher (Chapel Hill: University of North Carolina Press, 2006). On the evolution of Union occupation policies in the South, see Stephen V. Ash, *When the Yankees Came: Conflict and Chaos in the Occupied South, 1861–1865* (Chapel Hill: University of North Carolina Press, 1995), chs. 1, 2; Mark Grimsley, *The Hard Hand of War: Union Military Policy toward Southern Civilians, 1861–1865* (New York: Cambridge University Press, 1995), chs. 2, 3. Grimsley notes that even the "hard war" orders issued by Union General John Pope in mid-July 1862, allowing soldiers to live off the land and abandoning the policy of allocating Federal soldiers to guard Confederate property against plunder by their own army, had little effect. Even if the Union army had abandoned its conciliatory policies toward the Southern citizenry by the summer of 1862, it continued to employ a policy of restraint. See 85–92.

65. Buck, *Shadows on My Heart*, 92; Matthella Page Harrison Diary, May 30, 1862, UVA.

66. Chase and Lee, *Winchester Divided*, 26; Sigismunda Stribling Kimball Diary, March 27, 1862; Joseph Waddell Diary, May 4, 1862.

67. On the nature of news reporting in the Confederacy, see Yael A. Sternhell, "Communicating War: The Culture of Information in Richmond During the American Civil War," *Past & Present* 202 (2009): 175–206. On the confusing reports following large battles, see J. Cutler Andrews, *The South Reports the Civil War* (Princeton: Princeton University Press, 1970); George C. Rable, *News from Fredericksburg* (Milwaukee: Marquette University Press, 2000), 52.

68. Joseph Waddell Diary, May 1, 29, 1862; Mary Lee Diary, June 29, 1862, pp. 158–159. On the role of rumors in shaping Confederates' perceptions of the war, see Jason Phillips, "The Grape Vine Telegraph: Rumors and Confederate Persistence," *Journal of Southern History* 72, no. 4 (2006): 753–788; George C. Rable, "Despair, Hope, and Delusion: The Collapse of Confederate Morale Reexamined," in *The Collapse of the Confederacy*, ed. Mark Grimsley and Brooks D. Simpson (Lincoln: University of Nebraska Press, 2001).

69. McDonald, *A Woman's Civil War*, 81; Mary Lee Diary, September 5, 1862, pp. 225–226.

70. John Peyton Clark Diary, July 14–16, 1862.

71. Fanny Braxton Diary, March 28, 1862; Hubbs, *Voices from Company D*, 104.

72. DeLeon, *Four Years in Rebel Capitals*, 191; Thomas Petty Diary, April 16, 1862.

73. Edward Warren to wife, May 25, 1862, Edward T. H. Warren Letters 1861–1864, LVA; Barton, "Sketch of a Battle at Winchester," 4; Watkins Kearns Diary, May 24, 1862, VHS.

74. Mary Lee Diary, May 27, 1862, p. 113; Randolph Fairfax to Bert, May 27, 1862, Fairfax Family Papers; Andrew W. Gillett to John C. Eakle, July 13, 1862, Andrew W. Gillett Letter, UVA.

75. William Randolph Smith Diary, March 23, 1862; Joseph B. Polley to Father, March 14, 1862, Joseph B. Polley Papers, CRC; Hubbs, *Voices from Company D*, 83.

76. Barton, "Sketch of a Battle at Winchester," 1; W. J. Pegram to Mother, September 7, 1862, section 1, Pegram-Johnson-McIntosh Family Papers, 1825–1941; Edwin Penick to wife, September 5, 1862, Edwin Anderson Penick Letters.

77. John Peyton Clark Diary, March 12, 1862; George M. Neese, *Three Years in the Confederate Horse Artillery* (New York: Neale, 1911), 121.

78. Sears, *To the Gates of Richmond*, 343, 345.

79. Jedediah Hotchkiss to dear brother, August 14, 1862, Jedediah Hotchkiss Papers, LC; James Dinwiddie to Wife, June 29, 1862, James Dinwiddie Letters 1862; George K. Harlow to Father and Family, July 3, 1862, Harlow Family Papers. On the reactions of soldiers in the immediate aftermath of a Civil War battle, see Joseph Allan Frank and George A. Reaves, *"Seeing the Elephant": Raw Recruits at the Battle of Shiloh* (New York: Greenwood Press, 1989), 119–127; Bell Irvin Wiley, *The Life of Johnny Reb, the Common Soldier of the Confederacy* (Indianapolis: Bobbs-Merrill, 1943), 74–75.

80. Isaac Hirsh Diary, September 4, 1862, LVA; J. W. Reid, *History of the Fourth Regiment of South Carolina Volunteers, from the Commencement of the War until Lee's Surrender* (Greenville, S.C.: Shannon & Co., Printers, 1892), 103.

81. Richard Waldrop to Father, January 19, 1862, folder 1, Richard Woolfolk Waldrop Papers.

82. Mary Lee Diary, May 25, 1862, p. 115; McDonald, *A Woman's Civil War,* 51; Joseph E. Shaner to Father, May 1862, Shaner Family Papers, VHS; Mathella Page Harrison Diary, May 25, 1862; Buck, *Shadows on My Heart,* 82.

83. Watkins Kearns Diary, May 24, 1862; Douglas, *I Rode with Stonewall,* 54–55, 56. Jedediah Hotchkiss quotes an official report by the Confederate Chief Commissary, Major W. J. Hawks, in which he stated that following the Union stampede he received from Winchester and Martinsburg 92,700 lbs. of cattle, 14,637 lbs. of bacon, 6,000 lbs. of hard bread, 2,400 lbs. of sugar, and 350 bushels of salt. Hotchkiss, *Make Me a Map of the Valley,* 49.

84. Andrew Gillett to John C. Eakle, July 13, 1862, Andrew W. Gillett Letter; John Thruston Thornton to wife, July 4, 1862, John Thruston Thornton Papers, UVA.

85. Benjamin Farinholt Diary, August 30, 1862; J. E. B. Stuart to Thomas Grimke Rhett, May 8, 1862, item 247, box 1, J. E. B. Stuart Papers.

86. Jedediah Hotchkiss to My afflicted wife, March 25, 1862, Hotchkiss Papers, VOTS, http://valley.lib.virginia.edu/papers/A2520; Major Frank Buckner Jones Diary, March 23, 1862, Louisa Crawford Collection, HL; Buck, *Shadows on My Heart,* 91.

87. James Richmond Boulware Diary, September 19, 1862, LVA; Jedediah Hotchkiss to dear wife, September 21, 1862, Hotchkiss Papers, VOTS.

88. William Roane Aylett to E. C. Hill, undated, section 24, Aylett Family Papers, VHS; William Roane Aylett to Charles Hill Ryland, section 24, Aylett Family Papers.

89. Richard Waldrop to Father, September 24, 1864, folder 2, Richard Woolfolk Waldrop Papers; Thomas Greene to Elsie, September 20, 1862, Greene Papers, VHS; Charles William McVicar Diary, October 9, 1864.

90. DeLeon, *Four Years in Rebel Capitals,* 194; Mary Lee Diary, November 6, 1862, p. 229.

91. Joseph Waddell Diary, June 6, 1862; September 23, 1862.

92. Ibid., May 4, 1862; May 5, 1862; May 28, 1862.

93. John Sale to Aunt, January 21, 1863, John F. Sale Papers.

3. Southerners on the Run

1. George P. Rawick, *The American Slave: A Composite Autobiography,* 19 vols. (Westport, Conn.: Greenwood, 1972), vol. 3, S.C. narr. pt. 3, 168.

2. Sally E. Hadden, *Slave Patrols: Law and Violence in Virginia and the Carolinas* (Cambridge, Mass.: Harvard University Press, 2001); Stephanie M. H. Camp, *Closer to Freedom: Enslaved Women and Everyday Resistance in the Plantation South* (Chapel Hill: University of North Carolina Press, 2004), 15–16; Anthony E. Kaye, *Joining Places: Slave Neighborhoods in the Old South* (Chapel Hill: University of North Carolina Press, 2007), 149–150; Phillip Troutman, "Grapevine in the Slave Market: African American Geographical Literacy and the 1841 Creole Revolt," in *The Chattel Principle: Internal Slave Trades in the Americas,* ed. Walter Johnson (New Haven, Conn.: Yale University Press, 2004), 220.

3. Charles L. Perdue Jr., Thomas E. Barden, and Robert K. Phillips, *Weevils in the Wheat: Interviews with Virginia Ex-Slaves* (Charlottesville: University of Virginia Press, 1976), 267, 235.

4. Ibid., 201.

5. Eugene D. Genovese, *Roll, Jordan, Roll: The World the Slaves Made* (New York: Pantheon Books, 1974), 648; Ervin L. Jordan, *Black Confederates and Afro-Yankees in Civil War Virginia* (Charlottesville: University of Virginia Press, 1995), 72; William A. Link, *Roots of Secession: Slavery and Politics in Antebellum Virginia* (Chapel Hill: University of North Carolina Press, 2003), 99. For some examples of woods as a temporary hiding place for slaves, see Perdue et al., *Weevils in the Wheat,* 42, 63, 67, 71, 75, 78, 117, 125, 153–154, 324.

6. On African Americans during the American Revolution, see Sylvia R. Frey, *Water from the Rock: Black Resistance in a Revolutionary Age* (Princeton, N.J.: Princeton University Press, 1991); Gary B. Nash, *The Forgotten Fifth: African Americans in the Age of Revolution* (Cambridge, Mass.: Harvard University Press, 2006); Simon Schama, *Rough Crossings: Britain, the Slaves, and the American Revolution* (New York: Ecco, 2006).

7. Estimates of the overall number of fugitive slaves in the South during the war are in W. E. B. Du Bois, *Black Reconstruction: An Essay toward a History of the Part Which Black Folk Played in the Attempt to Reconstruct Democracy in America, 1860–1880* (New York: Russell & Russell, 1935), 66; Joel Williamson, *After Slavery: The Negro in South Carolina during Reconstruction, 1861–1877* (Chapel Hill: University of North Carolina Press, 1965), 3; Genovese, *Roll, Jordan, Roll,* 97; David W. Blight, *A Slave No More: Two Men Who Escaped to Freedom: Including Their Own Narratives of Emancipation* (Orlando, Fla.: Harcourt, 2007), 160. Steven Hahn and others have argued for the marginality of movement in the black South during the Civil War, since the great majority of slaves had no access to the Union army and thus could not flee. Yet Hahn too notes the great impact of the runaways on the fabric of slavery and on its chances of survival even in the event that the South had won the war: "In parts of the South, owing to shifting troop movements, the boundaries were regularly traversed; more generally the rebellion-by-flight of some slaves and the opportunities that it created came to exert an increasingly powerful influence on the day-to-day lives and struggles of virtually all

others. Haphazardly and unevenly as the process developed, the relation of master and slave behind Confederate lines was being renegotiated in ways far more fundamental than those envisioned by southern white reformers in the churches and state assemblies." Steven Hahn, *A Nation under Our Feet: Black Political Struggles in the Rural South, from Slavery to the Great Migration* (Cambridge, Mass.: Belknap Press of Harvard University Press, 2003), 83.

8. Robert Francis Engs, *Freedom's First Generation: Black Hampton, Virginia, 1861–1890* (Philadelphia: University of Pennsylvania Press, 1979), 18–22; Louis S. Gerteis, *From Contraband to Freedman: Federal Policy toward Southern Blacks, 1861–1865* (Westport, Conn.: Greenwood Press, 1973), 11–18. While the Fortress Monroe incident signals the beginning of Union intervention in slavery, some escapes took place even earlier. On Gwyns Island in the Chesapeake Bay, slaves were reported leaving on May 12, 1861. Mary T. Hunley Diary, May 12, 1861, p. 1, SHC.

9. Ira Berlin, *The Destruction of Slavery*, ser. 1, vol. 1, of *Freedom: A Documentary History of Emancipation, 1861–1867* (Cambridge, U.K.: Cambridge University Press, 1985), 61.

10. For a recent analysis of emancipation's uneven and shifting patterns, see Edward L. Ayers and Scott Nesbit, "Seeing Emancipation: Scale and Freedom in the American South," *Journal of the Civil War Era* 1, no. 1 (2011): 1–23. For interactive maps of the wartime emancipation process, see the University of Richmond's Digital Scholarship Lab, "Hidden Patterns of the Civil War," http://dsl .richmond.edu/civilwar/vizemanc.html.

11. Williamson, *After Slavery*, 4–5; Julie Saville, *The Work of Reconstruction: From Slave to Wage Laborers in South Carolina, 1860–1870* (Cambridge, U.K.: Cambridge University Press, 1994), 37.

12. John W. Blassingame, *Slave Testimony: Two Centuries of Letters, Speeches, Interviews, and Autobiographies* (Baton Rouge: Louisiana State University Press, 1977), 359.

13. Berlin, *Destruction of Slavery*, doc. 6, p. 81; Bell Irvin Wiley, *Southern Negroes, 1861–1865* (New York: Rinehart, 1953), 9.

14. John Peyton Clark Diary, July 28, 1862, Louisa Crawford Collection, SBJ.

15. Edmund Ruffin, *The Diary of Edmund Ruffin*, ed. William Kauffman Scarborough, 3 vols. (Baton Rouge: Louisiana State University Press, 1972), 2:338; Wiley, *Southern Negroes*, 9.

16. William Patterson Smith to Christopher, August 12, 1862, box 10, William Patterson Smith Papers, DL; C. L. Lumpkin to William Patterson Smith, October 6, 1862, box 10, William Patterson Smith Papers.

17. Kate Stone, *Brokenburn: The Journal of Kate Stone, 1861–1868*, ed. John Q. Anderson (Baton Rouge: Louisiana State University Press, 1995), 171; Isaac Shoemaker Diary, March 3, 1864, DL.

18. Edmund L. Drago, "How Sherman's March through Georgia Affected the Slaves," *Georgia Historical Quarterly* 57 (1973): 361–375; Leslie A. Schwalm, *A*

Hard Fight for We: Women's Transition from Slavery to Freedom in South Carolina (Urbana: University of Illinois Press, 1997), 125.

19. Rawick, *American Slave,* vol. 15, N.C. narr. pt. 2, 428.

20. Ibid., vol. 7, Oklahoma and Miss. narr., pt. 1, 338.

21. Berlin, *Destruction of Slavery,* 675–676.

22. Rawick, *American Slave,* vol. 7, Oklahoma and Miss. narr., pt. 1, 181.

23. Ibid., 299.

24. Stone, *Brokenburn,* 126; Henry Lee Swint, Lucy Chase, and Sarah Chase, *Dear Ones at Home: Letters from Contraband Camps* (Nashville, Tenn.: Vanderbilt University Press, 1966), 42.

25. Leon F. Litwack, *Been in the Storm So Long: The Aftermath of Slavery* (New York: Knopf, 1979), 34–35; Clarence L. Mohr, *On the Threshold of Freedom: Masters and Slaves in Civil War Georgia* (Athens: University of Georgia Press, 1986), 100–113; John Cimprich, "Slave Behavior During the Federal Occupation of Tennessee 1862–1865," *Historian* 44, no. 3 (1982): 335–346; Schwalm, *Hard Fight for We,* 108–113.

26. Fanny Braxton Diary, August 13, 1862, p. 72, VHS; Ruth H. Hairston to Cousin Betty, January 25, 1863, folder 10, series 1.2, Hairston-Wilson Papers, SHC. On the destabilization of the slave-master relationship in the wake of refugeeing, see also David Blight's introduction in *A Slave No More: Two Men Who Escaped to Freedom: Including Their Own Narratives of Emancipation* (Orlando, Fla.: Harcourt, 2007), 157; Armstead L. Robinson, *Bitter Fruits of Bondage: The Demise of Slavery and the Collapse of the Confederacy, 1861–1865* (Charlottesville: University of Virginia Press, 2005), 138.

27. On slave impressment see Stephanie McCurry, *Confederate Reckoning: Power and Politics in the Civil War South* (Cambridge, Mass.: Harvard University Press, 2010), 263–288; Lynda J. Morgan, *Emancipation in Virginia's Tobacco Belt, 1850–1870* (Athens: University of Georgia Press, 1992), 79–104.

28. John Peyton Clark Diary, August 18, 1862. See also Shoemaker Diary, March 3, 7–8, 1864; Mrs. Hugh Lee Diary 1862–1865, hereafter cited as Mary Lee Diary, June 4, 1862, p. 129, SBJ.

29. Berlin, *Destruction of Slavery,* doc. 106, p. 303.

30. Cimprich, "Slave Behavior," 341.

31. Perdue et al., *Weevils in the Wheat,* 239–240.

32. Rawick, *American Slave,* vol. 7, Oklahoma and Miss. narr., pt. 1, 202.

33. Blassingame, *Slave Testimony,* 451–452, 456, 546; Berlin, *Destruction of Slavery,* doc. 121, p. 325. See also Genovese, *Roll, Jordan, Roll,* 150; Litwack, *Been in the Storm So Long,* 52; Benjamin Quarles, *The Negro in the Civil War* (Boston: Little, Brown, 1953), 62.

34. Perdue et al., *Weevils in the Wheat,* 64.

35. Hadden, *Slave Patrols,* 183–184; Schwalm, *Hard Fight for We,* 105; Litwack, *Been in the Storm So Long,* 56; Jordan, *Black Confederates and Afro-Yankees,* 72, 75–82.

36. Schwalm, *Hard Fight for We*, 106–107; Stephen V. Ash, *When the Yankees Came: Conflict and Chaos in the Occupied South, 1861–1865* (Chapel Hill: University of North Carolina Press, 1995), 162–165.

37. Berlin, *Destruction of Slavery*, doc. 319, p. 794; James L. Roark, *Masters without Slaves: Southern Planters in the Civil War and Reconstruction* (New York: Norton, 1977), 74; Litwack, *Been in the Storm So Long*, 57; Ash, *When the Yankees Came*, 163; Mohr, *On the Threshold of Freedom*, 214–220.

38. Blassingame, *Slave Testimony*, 451.

39. Rawick, *American Slave*, vol. 7, Oklahoma and Miss. narr., pt. 1, 16.

40. Berlin, *Destruction of Slavery*, doc. 19, p. 115; Saville, *The Work of Reconstruction*, 35–36.

41. Berlin, *Destruction of Slavery*, doc. 20, p. 116; Blassingame, *Slave Testimony*, 361.

42. Berlin, *Destruction of Slavery*, doc. 201, p. 525.

43. Blight, *Slave No More*, 203.

44. Mary Lee Diary, June 4, 1862, p. 129.

45. Charles A. Wilder to Edwin M. Stanton, September 1863, folder 32, box 70, series 5, Loomis-Wilder Family papers, MAYU; Berlin, *Destruction of Slavery*, doc. 214, p. 570.

46. Schwalm, *Hard Fight for We*, 122, 125; Drago, "How Sherman's March through Georgia Affected the Slaves," 361–375.

47. Unknown woman to sister, October 26, 1862, folder 1862, box 32, Campbell Family Papers, DL.

48. Thavolia Glymph, "This Species of Property: Female Slave Contrabands in the Civil War," in *A Woman's War: Southern Women, Civil War, and the Confederate Legacy*, ed. Edward D. C. Campbell et al. (Richmond: Museum of the Confederacy, University Press of Virginia, 1996), xv, 264. See also Wilma A. Dunaway, *The African American Family in Slavery and Emancipation* (Cambridge: Cambridge University Press, 2003), ch. 6; Michelle A. Krowl, "African American Women and the United States Military in Civil War Virginia," in *Afro-Virginian History and Culture*, ed. John Saillant (New York: Garland, 1999), 173–210.

49. Rawick, *American Slave*, vol. 7, Oklahoma and Miss. narr., pt. 1, 189.

50. Mohr, *On the Threshold of Freedom*, 113; Gregg L. Michel, "From Slavery to Freedom: Hickory Hill, 1850–80," in *The Edge of the South: Life in Nineteenth-Century Virginia*, ed. Edward L. Ayers and John C. Willis (Charlottesville: University of Virginia Press, 1991), x, 256.

51. William L. Furlow, Request for Leave of Absence, box 150, Edward S. Willis Papers, BR; Stone, *Brokenburn*, 35.

52. Mary Lee Diary, June 26, 1862, p. 155; July 27, 1862, p. 186.

53. Litwack, *Been in the Storm So Long*, 54.

54. Mark A. Weitz, *More Damning Than Slaughter: Desertion in the Confederate Army* (Lincoln: University of Nebraska Press, 2005), ix. In an earlier work

Weitz defines desertion as "a voluntary, illegal departure from service with the intent never to return." Mark A. Weitz, *A Higher Duty: Desertion among Georgia Troops during the Civil War* (Lincoln: University of Nebraska Press, 2000), 35. This chapter is concerned with men who answered the definition of deserters but also with all other men who moved in and out of the army without permission while intending to return. Historians of Confederate desertion have often focused on the motivations of men to leave the army and on the impact of desertion on the South's defeat in the war. Though these are important issues, they are not the main interest of our discussion here. This study centers on desertion as a form of wartime flight and on the conflicts within the Confederate army over the white man's freedom of movement.

55. OR, ser. 4, vol. 2, 995. For additional figures of desertion in different units in the army, see Weitz, *More Damning Than Slaughter*, 269; Ella Lonn, *Desertion during the Civil War* (New York: Century, 1928), 27–30; Brian Holden Reid and John White, "'A Mob of Stragglers and Cowards': Desertion from Union and Confederate Armies, 1861–1865," *Journal of Strategic Studies* 8, no. 1 (1985): 64–77; Rand Dotson, "The Grave and Scandalous Evil Infected to Your People: The Erosion of Confederate Loyalty in Floyd County, Virginia," *Virginia Magazine of History and Biography* 108, no. 4 (2000): 393–434.

56. For an interpretation of desertion as a form of class-based resistance to the war, see Robinson, *Bitter Fruits of Bondage*, 189–247. For an opposing view, arguing that desertion was not the result of class resentment and that the Confederate army succeeded in binding together soldiers of different social classes, see Aaron Sheehan-Dean, "Justice Has Something to Do with It: Class Relations and the Confederate Army," *Virginia Magazine of History and Biography* 113, no. 4 (2005): 340–377. For an analysis of desertion that stresses the centrality of age and the physical condition of soldiers, see Kevin Conley Ruffner, "Civil War Desertion from a Black Belt Regiment: An Examination of the 44th Virginia Infantry," in *The Edge of the South: Life in Nineteenth Century Virginia*, ed. Edward L. Ayers and Colin C. Willis (Charlottesville: University of Virginia Press, 1991), 79–108.

57. OR, ser. 1, vol. 19, pt. 2, 629.

58. Ibid., 622.

59. James Leavett Powell, "Reminiscences," VHS.

60. Petition by a group of prisoners from the 44th Virginia Infantry, January 17, 1862, box 150, Edward Willis Papers, BR. On early policies of the Confederate government regarding absenteeism, see William Blair, *Virginia's Private War: Feeding Body and Soul in the Confederacy, 1861–1865* (New York: Oxford University Press, 1998), 64–65; Peter S. Carmichael, "So Far from God and So Close to Stonewall Jackson: The Executions of Three Shenandoah Valley Soldiers," *Virginia Magazine of History and Biography* 111, no. 1 (2003): 33–66; Edward L. Ayers, *In the Presence of Mine Enemies: War in the Heart of America, 1859–1863* (New York: Norton, 2003), 246.

61. Watkin Kearns Diary, March 25, June 18, 1862, VHS; James Bradfield Diary, typescript, July 10, 1862, SBJ. The frequent absences of Bradfield from his command did not prevent him from being appointed provost marshal for his unit in June 1862. Bradfield Diary, June 7, 1862.

62. Robert H. Depriest to Mary, August 23, 1863, Robert H. Depriest Letters, LVA; OR, ser. 4, vol. 2, 769.

63. Michael Freeze to wife, April 13, 1863, Michael Freeze Letters, SBJ; Francis McCelanaham to Captain (?), November 13, 1863, box 72, JWE; Henry G. Reynolds to Captain Pearce, November 18, 1863, box 70, JWE.

64. Joshua J. McKinney to Goode, folder 2, box 71, JWE; R. C. Walker to the Engineer in charge, March 1864, folder 2, box 71, JWE; James H. Skinner to Edward Johnson, April 9, 1862, folder 12, box 152, Edward Willis Papers, BR.

65. Eliza H. Minnally to General, November 13, 1863, box 72, JWE; Mrs. Frankling Brickle to General Wise, April 23, 1864, folder 5, box 74, JWE.

66. Robert T. Wilson to niece, December 17, 1864, Robert Wilson Papers, CRC.

67. The clash between army discipline and soldiers' notions of their rights as free men was by no means a new phenomenon. See Ricardo A. Herrera, "Self Governance and the American Citizen as Soldier, 1775–1861," *Journal of Military History* 65, no. 1 (2001): 21–52; Wayne E. Lee, "Mind and Matter—Cultural Analysis in American Military History: A Look at the State of the Field," *Journal of American History* 93, no. 4 (2007): 1116–1142. For an example of problems of discipline and obedience in a non-U.S. context, see Gervase Phillips, "'To Cry 'Home! Home!': Mutiny, Morale, and Indiscipline in Tudor Armies," *Journal of Military History* 65, no. 2 (2001): 313–332.

68. Evidence for the implementation of the sixty-day regulation can be found in dozens of applications in folders 1–5, box 70, JWE.

69. Richard Woolfolk Waldrop to father, September 24, 1864, folder 2, Richard Woolfolk Waldrop Papers, SHC.

70. Kenneth Radley, *Rebel Watchdog: The Confederate States Army Provost Guard* (Baton Rouge: Louisiana State University Press, 1989), 154.

71. Samuel Walkup Diary, March 4, 1865, DL; Lee quoted in Lonn, *Desertion during the Civil War*, 28.

72. John F. Sale to Mother and Aunt E., October 19, 1862, John F. Sale Letters, LVA.

73. OR, ser. 4, vol. 2, 769. See also Aaron W. Marrs, "Desertion and Loyalty in the South Carolina Infantry," *Civil War History* 50, no. 1 (2004): 47–65; Peter S. Bearman, "Desertion as Localism: Army Unit Solidarity and Group Norms in the American Civil War," *Social Forces* 70, no. 2 (1991): 321–342; Carmichael, "So Far from God," 40–42.

74. Report of Conscript Office, Richmond, VA, February 4, 1864, folder 20, box 141, BR; Joseph Jerry to Dear Major, July 10, 1863, folder 5, box 1, Isaac Howell Carrington Papers, DL.

75. James A. Seddon, "Communication of the Secretary of War relative to the 'domestic passport system' now enforced upon citizens traveling in some parts of the Confederate States outside of the lines of the armies" (Richmond: Confederate States of America War Department, 1864), 8; Watson D. Williams to Laura, February 27, 1863, Watson Dugat Williams Papers, CRC.

76. "A Bill to regulate Furloughs and Discharges to Soldiers in Hospitals," April 4, 1863, House of Representatives, Richmond, Va., Confederate States of America Collection, General Collection, BRB.

77. Weitz, *More Damning Than Slaughter,* 103, 261. See also Richard Bardolph, "Confederate Dilemma: North Carolina Troops and the Deserter Problem, Part 1," *North Carolina Historical Review* 66 (1989): 61-86; Marrs, "Desertion and Loyalty in the South Carolina Infantry," 59.

78. OR, ser. 1, vol. 11, pt. 3, 506; Alexander Haskell Brown Record Book 1862, July 20, 1862, SHC; Page to General Wise, August 16, 1862, box 72, JWE; W. B. Ballard to Brigadier General Wise, August 23, 1862, folder 7, box 70, JWE.

79. James P. Pate, *When This Evil War Is Over: The Correspondence of the Francis Family, 1860-1865* (Tuscaloosa: University of Alabama Press, 2006), 85.

80. Charles Minnigerode to Thomas H. Owen, February 2, 1865, folder 48, box 141, BR; William C. Scott to General Edward Johnson, February 7, 1862, box 150, Edward Willis Papers, BR.

81. Edwin Anderson Penick to wife, July 23, 1862, Edwin Anderson Penick Letters, 1862, VHS; E. J. B. McMillan to Captain Pierce, folder 1, box 70, JWE; Geo. W. Abbot to Captain Pearce, November 19, 1863, Box 72, JWE; R. H. Spencer to Captain Pierce, January 22, 1864, folder 2, box 71, JWE.

82. Weitz, *More Damning Than Slaughter,* 87.

83. Richard Bardolph, "Inconstant Rebels: Desertion of North Carolina Troops in the Civil War," *North Carolina Historical Review* 41, no. 2 (1964): 163-189; Blair, *Virginia's Private War,* 65; Ruffner, "Civil War Desertion from a Black Belt Regiment," 96; Bardolph, "Confederate Dilemma, Part 1," 70.

84. William A. Tesh to Family, August 19, 1863, William A. Tesh Letters, DL; Alexander Haskell Brown Record Book, July 10, 1862.

85. N. B. Street to Captain Peirce, November 13, 1863, folder 2, box 71, JWE; George W. Hull to Edward Jackson, March 7, 1862, box 150, Edward Willis Papers, BR; William Abeggett to Captain Pierce, March 19, 1864, folder 2, box 71, JWE; N. E. Hayes to Captain Pierce, Sept. 8 (no year), folder 4, box 71, JWE.

86. On discipline in the Confederate army and the centrality of the common soldier's sense of independence, see David Herbert Donald, "Died of Democracy," in *Why the North Won the Civil War,* ed. David Herbert Donald (Baton Rouge: Louisiana State University Press, 1960), 81-92; David Herbert Donald, "The Confederate as a Fighting Man," *Journal of Southern History* 25 (1959): 178-193; Charles E. Brooks, "The Social and Cultural Dynamics of Soldiering in Hood's Texas Brigade," *Journal of Southern History* 67, no. 3 (2001): 535-572. On the

Southern man as master, see Stephanie McCurry, *Masters of Small Worlds: Yeo-man Households, Gender Relations, and the Political Culture of the Antebellum South Carolina Low Country* (New York: Oxford University Press, 1995).

87. OR, ser. 4, vol. 2, 14; J. M. Page to General Wise, August 21, 1862, box 72, JWE.

88. Lonn, *Desertion during the Civil War,* 78–83; Blair, *Virginia's Private War,* 67–68; Radley, *Rebel Watchdog,* 94–95, 153; Weitz, *More Damning Than Slaugh-ter,* 101, 239; Bardolph, "Confederate Dilemma, Part 1," 182; Bessie Martin, *Deser-tion of Alabama Troops from the Confederate Army* (New York: Columbia Univer-sity Press, 1932), 197–205.

89. Rawick, *American Slave,* vol. 6, Alabama narr., 270; William A. Tesh to Family, August 19, 1863, William A. Tesh Letters.

90. Ujanirtus Allen, *Campaigning with "Old Stonewall": Confederate Captain Ujanirtus Allen's Letters to His Wife,* ed. Randall Allen and Keith S. Bohannon (Baton Rouge: Louisiana State University Press, 1998), 124.

91. "Officers in Richmond," *Richmond Enquirer,* April 15, 1863; Special Orders no. 97, John A. Coke Papers, NYHS.

92. J. B. Jones, *A Rebel War Clerk's Diary at the Confederate States Capital* (Philadelphia: Lippincott, 1866), 2:317. See also Emma Mordecai Diary, October 8, 1864, Mordecai Family Papers, SHC.

93. As the problem of desertion worsened the Bureau of Conscription was as-signed the responsibility for hunting down deserters as part of its larger task of providing the army with manpower. General Order no. 1 from Samuel Cooper, the Adjutant General of the Confederate army, read, "Enrolling officers are required to be vigilant in the discharge of their duties within the district confided to them, not only in respect to the enrollment of conscripts, but also in the apprehension and arrest of stragglers and deserters from the army." OR, ser. 4, vol. 2, 295. While avoiding conscription and deserting the army were two very different offenses, they both resulted in men withholding their services from the army. See also Al-bert Burton Moore, *Conscription and Conflict in the Confederacy* (New York: Mac-millan, 1924).

94. John Robert Lowery to Mother, August 25, 1862, folder 2, John Robert Low-ery Papers, SHC.

95. Charles J. Hutson to Father, November 7, 1863, Charles J. Hutson Papers, GLC.

96. Edward Willis to Walter H. Taylor, February 28, 1864, folder 70, box 152, Edward Willis Papers, BR; OR, ser. 4, vol. 2, 675.

97. L. S. Wright and B. S. E. Wright to Family, November 27, 1863, Wright Family Papers, DL. See also *Fear in North Carolina: The Civil War Journals and Letters of the Henry Family,* ed. Karen L. Clinard and Richard Russell (Asheville, N.C.: Reminiscing Books, 2008), 114, 199, 204, 244; William Elliott Jr. to My Dear Mother, April 12, 1863, Elliott and Gonzales Family Papers, DOCS, http://doc-south.unc.edu/imls/gonzales/gonzales.html. For recent discussions of dissent and internal conflict in these areas of the Confederacy, see Daniel E. Sutherland, *A

Savage Conflict: The Decisive Role of Guerillas in the American Civil War (Chapel Hill: University of North Carolina Press, 2009); Victoria E. Bynum, *Shadow of the Civil War: Southern Dissent and Its Legacies* (Chapel Hill: University of North Carolina Press, 2010).

98. Mary P. Davis to Cousin Ben, August 9, 1863, Mary P. Davis Papers, DL.

99. G. Ward Hubbs, *Voices from Company D: Diaries by the Greensboro Guards, Fifth Alabama Infantry Regiment, Army of Northern Virginia* (Athens: University of Georgia Press, 2003), 194.

100. On the South's rival geographies, see Camp, *Closer to Freedom*, 135–137; John Michael Vlach, *Back of the Big House: The Architecture of Plantation Slavery* (Chapel Hill: University of North Carolina Press, 1993), 12–17.

101. Rawick, *American Slave*, vol. 9, N.C. narr. part 1, 220.

102. Mary A. Harper to John Lane Stuart, January 12, 1863, John Lane Stuart Papers 1852–1863, DL.

103. OR, ser. 4, vol. 2, 675.

104. Rawick, *American Slave*, vol. 7, Oklahoma and Miss. narr., pt. 2, 5.

105. OR, ser. 1, vol. 53, 64.

106. Rawick, *American Slave*, supp. ser. 2, vol. 9, pt. 8, Texas narr., 3484.

107. Charles William McVicar Diary, May 2, 1864, LVA; Joseph LeConte and Caroline Eaton LeConte, *'Ware Sherman: A Journal of Three Months' Personal Experience in the Last Days of the Confederacy* (Berkeley: University of California Press, 1937), 24–25; Perdue et al., *Weevils in the Wheat*, 150.

108. OR, ser. 1, vol. 39, pt. 1, 235; ? to Son, April 3, 1865, box 3, folder 1865–1866, MacRae Family Papers, 1862–1878, DL; Frank A. Montgomery, *Reminiscences of a Mississippian in Peace and War* (Cincinnati: Robert Clarke, 1901), 45.

109. Alexander Haskell Brown Record Book 1862, July 25, 1862; John Robert Bagby to Betty, April 16, 1863, section 4, Bagby Family Papers, VHS.

110. Female labor, both black and white, was of great importance to the Confederacy as well. Yet because women did not serve in combat and were not impressed into service building fortifications or working in factories, their labor was perceived as less critical than men's.

111. McCurry, *Confederate Reckoning*, ch. 7; Schwalm, *Hard Fight for We*, 82–83; Wiley, *Southern Negroes*, 114–121.

112. OR, ser. 4, vol. 2, 421.

113. As one historian of black mobility after the Civil War has argued, "Central to slavery had been the ability of masters to control black movement; central to freedom was the right of former bondsmen to pick up and move when they wished. Long after emancipation, southern whites continued to believe that they had every right to limit black freedom in virtually every way they chose, and the fifty years after the Civil War were marked by a continuing struggle over how much freedom of movement blacks should have." William Cohen, *At Freedom's Edge: Black Mobility and the Southern White Quest for Racial Control, 1861–1915*

(Baton Rouge: Louisiana State University Press, 1991), 3. On vagrancy laws and the suppression of black movement during Reconstruction, see Eric Foner, *Reconstruction: America's Unfinished Revolution, 1863–1877* (New York: Harper & Row, 1988), 200–201; Amy Dru Stanley, *From Bondage to Contract: Wage Labor, Marriage, and the Market in the Age of Slave Emancipation* (New York: Cambridge University Press, 1998), 124–126; Hadden, *Slave Patrols,* 191–192.

114. Drew Gilpin Faust, "Christian Soldiers: The Meaning of Revivalism in the Confederate Army," *Journal of Southern History* 53, no. 1 (1987): 63–90. While Faust argues that serving in the Confederate army was akin to work in a factory, it is my contention that another framework of comparison for soldiering is agricultural labor in its Southern form.

115. Jedediah Hotchkiss, *Make Me a Map of the Valley: The Civil War Journal of Stonewall Jackson's Topographer,* ed. Archie P. McDonald (Dallas: Southern Methodist University Press, 1973), 96; Randolph Fairfax to Mamma, January 31, 1862, Fairfax Family Papers, LVA. See also John Robert Lowery to Mother and Francis, September 14, 1862, folder 2, John Robert Lowery Papers; Edwin Anderson Penick to Family, April 19, 1862, Edwin Anderson Penick Letters; William T. Kinzer Diary, vol. 5, November 17, 1861, VHS; Thomas Greene to Elsie, July 17, 1864, section 17, Greene Family Papers, VHS; Hubbs, *Voices from Company D,* 78, 85, 211.

116. Ella Lonn explains the terms: "*Bucking* was the name applied to tying a soldier's hands together at the wrists and slipping them down over his knees where they were held in place by running a stick under the knees and over the arms.... *Gagging* was the suggestive name applied to fastening a bayonet in the mouth by trying it with a string which passed behind the neck." Lonn, *Desertion during the Civil War,* 57.

117. Ibid., 58; Bardolph, "Confederate Dilemma, Part 1," 198; Carmichael, "So Far from God," 45; Faust, "Christian Soldiers," 79.

118. OR, ser. 4, vol. 2, 49; Samuel Walkup Diary, June 23, 1863; Eldred J. Simkins to Eliza Simkins, September 2, 1864, file 180, Simkins Family Papers, HL. Charles E. Brooks has found staunch resistance of soldiers to punishment reminiscent of slavery. Brooks, "The Social and Cultural Dynamics of Soldiering," 558–559. For punishment in the U.S. Army before the Civil War, see Mark A. Vargas, "The Military Justice System and the Use of Illegal Punishments as Causes of Desertion in the U.S. Army, 1821–1835," *Journal of Military History* 55, no. 1 (1991): 1–19.

119. Michael R. Reed to Minerva Sparks Reed, March 20, 1863, Sparks Family Papers, 1856–1897, HL; John Harper to John Lane Stuart, March 22, 1863, John Lane Stuart Papers. See also Martin Diller Coiner to Katherine Margaret (Coiner) Palmer, August 21, 1862, section 3, Coiner Family Papers, VHS.

120. Quoted in Roark, *Masters without Slaves,* 74.

121. John Robert Lowery to Mother, April 11, April 27, 1863, John Robert Lowery Papers; Eldred J. Simkins to Eliza Josephine Trescot Simkins, March 21, 1865, file 204, Simkins Family Papers. His own brother also deserted the march.

122. Edward S. Willis to Gabriel James Raines, January 31, 1863; John B. Weems to Gabriel James Raines, February 19, 1863, folder 136, box 152, Edward Willis Papers, BR. Historians generally agree on the failure of the hunt for deserters. Bardolph defined it as a "sprawling, wide-ranging, and remarkably unsuccessful enterprise" ("Confederate Dilemma, Part 1," 181). See also Blair, *Virginia's Private War*, 88–89; Weitz, *More Damning Than Slaughter*, 236, 270.

123. Seddon, "Communication of the Secretary of War relative to the 'domestic passport system,'" 2.

124. Ibid., 2–3.

125. Ibid., 5.

126. Passport Books, vols. 101–109, 111–129, 141–150, ch. 9, RG 109, NA.

127. Seddon, "Communication of the Secretary of War relative to the 'domestic passport system,'" 7.

128. Arrival at Richmond Reported to the Provost Marshal General's Office, 1862–1863, vol. 186, ch. 9, RG 109, NA.

129. Seddon, "Communication of the Secretary of War relative to the 'domestic passport system,'" 4, 6.

130. Johnson Hagood, *Memoirs of the War of Secession*, ed. U. R. Brooks (Columbia, S.C.: State Co., 1910), 71; Alexander Haskell Brown, Record Book, May 21, 1862.

131. For some examples of the workings of this system, see Special Orders no. 28, H.Q. 1st Division, Culpeper, March 25, 1862, folder 5, box 1, Isaac Howell Carrington Papers; P. Jervey to General Wise, January 13, 1864, folder 6, box 74, JWE; M. K. Aiken to Captain Pearce, March 13, 1864, folder 6, box 74, JWE; M. H. Browning to General Wise, December 30, 1863, folder 6, box 74, JWE.

132. Arthur James Lyon Fremantle, *The Fremantle Diary: Being the Journal of Lieutenant Colonel James Arthur Lyon Fremantle, Coldstream Guards, on His Three Months in the Southern States* (Boston: Little, Brown, 1954), 107, 185–186; W. C. Corsan, *Two Months in the Confederate States: An Englishman's Travels through the South*, ed. Benjamin H. Trask (Baton Rouge: Louisiana State University Press, 1996), 41.

133. A. J. Deyrite, March 11, 1865, folder March 1865, box 6, RG 109, NA; Robert Hill & Sons to chief clerk at Passport Office, December 15, 1864, folder December 1864, box 2, RG 109, NA.

134. E. S. (? name unclear) to Major Carrington, November 14, 1864, folder November 1864, box 2, RG 109, NA.

135. Clement Young, December 15, 1864, folder December 1864, box 2, RG 109, NA.

136. Mrs. Susan Hogue, January 31, 1865, folder January 1865, box 3, RG 109, NA; Pass given to Mast. E. Richardson, January 18, 1865, folder January 1865, box 3, RG 109, NA.

137. Earnest Bolton, November 14, 1864, folder November 1864, box 1, RG 109, NA.

138. James C. Tyler, December 15, 1864, folder December 1864, box 2, RG 109, NA; John W. Hall, January 31, 1865, folder January 1865, box 3, RG 109, NA; R. E. Ripley to Maj. I. H. Carrington, January 24, 1865, folder January 1865, box 3, RG 109, NA; J. R. Anderson to Major Carrington, January 25, 1865, folder January 1865, box 3, RG 109, NA.

139. Judith White Brockenbrough McGuire, *Diary of a Southern Refugee, During the War* (Richmond, Va.: J. W. Randolph & English, 1889), 76.

140. Nelson D. Lankford, *Richmond Burning: The Last Days of the Confederate Capital* (New York: Viking, 2002), 19; Mark E. Neely, *Southern Rights: Political Prisoners and the Myth of Confederate Constitutionalism* (Charlottesville: University of Virginia Press, 1999), 3–4.

141. Seddon, "Communication of the Secretary of War relative to the 'domestic passport system,'" 7.

142. Robert S. Cosby, January 23, 1865, folder January 1865, box 3, RG 109, NA; (?) Moore, January 25, 1865, folder January 1865, box 3, RG 109, NA.

143. Robert Winter, March 27, 1865, folder March 1865 Negroes, box 3, RG 109, NA.

144. Marion Stewart, December 30, 1864, folder December 1864, box 3, RG 109, NA.

145. OR, ser 1, vol. 12, pt. 3, 864.

146. See, for example, Stonewall Jackson's use of information provided by civilian travelers in OR, ser. 1, vol. 12, pt. 3, 881, 882.

147. Harriett H. Griffith Diary, March 9, 12, 22, 1862, box 1, Harriett Hollingsworth Griffith Collection, SBJ; Julia Chase and Laura Lee, *Winchester Divided: The Civil War Diaries of Julia Chase and Laura Lee*, ed. Michael G. Mahon (Mechanicsburg, PA: Stackpole Books, 2002), 21, 29, 30, 130, 132.

148. Mary Lee Diary, July 27, 1862, p. 186; Lucy Rebecca Buck, *Shadows on My Heart: The Civil War Diary of Lucy Rebecca Buck of Virginia*, ed. Elizabeth R. Baer (Athens: University of Georgia Press, 1997), 61.

149. Gettie (Margaretta) Miller Diary, Godfrey Miller Collection, SBJ, March 24, 1862, M345, Roll 291, UPMF.

150. Mary Lee Diary, August 27, 1862, pp. 215–216; Chase and Lee, *Winchester Divided*, 77; M345, Roll 233, UPMF.

151. M416, Roll 4, UPMF.

152. Ibid.; Chase et al., *Winchester Divided*, 50.

153. Buck, *Shadows on My Heart*, 61; John Peyton Clark Diary, March 20, 1862.

154. Robert Young Conrad to Powell Conrad, March 19, 1862, Conrad Family Papers, VHS; Chase and Lee, *Winchester Divided*, 30; Cornelia Peake McDonald, *A Woman's Civil War: A Diary, with Reminiscences of the War, from March 1862*, ed. Minrose Gwin (Madison: University of Wisconsin Press, 1992), 123; Mary Lee Diary, August 14, 1862, p. 203.

155. Matthella Page Harrison Diary, March 31, 1863, May 25, 1863, UVA; Gettie (Margaretta) Miller Diary, April 3, 1863.

156. M416, Roll 57, UPMF.

157. Chase et al., *Winchester Divided,* 182–185; Sheila R. Phipps, *Genteel Rebel: The Life of Mary Greenhow Lee* (Baton Rouge: Louisiana State University Press, 2004), 200–206.

158. Emma Mordecai Diary, May 29, 1864.

159. George C. Rable, *Civil Wars: Women and the Crisis of Southern Nationalism* (Urbana: University of Illinois Press, 1989), 183.

160. Ibid., 182–183.

161. Elizabeth Pendleton Hardin, *The Private War of Lizzie Hardin: A Kentucky Confederate Girl's Diary of the Civil War in Kentucky, Virginia, Tennessee, Alabama, and Georgia,* ed. G. Glenn Clift (Frankfort: Kentucky Historical Society, 1963), 33; Munroe Crane, *The Great Panic: Being Incidents Connected with Two Weeks of the War in Tennessee* (Nashville, Tenn.: Johnson & Whiting, 1862), 11.

162. Chase and Lee, *Winchester Divided,* 19–20; Hotchkiss, *Make Me a Map of the Valley,* 4; Anzolette E. Pendleton to husband, April 23, 1862, April 27, 1862; Anzolette E. Pendleton to son, April 27, 1862, folder 21, box 2, William Nelson Pendleton Papers, SHC.

163. Joseph Waddell Diary, April 22, 1862, VOTS, http://valley.lib.virginia.edu/papers/AD1500.

164. Fannie Braxton Diary, March 14, 1862, p. 18; Susan Leigh Blackford and Charles Minor Blackford, *Letters from Lee's Army, or, Memoirs of Life in and out of the Army in Virginia during the War between the States,* ed. Charles Minor Blackford III (Lincoln: University of Nebraska Press, 1998), 137.

165. Margaret Ann "Meta" Morris Grimball Diary, May 12, 1862, DOCS, http://docsouth.unc.edu/fpn/grimball/grimball.html; Emma LeConte, *When the World Ended: Diary* (New York: Oxford University Press, 1957), 30.

166. McDonald, *A Woman's Civil War,* 166. See also Mary Elizabeth Mitchell Journal, 49, SHC; Elizabeth Avery Meriwether, "Recollections of Ninety Two Years," 28, SHC.

167. Katherine Polk Gale, "Recollections of Life in the Southern Confederacy," 16, Gale and Polk Family Papers, 1815–1895, SHC.

168. Fremantle, *Diary,* 100–101; Katherine Polk Gale, "Recollections," 16.

169. John Sale to Aunt, January 31, 1863, John F. Sale Letters; ? to Son, April 3, 1865, MacRae Family Papers, Box 3, Folder 1865–1866.

170. Ruth H. Hairston to Cousin Bettie, January 25, 1863, Hairston-Wilson Family Papers, folder 10, ser. 1.2, SHC.

171. Katherine Polk Gale, "Recollections," 15–21; Mary Elizabeth Mitchell Journal, 53; Emma Mordecai Diary, July 4, 1864; McGuire, *Diary of a Southern Refugee,* 238–241. For an analysis of settlement patterns among refugees through-

out the Confederacy, see Mary Elizabeth Massey, *Refugee Life in the Confederacy* (Baton Rouge: Louisiana State University Press, 1964), 68–92.

172. Ash, *When the Yankees Came,* 20, 178–180; Joan E. Cashin, "Into the Trackless Wilderness: The Refugee Experience in the Civil War," in *A Woman's War: Southern Women, Civil War, and the Confederate Legacy,* ed. Edward D. C. Campbell et al. (Richmond: Museum of the Confederacy and University Press of Virginia, 1996), xv, 264; Rable, *Civil Wars,* 187.

173. Jorantha Semmes to Benedict Joseph Semmes, July 20, 1863, folder 9, Semmes Family Papers, SHC; Joseph Waddell Diary, March 14, 1865; Eliza Simkins to Eldred Simkins, September 8, 1864, file 291, Simkins Family Papers.

174. Cashin, "Into the Trackless Wilderness," 36; Massey, *Refugee Life in the Confederacy,* 28–29; Ash, *When the Yankees Came,* 18–19; Rable, *Civil Wars,* 184–185.

175. Ruffin, *Diary,* 2:410; Fremantle, *Diary,* 72; Frances Hewitt Fearn, *Diary of a Refugee,* ed. Rosalie Urquhart (New York: Moffat, Yard, 1910), 15, DOCS, http://docsouth.unc.edu/fpn/fearn/fearn.html.

176. Stone, *Brokenburn,* 191.

177. On the implications of the refugee experience on class relations in white society, see Cashin, "Into the Trackless Wilderness," 48–49; Rable, *Civil Wars,* 184; Drew Gilpin Faust, *Mothers of Invention: Women of the Slaveholding South in the American Civil War* (Chapel Hill: University of North Carolina Press, 1996), 41–44.

178. Rawick, *American Slave,* vol. 7, Oklahoma and Miss. narr., pt. 1, 222.

179. Catherine Clinton, *The Plantation Mistress: Woman's World in the Old South* (New York: Pantheon Books, 1982), 164–165; Elizabeth Fox-Genovese, *Within the Plantation Household: Black and White Women of the Old South* (Chapel Hill: University of North Carolina Press, 1988), 70; Jane Turner Censer, *The Reconstruction of White Southern Womanhood, 1865–1895* (Baton Rouge: Louisiana State University Press, 2003), 21; Cashin, "Into the Trackless Wilderness," 29. On the gendered conventions of travel in the antebellum North, see Patricia Cline Cohen, "Safety and Danger: Women on American Public Transport 1790–1850," in *Gendered Domains: Rethinking Public and Private in Women's History,* ed. Dorothy O. Helly and Susan M. Reverby (Ithaca, N.Y.: Cornell University Press, 1992).

180. Edward T. H. Warren to Wife, April 2, 1862, Edward T. H. Warren Letters 1861–1864, UVA. For examples of men who did try to manage their family's departure while they were in the army, see Ellen Hobson Bagby Matthews to Father, April 11, 1862, section 6, George William Bagby Papers 1828–1883, VHS; Anzolette E. Pendleton to husband, April 23, 1862, folder 21, box 2, William Nelson Pendleton Papers; John Nadenbousch to wife, March 4, 1862, John Quincy Adams Nadenbousch Letters, Soldiers Letters Collection, MOC.

181. Jorantha Semmes to Benedict Joseph Semmes, July 20, 1863, folder 9, Semmes Family Papers; Emily Lovell to Mansfield Lovell, October 29, 1862, folder 103, box 6, Mansfield Lovell Papers; Emily Lovell to Mansfield Lovell, November 4, 1862, folder 104, box 6, Mansfield Lovell Papers.

182. Jorantha Semmes to Benedict Joseph Semmes, September 20, 1863, folder 9, Semmes Family Papers; Emily Lovell to Mansfield Lovell, November 15, 1862, folder 107, box 6, Mansfield Lovell Papers. On the preservation of Southern patriarchy during the war, see Ash, *When the Yankees Came,* 203; Faust, *Mothers of Invention;* Rable, *Civil Wars.* For an opposing view, see LeeAnn Whites, *The Civil War as a Crisis in Gender: Augusta, Georgia, 1860–1890* (Athens: University of Georgia Press, 1995).

183. Stone, *Brokenburn,* 191, 199.

184. Quoted in Litwack, *Been in the Storm So Long,* 112. For a shorter version of this song, see Rawick, *American Slave,* vol. 2, S.C. narr. part 2, 197. On the origins of this song, see Kate Masur, "'A Rare Phenomenon of Philological Vegetation': The Word 'Contraband' and the Meanings of Emancipation in the United States," *Journal of American History* 93, no. 4 (2007): 42–43.

185. On flight and gender in slavery, see John Hope Franklin and Loren Schweninger, *Runaway Slaves: Rebels on the Plantation* (New York: Oxford University Press, 1999), 210–212; Michael P. Johnson, "Runaway Slaves and the Slave Communities in South Carolina, 1799 to 1830," *William and Mary Quarterly* 38 (1981): 418–441; Camp, *Closer to Freedom,* 28, 36–37.

186. For a recent study of the connections between black women's and white women's experiences, see Thavolia Glymph, *Out of the House of Bondage: The Transformation of the Plantation Household* (Cambridge, U.K.: Cambridge University Press, 2008), especially 132–133.

187. Stone, *Brokenburn,* 191; Isaac Shoemaker Diary, March 3, 1864.

188. Rawick, *American Slave,* vol. 7, Oklahoma and Miss. narr., pt. 1, 306.

4. Dissolution in Motion

1. Samuel C. J. Moore to Dear Sir, February 22, 1865, section 1, Civil War Miscellaneous Papers, Thornton Tayloe Perry collection, VHS; Eldred J. Simkins to Eliza, March 21, 1865, file 204, Simkins Collection, HL; Floride Clemson, *A Rebel Came Home: The Diary of Floride Clemson Tells of Her Wartime Adventures in Yankeeland, 1863–64, Her Trip Home to South Carolina, and Life in the South during the Last Few Months of the Civil War and the Year Following* (Columbia: University of South Carolina Press, 1961), 76; J. B. Jones, *A Rebel War Clerk's Diary at the Confederate States Capital* (Philadelphia: Lippincott, 1866), 2:408. The idea that the war would end in one grand battle was typical for an era that thought of war in Napoleonic terms. Even after four years of a greatly changed military reality, both civilians and soldiers continued to expect an Austerlitz of their own. For the great impact of the Napoleonic Wars and their legacy on Civil War thinking, see especially Russell Frank Weigley, *The American Way of War: A History of United States Military Strategy and Policy* (Bloomington: Indiana University Press, 1977), ch. 6, and the more recent

Russell Frank Weigley, *A Great Civil War: A Military and Political History, 1861–1865* (Bloomington: University of Indiana Press, 2000). For a discussion of this idea in a broader context of nineteenth-century warfare, see John A. Lynn, *Battle: A History of Combat and Culture* (Boulder, Colo.: Westview Press, 2003), ch. 6.

2. OR, ser. 1, vol. 34, pt. 1, 38; Brig. Gen. Shoupe Diary, July 25, 1864–January 16, 1865, John Bell Hood Papers, 1862–1864, box 1, RG 109, NA. See also Wiley Sword, *Embrace an Angry Wind: The Confederacy's Last Hurrah: Spring Hill, Franklin, and Nashville* (New York: HarperCollins, 1992), chs. 13–14; Jack H. Lepa, *Breaking the Confederacy: The Georgia and Tennessee Campaigns of 1864* (Jefferson, N.C.: McFarland, 2005), ch. 19.

3. Samuel Rush Watkins, *"Co. Aytch"* (Chattanooga, Tenn.: Times Printing Company, 1900), 128; Douglas Cater to Dear Cousin, January 12, 1865, Douglas Cater and Rufus W. Cater Papers, 1859–1865, LC.

4. Benedict Joseph Semmes to Jorantha Semmes, January 12, 1865, folder 9, Semmes Family Papers, SHC; Emma Holmes, *The Diary of Miss Emma Holmes, 1861–1866*, ed. John F. Marszalek (Baton Rouge: Louisiana State University Press, 1979), 394.

5. Benedict Joseph Semmes to Jorantha Semmes, January 12, 1865, folder 9, Semmes Family Papers, SHC; J. B. Jones, *Rebel War Clerk's Diary*, 2:361–362.

6. Mark Grimsley, "Learning to Say 'Enough': Southern Generals and the Final Weeks of the Confederacy," in *The Collapse of the Confederacy*, ed. Mark Grimsley and Brooks D. Simpson (Lincoln: University of Nebraska Press, 2001), 71. See also Robert C. Black, *The Railroads of the Confederacy* (Chapel Hill: University of North Carolina Press, 1952), 272–274.

7. Rawleigh William Downman to Dear Wife, October 20, 1864, section 10, Downman Family Papers, VHS; Rawleigh William Downman to Dearest Wife, January 5, 1865, section 10, Downman Family Papers; OR, ser. 1, vol. 48, pt. 1, 625; Silas Chandler to Dear Wife, February 21, 1865, Silas Chandler Letters, LVA; Jefferson Headrick to Brother, February 27, 1865, Frank Family Letters, SHC. This ended up being the fate also of Joseph Johnston's army, who surrendered to William T. Sherman on April 26. Four days before, the Confederacy's postmaster wrote in an official message to Jefferson Davis, "The army under the command of General Johnston has been reduced to fourteen or fifteen infantry and artillery and cavalry, and this force is from demoralization and despondency melting away rapidly by the troops abandoning the army and returning to their houses singly and in numbers large and small." John H. Reagan to Jefferson Davis, April 22, 1865, folder 29, box 3, Jefferson Davis Papers, RG 109, NA.

8. OR, ser. 1, vol. 46, pt. 3, 1353.

9. Ella Lonn, *Desertion during the Civil War* (New York: Century, 1928), 23–29; Mark A. Weitz, *More Damning Than Slaughter: Desertion in the Confederate*

Army (Lincoln: University of Nebraska Press, 2005), 277–283; William Marvel, *Lee's Last Retreat: The Flight to Appomattox* (Chapel Hill: University of North Carolina Press, 2002), 5–6; J. Tracy Power, *Lee's Miserables: Life in the Army of Northern Virginia from the Wilderness to Appomattox* (Chapel Hill: University of North Carolina Press, 1998), 255–260.

10. Joseph Waddell Diary, March 28, 1865, VOTS, http://valley.lib.virginia.edu /papers/AD1500.

11. James M. McPherson, *Battle Cry of Freedom: The Civil War Era* (Oxford: Oxford University Press, 1988), 844–848; Power, *Lee's Miserables*, 270–281; Jay Winik, *April 1865: The Month That Saved America* (New York: HarperCollins, 2001), 123–147; Michael Golay, *A Ruined Land: The End of the Civil War* (New York: Wiley, 1999), ch. 5; Marvel, *Lee's Last Retreat*, 27–181.

12. Robert E. Lee's dispatch to Jefferson Davis on April 12, 1865, lists 7,892 infantry and 2,100 cavalry soldiers as having been present for duty on April 9. OR, ser. 1, vol. 46, 1266–1267. These numbers have never been verified, and the strength of the Army of Northern Virginia during the Appomattox campaign has always been a fiercely contested issue. Union veterans often accused their Confederate peers of misrepresenting the number of Southern soldiers who surrendered at Appomattox as being smaller than it actually was in order to portray a picture of overwhelming Northern strength. For discussions of the size of the Confederate army at Appomattox, see Marvel, *Lee's Last Retreat*, 201–205; Chris Calkins, *The Final Bivouac: The Surrender Parade at Appomattox and the Disbanding of the Armies, April 10–May 20, 1865* (Lynchburg, Va.: H. E. Howard, 1988), 201–221; Power, *Lee's Miserables*, 404–405n144. The same gaps between the number of men who were with their commands during the final ceasefire and the ones who were eventually paroled existed in every part of the Confederacy. Joseph E. Johnston's army numbered 20,000 men when he surrendered, but more than 89,000 soldiers eventually surrendered to Federal authorities in the states of the Deep South. The total number of men who were paroled by the Union is 174,223. See OR, ser. 2, vol. 8, 828–829; Grimsley, "Learning to Say 'Enough,'" 69.

13. For detailed returns of different units in the Army of Northern Virginia on April 8, 1865, see folder 26, Robert E. Lee Headquarters Papers 1850–1876, VHS. See also William B. Holberton, *Homeward Bound: The Demobilization of the Union and Confederate Armies, 1865–1866* (Mechanicsburg, Pa.: Stackpole Books, 2000), 18; Marvel, *Lee's Last Retreat*, 206.

14. Llewellyn Traherne Basset Saunderson, April 7, Diary March 17–April 14, 1865, VHS. See also Kena King Chapman Diary, April 11, 1865, SHC; Charles Cheves Haskell, "Reminiscences of the Confederate War, 1861–1865," 119, VHS; Joseph Banks Lyle Diary, April 7, 1865, VHS; James Eldred Phillips Diary, April 3–8, 1865, VHS; John Baxter Moseley Diary, April 3–5, 1865, VHS; Thomas Pollock Devereux, "Reminiscences," SHC; J. R. Sheldon, "Last March of the Army of Lee," 2–4, VHS.

15. Henry T. Bahnson, "Recollections," notebook 3, 15–16, SHC. See also George Philip Clarke Diary, April 6, 1865, LVA; Sheldon, "Last March," 5–9.

16. James E. Whitehorne Diary, April 4, 1865, SHC. See also Edward Alexander Moore, *The Story of a Cannoneer under Stonewall Jackson in Which Is Told the Part Taken by the Rockbridge Artillery in the Army of Northern Virginia* (New York: Neale, 1907), 301; Samuel Howard Gray, *A Confederate Diary of the Retreat from Petersburg, April 3–20, 1865*, ed. Richard Barksdale Harwell (Atlanta: Library, Emory University, 1953).

17. John S. Wise, *The End of an Era* (Boston: Houghton Mifflin, 1899), 433; James E. Whitehorne Diary, April 4, 1865.

18. George Philip Clarke Diary, April 7, 1865; William Gordon McCabe to Miss Mary, April 7, 1865, section 17, Early Family Papers, VHS.

19. Movements before April 2 suggested what would happen when the army became mobile again: 512 men deserted Pickett's division in the course of a single bloodless march a few weeks prior to the Appomattox campaign. OR, ser. 1, vol. 46, pt. 3, 1353.

20. Christopher Q. Tompkins, April 7, 1865, in "The Occupation of Richmond, 1865," reprinted in *Virginia Magazine of History and Biography* 73 (1965): 192. See also Jedediah Hotchkiss, *Make Me a Map of the Valley: The Civil War Journal of Stonewall Jackson's Topographer*, ed. Archie P. McDonald (Dallas: Southern Methodist University Press, 1973), 266.

21. Mary Alice Downman to Beloved Husband, April 10, 1865, section 10, Downman Family Papers. See also Anne Jennings Wise Hobson Diary, April 10, 1865, VHS.

22. Mary Elizabeth Mitchell Journal, May 13, 1865, SHC; Susan R. Jervey, *Two Diaries from Middle St. John's, Berkeley, South Carolina, February–May 1865*, 24, DOCS, http://docsouth.unc.edu/fpn/jervey/jervey.html.

23. George P. Rawick, *The American Slave: A Composite Autobiography*, 19 vols. (Westport, Conn.: Greenwood, 1972), vol. 8, Arkansas narr., pt. 1, 107.

24. Rawick, *American Slave*, vol. 4, Texas narr., pt. 2, 191.

25. Holberton, *Homeward Bound*, 87–90. For soldiers who benefited from free transport, see Edward Chaffers, to mother, June 5, 1865, Southern Women's Collection, box 4, MOC; Henry Robinson Berkeley Diary, June 24, 1865, VHS. Among those observing the depredations committed by returning soldiers on civilians were members of the presidential retinue. See Stephen R. Mallory Diary and reminiscences, 1861–1867, SHC; John Taylor Wood Diary, April 15, folders 9–10, John Taylor Wood Papers, SHC.

26. Robert Pooler Myers Diary, April 14, 1865, MOC.

27. Kena King Chapmen Diary, April 14, 16, 1865, SHC; Bahnson, "Recollections," 29.

28. Isaac Coles, Recollections of 1861–1865, box 9, Pocket Plantation Records, UVA; Holmes, *The Diary of Miss Emma Holmes*, 439; Noah Andre Trudeau, *Out*

of the Storm: The End of the Civil War, April–June 1865 (Boston: Little, Brown, 1994), 382.

29. (?) Mordecai to Mrs. Butler, August 21, 1865, section 3, Edgar E. McDonald Papers, VHS.

30. Rawick, *American Slave,* vol. 3, S.C. narr., pt. 4, 14; vol. 8, Arkansas narr., pt. 1, 286; suppl. series. 2, vol. 9, pt. 8, Texas narr., 3484.

31. Rawick, *American Slave,* vol. 7, Oklahoma and Miss. narr., pt. 1, 340; suppl. ser. 2, vol. 3, Texas narr., 258; vol. 6, Alabama narr., 270; vol. 14, N.C. narr., pt. 1, 128.

32. Rawick, *American Slave,* vol. 7, Oklahoma and Miss. narr., pt. 1, 305; vol. 9, Arkansas narr., 152; vol. 4, Texas narr., pt. 1, 215.

33. Rawick, *American Slave,* vol. 7, Oklahoma and Miss. narr., pt. 1, 273.

34. Rawick, *American Slave,* vol. 7, Oklahoma and Miss. narr., pt. 2, 53.

35. Leon F. Litwack, *Been in the Storm So Long: The Aftermath of Slavery* (New York: Knopf, 1979), 297; Peter Kolchin, *First Freedom: The Responses of Alabama's Blacks to Emancipation and Reconstruction* (Westport, Conn.: Greenwood Press, 1972), 4; William Cohen, *At Freedom's Edge: Black Mobility and the Southern White Quest for Racial Control, 1861–1915* (Baton Rouge: Louisiana State University Press, 1991), 3–5; Joel Williamson, *After Slavery: The Negro in South Carolina during Reconstruction, 1861–1877* (Chapel Hill: University of North Carolina Press, 1965), 33.

36. Tompkins, "The Occupation of Richmond, 1865," 192.

37. Emma Mordecai Diary, May 4, 1865, Mordecai Family Papers, SHC.

38. There is a range of opinions among historians about the extent and scale of black migration in the postemancipation South. Peter Kolchin claims that in Alabama a majority of the formerly enslaved population left the plantations, at least temporarily. Eric Foner argues that most freed people did not leave their place of bondage at all during 1865, yet he also describes a massive wave of black mobility immediately after the war. Leon Litwack says ambiguously that "large numbers" stayed in the plantations, yet he too describes in vivid detail the departure of slaves in 1865. Scott Nesbit has recently demonstrated through his study of postemancipation marriage patterns that former slaves migrated away from the counties where they were born when they got married shortly after the war. Susan O'Donovan has suggested that the great majority of slaves stayed put in the immediate aftermath of defeat and that the myth of freed people's movement was largely the creation of slaveholders. However, her study focuses on southwestern Georgia, an area that saw little fighting throughout the war. She does note that in parts of the South where armies were active, like the Mississippi Valley, the Upper South, and the path of Sherman's march, "war had swept a good many black people out of their cabins and away from their masters' plantations." In her study of African Americans in the Appalachians, Wilma A. Dunaway also argues that most slaves in this particular area stayed with their former owners for years after emancipation, though she too cites evidence showing that many reacted to news

of emancipation by setting out for brief excursions to explore their immediate surroundings. See Kolchin, *First Freedom*, 6; Eric Foner, *Reconstruction: America's Unfinished Revolution, 1863–1877* (New York: Harper & Row, 1988), 81; Litwack, *Been in the Storm So Long*, 297–332; Scott Nesbit, "Scales Intimate and Sprawling," *Southern Spaces*, July 19, 2011, http://southernspaces.org/2011/scales -intimate-and-sprawling-slavery-emancipation-and-geography-marriage -virginia; Susan E. O'Donovan, *Becoming Free in the Cotton South* (Cambridge, Mass.: Harvard University Press, 2007), 119–121, quote on 119; Wilma A. Dunaway, *The African-American Family in Slavery and Freedom* (Cambridge: Cambridge University Press, 2003), 215–226.

39. Rawick, *American Slave*, vol. 15, N.C. narr., pt. 2, 181.

40. Steven Hahn et al., *Land and Labor, 1865*, Freedom: A Documentary History of Emancipation, ser. 3, vol. 1 (Chapel Hill: University of North Carolina Press, 2008), doc. 289, p. 975.

41. John Richard Dennett, *The South As It Is: 1865–1866* (New York: Viking Press, 1965), 364.

42. Rawick, *American Slave*, vol. 7, Oklahoma and Miss. narr., pt. 2, 62; part 1, 51.

43. Tompkins, "The Occupation of Richmond, 1865," 192; William Harwar Parker, *Recollections of a Naval Officer, 1841–1865* (New York: C. Scribner's Sons, 1883), 370.

44. Dennett, *South As It Is*, 364.

45. On black migration patterns in the postemancipation South, see Hahn, *Land and Labor, 1865*, 82–83, 602; Foner, *Reconstruction*, 81–82; Litwack, *Been in the Storm So Long*, 310–322; John Thomas O'Brien, *From Bondage to Citizenship: The Richmond Black Community, 1865–1867* (New York: Garland, 1990), 85–94; Kolchin, *First Freedom*, 23; Howard N. Rabinowitz, *Race Relations in the Urban South, 1865–1890* (New York: Oxford University Press, 1978), 16–26; Cohen, *At Freedom's Edge*, 44–45; Orville Vernon Burton, "The Rise and Fall of Afro-American Town Life: Town and Country in Reconstruction Edgefield, South Carolina," in *Toward a New South? Studies in Post–Civil War Southern Communities*, ed. Orville Vernon Burton and Robert C. McMath (Westport, Conn.: Greenwood Press, 1982).

46. Williamson, *After Slavery*, 39–40; Litwack, *Been in the Storm So Long*, 297; Foner, *Reconstruction*, 81; Kolchin, *First Freedom*, 20; Hahn, *Land and Labor, 1865*, 23–24; Dunaway, *The African-American Family in Slavery and Freedom*, 221.

47. Hahn, *Land and Labor, 1865*, doc. 172B, p. 655.

48. Edmund Ruffin, *The Diary of Edmund Ruffin*, ed. William Kauffman Scarborough, 3 vols. (Baton Rouge: Louisiana State University Press, 1972), 3:869; John Kimberly to Bettie Kimberly, April 23, 1865, folder 58, John Kimberly Papers, SHC; Emma Mordecai Diary, May 5, 1865; Joseph Waddell Diary, May 2, 1865.

49. Hahn, *Land and Labor, 1865*, doc. 14, p. 118; doc. 12, p. 102.

50. "Report of cases heard and decided by Provost Marshal Greene County VA for the week ending Saturday September 23rd, 1865," folder 16, box 23, BR.

51. Sally E. Hadden, *Slave Patrols: Law and Violence in Virginia and the Carolinas* (Cambridge, Mass.: Harvard University Press, 2001), 192–193; Hahn, *Land and Labor, 1865*, 186–187; Kolchin, *First Freedom*, 5–6; Foner, *Reconstruction*, 81, 152–153.

52. Hahn, *Land and Labor, 1865*, doc. 45A, pp. 237–239n; doc. 33, p. 167.

53. William H. Sims to Phebe Howson, May 25, 1865, section 8, Bailey Family Papers, VHS; Joseph Waddell Diary, May 30, 1865; J. T. Trowbridge, *The South: A Tour of Its Battlefields and Ruined Cities* (New York: Arno Press, 1969), 155. On the efforts of the Ruffin family to turn out their former bondspeople, see Ruffin, *Diary*, 3:869; Frank G. Ruffin to Brigadier General M. R. Patrick, May 8, 1865, folder 14, box 80, BR.

54. Charles L. Perdue et al., *Weevils in the Wheat: Interviews with Virginia Ex-Slaves* (Bloomington: Indiana University Press, 1980), 126; Rawick, *American Slave*, vol. 8, Arkansas narr., pt. 1, 349; vol. 2, S.C. narr., pt. 1, 5.

55. Rawick, *American Slave*, suppl. ser. 2, vol. 3, Texas narr., 760.

56. Hahn, *Land and Labor, 1865*, doc. 156, p. 617.

57. (?) Mordecai to Mrs. Butler, August 21, 1865, section 3, Edgar E. McDonald Papers; John Kimberly to Bettie Kimberly, April 23, 1865, folder 58, John Kimberly Papers; Susan Hoge to Mrs. Howard, October 28, 1865, section 34, Hoge Family Papers, VHS.

58. Rawick, *American Slave*, vol. 2, S.C. narr., pt. 1, 5; vol. 7, Oklahoma and Miss. narr., pt. 2, 40–41.

59. Hahn, *Land and Labor, 1865*, doc. 22, p. 147.

60. Ibid., doc 52A, p. 267n.; doc. 35, pp. 198–199.

61. Ibid., doc. 44, p. 237n; doc. 38, p. 214.

62. Ibid., doc. 37D, p. 212; doc. 52E, pp. 271–272.

63. Ibid, doc. 52D, p. 271; doc. 52H, p. 277.

64. Ibid., doc. 21, p. 144; doc. 38, p. 214.

65. Ibid., doc. 42, p. 225; doc. 148, p. 585n.

66. On July 25, 1865, in response to both white planters' and some Northern officials' efforts to forcibly prevent freed people from moving, Secretary of War Edwin M. Stanton issued General Order no, 129, which annulled any system of passes for freedom and forbade "any restraints or punishments not imposed on other classes." Ibid., doc. 48, p. 259.

67. John W. Blassingame, *Slave Testimony: Two Centuries of Letters, Speeches, Interviews, and Autobiographies* (Baton Rouge: Louisiana State University Press, 1977), 568; Elizabeth Pendleton Hardin, *The Private War of Lizzie Hardin: A Kentucky Confederate Girl's Diary of the Civil War in Kentucky, Virginia, Tennessee, Alabama, and Georgia*, ed. G. Glenn Clift (Frankfort: Kentucky Historical Society, 1963), 231; Anne Hobson Diary, April 10, 1865; John Kimberly to Bettie Kimberly, April 23, 1865, folder 58, John Kimberly Papers; M416, Roll 57, UPMF.

68. Benedict Joseph Semmes to wife, August 10, 1863, folder 9, Semmes Family Papers.

69. Jones, *Rebel War Clerk's Diary*, 2:427.

70. Notes of John Bell Hood about the spring campaign of 1865, Civil War Collection, HL.

71. For examples of this sentiment, see Jones, *Rebel War Clerk's Diary*, 2:418; Eldred J. Simkins to Eliza Josephine Trescot Simkins, March 21, 1865, file 204, Simkins Family Papers.

72. White Southerners were by no means unique in this approach. The geographer Yi-Fu Tuan argues that modern societies hold on to ideas of mythical space, "a fuzzy area of defective knowledge surrounding the empirically known; it frames pragmatic space." Yi-fu Tuan, *Space and Place: The Perspective of Experience* (Minneapolis: University of Minnesota Press, 1977), 86.

73. Stephen V. Ash, *When the Yankees Came: Conflict and Chaos in the Occupied South, 1861–1865* (Chapel Hill: University of North Carolina Press, 1995).

74. Eldred J. Simkins to Eliza Simkins, March 21, 1865, file 204, Simkins Family Papers.

75. John C. Rutherford to wife, January 18, 1865, box 5, Rutherford Family Papers, DL; Anne Hobson Diary, April 10, 1865; James E. Whitehorne Diary, March 31, 1865.

76. Parker, *Recollections*, 351; Charles R. Chewning Diary, April 2, 1865, SBJ.

77. Wise, *The End of an Era*, 415; Charles Chewning Diary, April 5, 1865.

78. "To the People of the Confederate States of America," OR, ser. 1, vol. 46, pt. 3, 1382–1383.

79. Historians have fiercely debated whether the purpose of the proclamation was to to incite the civilian population into guerrilla warfare. See Emory M. Thomas, *The Confederate Nation, 1861–1865* (New York: Harper & Row, 1979), 301; Winik, *April 1865*, 147–150; William C. Davis, *An Honorable Defeat: The Last Days of the Confederate Government* (New York: Harcourt, 2001), 80–84; Michael B. Ballard, *A Long Shadow: Jefferson Davis and the Final Days of the Confederacy* (Jackson, Miss.: University Press of Mississippi, 1986), 56–57. For a persuasive and opposing view, arguing that Davis was committed to continuing the fight with regular armies, see William B. Feis, "Jefferson Davis and the 'Guerilla Option': A Reexamination," in *The Collapse of the Confederacy*, ed. Mark Grimsley and Brooks D. Simpson (Lincoln: University of Nebraska Press, 2001). See also Herman Hattaway and Richard E. Beringer, *Jefferson Davis, Confederate President* (Lawrence: University Press of Kansas, 2002), 395–396; William J. Cooper, *Jefferson Davis, American* (New York: Knopf, 2000), 526–527.

80. Varina Davis to Jefferson Davis, April 7, 1865, *The Papers of Jefferson Davis*, vol. 11, ed. Lynda L. Crist, Barbara J. Rozek, and Kenneth H. Williams (Baton Rouge: Louisiana University Press, 2003), 514; Wise, *The End of an Era*, 414.

81. Jones, *Rebel War Clerk's Diary*, 2:413; Francis Richard Lubbock, *Six Decades in Texas: Or, Memoirs of Francis Richard Lubbock, Governor of Texas in War Time, 1861–63. A Personal Experience in Business, War, and Politics*, ed. Cadwell Walton Raines (Austin, Texas: B. C. Jones, 1900), 565.

82. George Alexander Martin Diary, April 2–May 20, 1865, VHS; Thomas Rowland to Mother, April 12, 1865, Thomas Rowland Letters, MOC.

83. Emma Le Conte, *When the World Ended: The Diary of Emma LeConte*, ed. Earl Schenck Miers (Lincoln: University of Nebraska Press, 1987), 96; Hardin, *The Private War of Lizzie Hardin*, 234; Mary Elizabeth Mitchell Journal, May 6, 1865, p. 66; Kate Stone, *Brokenburn: The Journal of Kate Stone, 1861–1868*, ed. John Q. Anderson (Baton Rouge: Louisiana State University Press, 1995), 341; George Alexander Martin Diary, May 4, 1865.

84. On the role of the military in bringing the end of the war, see Grimsley, "Learning to Say 'Enough.'"

85. John Taylor Wood Diary, April 21, 1865.

86. "The Journey of President Davis to Richmond," *Richmond Enquirer*, May 30, 1861.

87. Robert Garlick Hill Kean, *Inside the Confederate Government: The Diary of Robert Garlick Hill Kean, Head of the Bureau of War* (New York: Oxford University Press, 1957), 207.

88. Halcott Pride Jones Diary, May 4, 1865, MOC.

89. George Alexander Martin Diary, May 4, 1865.

90. On the flight of the Confederate government, see *The Papers of Jefferson Davis*, vol. 11, 492–585; John Taylor Wood Diary, April 2–May 16, 1865; Stephen Mallory, Reminiscences; Lubbock, *Six Decades in Texas*, 563–573; Parker, *Recollections*, 351–368; Given Campbell, Memorandum of a Journal Kept Daily During the Last March of Jefferson Davis, LC; John H. Reagan, *Memoirs: With Special Reference to Secession and the Civil War* (New York: Neale, 1906), 197–220; Anna Holmes Trenholm Diary, April–June 1865, SHC. See also W. H. Swallow, "The Retreat of the Confederate Government from Richmond to the Gulf," *Magazine of American History* 15 (1886); A. J. Hanna, *Flight into Oblivion* (New York: Johnson Publishing Company, 1938); Davis, *An Honorable Defeat*, 62–306; Ballard, *A Long Shadow*, 43–144; Hattaway and Beringer, *Jefferson Davis, Confederate President*, 391–430; Cooper, *Jefferson Davis, American*, 523–534; Davis, *The Long Surrender*, 30–32, 61–148; Nelson Lankford, *Richmond Burning: The Last Days of the Confederate Capital* (New York: Penguin, 2002), 77–79, 91, 104–105; Joan E. Cashin, *First Lady of the Confederacy: Varina Davis's Civil War* (Cambridge, Mass: Harvard University Press, 2006), 157–163. Eventually, almost all members of the Confederate government were caught and brought under custody. The two exceptions were John C. Breckinridge and Judah P. Benjamin, who succeeded in getting to Cuba.

Epilogue

1. Napier Bartlett, *A Soldier's Story of the War; Including the Marches and Battles of the Washington Artillery, and of Other Louisiana Troops* (New Orleans: Clark & Hofeline, 1874), 5–6.

2. John Lowe, "'The Unvanquished': Faulkner's Nietzschean Skirmish with the Civil War," *Mississippi Quarterly* 46, no. 3 (1993): 407–436.

3. Don H. Doyle, "Faulkner's Civil War in Fiction, History, and Memory," in *Faulkner and War: Faulkner and Yoknapatawpha, 2001*, ed. Noel Polk and Ann J. Abadie (Jackson: University of Mississippi Press, 2004), 4. See also Don H. Doyle, *Faulkner's County: The Historical Roots of Yoknapatawpha* (Chapel Hill: University of North Carolina Press, 2001).

4. William Faulkner, *The Unvanquished* (New York: Random House, 1938), 94.

5. Ibid., 92.

6. Ibid., 110.

7. Ibid., 109.

8. Ibid., 107–108.

9. Ibid., 170–171.

10. Ibid., 159.

Acknowledgments

One of the greatest pleasures of bringing a book to completion is finally having an opportunity to publicly thank the individuals and institutions who helped me along the way. My single greatest debt is to the people who mentored me as a graduate student at Princeton and who have kept on teaching, inspiring, and encouraging me ever since. James McPherson, the foremost authority on the American Civil War, offered unmatched knowledge, staunch support, and rigorous engagement. He believed in this project even when I wavered, and he provided me with the firm backing so few young scholars ever receive. This book would not have come to fruition without him. Daniel Rodgers transformed my thinking about cultural history and has made me a better scholar in so many ways. His rare mind and exceptional generosity were nothing short of crucial throughout this long process, and I am appreciative beyond words of the time, energy, and thought he has devoted, and still devotes, to me and my work.

So many other professors, friends, and colleagues deserve my deepest thanks. Christine Stansell provided penetrating critiques of my writing and taught me much about gender, history, and life. Jay Winter treats me as if I were one of his own graduate students: always ready to read and comment, always pushing me to think harder and faster, always providing a role model as a cultural historian of war. Moshe Sluhovsky's tough love has been essential from my time as an undergraduate student and all the way to my postdoctoral days. Stephanie McCurry's profound insights were extremely important for the evolution of my thinking about the South.

Others who taught me a great deal include Menahem Blondheim, Robert Darnton, Elizabeth Lunbeck, Philip Nord, Nell Irvin Painter, Anson Rabinbach, Sean Wilentz, and Shira Wolosky. For reading, listening, and offering fantastically useful comments on various segments and drafts of this book, I am grateful to Gretchen Boger, W. Fitzhugh Brundage, Christina Burnett, Erica Gilles, Joseph Glatthaar, Chin Jou, Ruth Hacohen, Eran Shalev, Zur Shalev, David Shulman, Dror Wharman, Michael Zakim, an anonymous reader for Harvard University Press, and Milette Shamir, who introduced me to *The Unvanquished*. Many thanks to the commentators and audiences at the Southern Historical Association, the American Historical Association, the European Southern Studies Forum, the American Studies Forum at Tel Aviv University, the migration workshop at Haifa University, the Modern America workshop at Princeton, the Gilder Lehrman Center for the Study of Slavery, Resistance and Abolition at Yale, and the history department colloquium at the Hebrew University of Jerusalem.

Apart from generosity in spirit, I have also benefited from tremendous generosity in funding. First and foremost, the Department of History and the graduate school at Princeton enabled me to enjoy years of uninterrupted study, for which I will forever be grateful. I have also been the lucky recipient of the Dan David scholarship, as well as postdoctoral fellowships from the Rothschild Foundation (Yad Hanadiv) and from the faculty of the Humanities at the Hebrew University. The Martin Buber Society of Fellows in the Humanities, also at the Hebrew University, provided not just munificent funding, but also a home, a community, and some relationships I plan to keep for life. Additional research funds were granted through a Keck-Mellon Fellowship from the Huntington Library, a Mellon Fellowship from the Virginia Historical Society, the program of African American studies at Princeton, the Gilder Lehrman Institute for the Study of American History, and the Gilder Lehrman Center for the Study of Slavery, Resistance and Abolition at Yale.

Like any other historian, I am entirely dependent on librarians and archivists who safeguard the material from which books are made. For their astounding professionalism, abundant patience, and much goodwill, I am grateful to the staffs of the Manuscript Division at the Library of Congress; the National Archives and Records Administration in Washington, D.C.; the Library of Virginia in Richmond; the Southern Historical Collection at the University of North Carolina at Chapel Hill; the Rare Books, Manuscripts, and Special Collections Library at Duke University; the Confederate Research Center at Hill College in Hillsboro, Texas; the Stuart Bell Junior Archives at the Handley Regional Library in Winchester, Virginia; the Beinecke Rare Book and Manuscript Library and the Manuscripts and Archives Department at Yale University; the Department of Rare Books and Special Collections at Princeton University Library; the Gilder Lehrman Collection in New York City; the New-York Historical Society; and the Special Collections Library at the University of Virginia, Charlottesville. Special thanks to the extraordinary Frances Pollard and the staff at the Virginia Historical Society, to John Rhodehmael and the staff of the Huntington Library, and to John Coski and his troops at the Eleanor S. Brockenbrough Library in the Museum of the Confederacy. Elizabeth Bennett, the history bibliographer at Princeton, had answers to all questions, large and small. Philip Schwartzberg drew the maps for this book with talent and expertise.

At Harvard University Press, I was extraordinarily lucky to be taken under the wing of Joyce Seltzer, who offered firm and astute guidance through the process of writing and rewriting a first book. Christine Dahlin and Judith Hoover saw the process through its final stages, with great care and meticulous attention to detail.

This book was written over the course of several years. Some were better, some were worse. Through it all I enjoyed the uniquely good company of many close friends, not all of whom can be named here. I am particularly indebted to Joshua Derman, Idit Froim, Guy Geltner, Erica Gilles, Faina Goldstein, Moran Haviv, Noa Hocherman, Tali Krakowsky, Tali Mentovitch, Katherine Moran, Yonatan Reguer, Natan Sachs, Danielle Shani, Yaniv Shirazi, and Will Slauter. I hope they know that I could not have managed without them.

I have also enjoyed much encouragement from my sister and brother-in-law, Tali and Noah Gerber. Most important, they have made me the proud and happy aunt of Neta, Daphna, and Simi.

Finally, my parents, Ziva and Zeev Sternhell. This is not the place to describe all they have given me and all that I owe them. Let it simply be said that they are my closest friends, my greatest allies, and that their love has sustained me during every minute of my life. I dedicate this book to them, with everlasting gratitude and affection.

Index